This Book is Fo

C000043183

- You've always wanted to write a book but have never got round to it.

- You're keen to write a book but don't know how you can turn your thoughts and ideas into one.

- People keep telling you that you should write a book but you haven't put pen to paper.

- You know someone who's writing a book and you want to give them the perfect gift.

- You're writing a book but it's stalling because you've lost your way.

- Your book is nearing publication but you don't have a powerful marketing plan in place to promote it.

- Marketing your book looks challenging and you don't know where to start.

- You've tried marketing your book but it hasn't delivered what you were hoping for.

- You want to relaunch your book with a new marketing plan in place.

- You want your book to position you as a thought leader and a key person of influence in your field.

- You want to produce a book that's destined for the big time; that will stay in the bestsellers for months if not years.

The ULTIMATE GUIDE to

WRITING & MARKETING

A BESTSELLING BOOK

on a shoestring budget

Dee Blick

Published by
Filament Publishing Ltd
16, Croydon Road, Waddon, Croydon,
Surrey, CR0 4PA, United Kingdom
Telephone +44 (0)20 8688 2598
Fax +44 (0)20 7183 7186
info@filamentpublishing.com
www.filamentpublishing.com

© Dee Blick 2015

The right of Dee Blick to be identified as the author
of this work has been asserted by her in accordance with the
Designs and Copyright Act 1988.

ISBN - 978-1-910125-04-5

Printed by PB Print UK

This book is subject to international copyright and may
not be copied in any way without the prior written
permission of the publishers.

Dedication

To Malcolm, Mum and Drew.
My three biggest supporters.

Contents

Chapter 21: How intelligent blogging can boost book sales.   347
- Get in the blogging habit and build momentum.
- Research blog sites popular with your readers and connect with editors and journalists subtly.
- Use your book as the basis of your blogs. Little tasters whet readers' appetites...

Chapter 22: How to tweet your way to book sales galore!   367
- Get into the spirit of Twitter: be sociable and engaging.
- Build relationships with your readers and other influential people and ask for reviews!
- Why it's important to tweet regularly - but not exclusively - about your book.

Chapter 23: How to pull off the perfect book launch.   393
- It's easy to create a buzz about your book launch when you know how.
- Why stick at one launch when you can have more? They'll help your book sales snowball.
- How to attract a sponsor and have a no-cost launch!

Chapter 24: How to get positive reviews and how to get professional reviewers to review your book.   409
- Rave reviews sell books - but don't be tempted to use fake ones!
- Ask regularly for reviews on Twitter, at book signings and at public speaking engagements.
- Step by step - how to approach professional reviewers.

About Dee Blick

Dee is a genuine number one bestselling author, a keen blogger, and a columnist with 10 copywriting awards to her credit. Her second book, *The Ultimate Small Business Marketing Book* was awarded a publishing deal in China. It also reached the top 150 of all books on Amazon and is required syllabus reading for marketing and business students at the University of Texas. Her third book, *The 15 Essential Marketing Masterclasses For Your Small Business* was published by global brand Wiley and has won several awards since it was published.

Dee has been a prolific and enthusiastic writer from a very young age winning her first writing award at the age of eleven. Today much of her time is spent writing sales letters, brochures, blogs and press releases and creating articles for magazines.

Dee is also a warm and animated professional speaker, coach, and trainer and enjoys nothing more than inspiring other authors to realise their dream of writing a bestselling book.

Dee's photo kindly taken by Frazer Visser of Hamilton Studios

Foreword

It's hard to try to sum up Dee Blick. If I had a quick go, I'd say she's charming and capable, erudite and plainly spoken, conscientious and hard working, diligent and creative, inspirational and mentoring, gracious and strategic. She's a (small) business marketing force of nature equally powerful in person or via phone, email and social media. Dee is also an author with an enviable track record of success in terms of utility, sales, reputation and reach. Dee writes in a straightforward conversational style – it's as if your gifted successful sister sat next to you to smooth and mentor your every step. The simplicity of her writing style regularly masks the thought, strategy, experience and hard work actually required to express her many ideas, advice and suggestions so succinctly.

They say that those who can't do, teach. Dee is the exception that proves this rule since she does and teaches with equal fluency as well as also bringing to bear her trademark *joie de vivre*. Dee definitely both walks the walk and talks the talk. Although a truism, it's no less correct that all overnight success is invariably the result of careful planning, relentless hard work, great customer service and, of course, a quality product. With Dee's advice ringing in your head (or guiding your progress), the future prospects for your writing already look brighter.

Of course, given the sheer number of books published every year, there is still always need for good fortune! However, even a blind man on a galloping horse would advise you apply the lessons, ideas and techniques contained within these pages if you want to find yourself well on the way to writing and marketing your own bestselling book. If this were a Police interrogation (rather than a foreword), I'd quickly confess (again) that Dee Blick exhibits and communicates great skills as a writer and marketer. She's a woman you'd want to listen to and learn from as well as look to for advice and guidance since she really knows her stuff (when it comes to both writing and marketing). Dee is hard working, enthusiastic and, very importantly and slightly unusually for highly successful marketers, doesn't BS.

Given her own publishing track record and achievements, Dee can really help you give full lustre to your ideas and voice as well as help you create your own unique but, nonetheless, saleable book. Dee will also help you plan, curate and structure it. Follow some or most of the advice included in the following pages (while adding your own passions) and I'm confident that Dee's ideas and process will help you write and deliver the best book you can. In addition, Dee's advice will help you market and promote it in a way that positions your book for sales success and that all important word-of-mouth acclaim. Don't take my word (or hers) for the Dee Blick phenomena – just search Google or Amazon: type in her name or "small business marketing" and see the results for yourself. Many try but few are chosen when it comes to writing any number one best seller, let alone then remaining at number 1 for the next three years! Her success is such that major global publisher Wiley/Capstone sought out the alchemy of her ideas and approach to add further sheen to their own already highly illustrious author roster.

Dee being Dee hasn't let success go to her head but continues to survive and thrive by being her own woman, applying her hard won but easily worn experience; while choosing the publishing routes to goal that best suit her needs, requirements and aims. Stranger still to report, the only real threat to Dee's status as Amazon's best selling small business marketing author currently appears to be other books written by Dee. I'd hate to be a rival author – I'd be sickened by the sales, irked by her charm and devastated by her strategic business acumen ("I don't wait for an opportunity – I'm there long before!"). Dee has so many five star Amazon reviews for her various titles they could almost be published as a book!

Anyways: congratulations!

You've already made a great start on the road to writing and marketing your own bestseller since you've started to read this book. To recount its virtues again: it's packed full of hard won tips, tricks, advice, suggestions, tried and tested formulas for your pending publishing success. It's a mix of powerful tasty ingredients that make it part primer, part safety net, part recipe book, part route map and part gourmet meal. Dee's chatty conversational style makes her guidance and advice easy to understand and apply. Dee writes in a way that feels like a face-to-face or phone conversation with a friend (albeit an expert one) or member of the family. So, fasten your seat belt and buckle in for your own publishing ride of a lifetime.

Jeff Scott, Book PR Publicist, Author and Writer

Introduction

I consider myself fortunate in that I was a born writer who became a marketer when I was 22. I have more than three decades of writing and marketing experience. However, these two skills didn't mean it was all plain sailing when I wrote my first book. In fact I made no end of mistakes simply because I didn't know any better. I was a naïve first time author, high on expectation but low on that all essential know-how! But of course every cloud has a silver lining and these early experiences and mistakes gave me an insider's understanding of the challenges authors face at every stage of the writing, publishing and marketing process.

Shortly after my second book had been published and it was riding high in the bestsellers I remember thinking that, one day, I would write a book covering every bit of information I would've welcomed wholeheartedly while writing my first book. The seed was sown and it was only a matter of time before this book worked its way to the top of my agenda.

It has to be said that writing this book has been a joyful experience, knowing that what I was sharing would (hopefully) help many thousands of authors worldwide. I had a very clear vision of what I wanted to accomplish and what I wanted to include. I know just how important it is for you to have the right facts, figures, tips and strategies to help you at every stage of your journey. The last thing you want is empty rhetoric, expensive marketing schemes and highfalutin' advice! I hope you'll see *The Ultimate Guide to Writing and Marketing a Bestselling Book - on a Shoestring Budget* as an indispensable guide and the next best thing to having me sitting with you, taking you through the process.

"Is this book just for non-fiction writers?"

I was asked this by a friend and it's a good question! This book is ideal for every stage of writing and marketing a work of non-fiction, but not so much for novelists where the first six chapters are likely to be less relevant.

However from Chapter 7 onwards the advice is just as relevant to novelists.

I say this because the non-fiction writer already knows the world they are writing about. They have navigated its pitfalls and plotted a successful course through it for some time. They have much of the subject matter in their subconscious ready to be mined for tips, case studies and other content.

A novelist has to create the world and the characters they're going to write about from scratch (and that's just as true for writers of genre fiction). They have very different challenges to deal with in the research, planning and writing phases. They have to know their genre and its conventions intimately; develop a believable, enticing and original-enough plot; create three-dimensional characters their readers will love (or love to hate); tell the story through a masterful use of the narrative delivery modes (action, dramatic summary, exposition, description, dialogue) and that's just the tip of a very large iceberg...

So if you're a non-fiction writer, all of this book will apply to you. If you're a novelist or fiction writer everything from Chapter 7 onwards is just as relevant to you as it is to non-fiction authors.

In every chapter I have endeavoured to cover the key dos and don'ts, illustrating many of the tips with real-life examples and useful templates. In five of the chapters I have also enlisted the help of some talented experts who also happen to be successful published authors. You can trust their advice because they most definitely practice what they preach! You can find out more about these experts at the back of this book.

So, how would I encourage you to use this book?

I have written it so that you can initially enjoy reading it from beginning to end before starting again, this time reading the chapters that are relevant to you, pad and pen to hand so you can record your thoughts and make notes of the actions you're going to take. The question 'how can this chapter be of benefit to me?' should never be far from your mind.

If you can use the book in this focused and practical manner, you will be well and truly on your way to creating a bestseller.

I wish you well and look forward to hearing of your progress.

Kind regards,
Dee Blick

PART ONE

Mainly for Non-Fiction Writers

CHAPTER 1

From Humble Beginnings...

"Your book won't sell because it's too expensive. Who's going to pay £13.99 for it when there are cheaper marketing books for small businesses?"

When I was told this by a businessman I'd been recommended to my heart sank. He sold business books for a living. I'd hoped that after speaking to me he would add my new book to the titles he was already promoting. Here I was with my very first book fresh from the printers and already it had been consigned to the author graveyard by a guy who was seemingly in the know.

So what did I do? Reduce the price of my book? Give up my dream of being a bestselling author? Decide he was right, that I'd been deluded in thinking that my childhood dream of becoming a successful author was possible?

I completely ignored his advice, dusted myself down and decided that when my book did make it into the bestsellers I would recall his grim comments with a grin.

Although shaken by his 'advice', I knew deep down he was wrong and so I could not allow his negativity to have any impact on me beyond the inevitable bruising of my ego.

You may experience something like this. You may well have the odd critic who's only too keen to tell you in no uncertain terms why your book won't sell; that your subject matter has been covered many times before. And what can you possibly bring to the table that's new and exciting anyway?

Ignore your critics. Blaze your trail to bestselling glory.

This is your journey. There's a book inside you which is why you're reading this one. You can spend the precious time you have on this planet being distracted by negative people so that your book never sees the light of day *or you can do what I have always done and believe in yourself wholeheartedly.*

And make sure to start writing.

I've wanted to write this book for some time now but over the past six years most of my spare time has been devoted to writing three small business marketing books. Indeed before writing this book I had to prove to myself that I was an author of integrity; that you could trust my advice on writing and marketing a bestselling book because I had become a bestselling author. And so for the record, I am a genuine Number One bestselling author not simply a clever marketer who has managed to sell enough books to propel me to the top of my category on Amazon only to tumble from this spot a day or so later.

It was only when my three books were more or less permanently in the top five bestsellers in Amazon's small business marketing category and I had a publishing deal in China that I could see how my story and approach to writing and marketing a book could help you if you're aiming for similar success.

As part of my research, I spent some time on Amazon UK evaluating all the titles on how to write a book. I couldn't find anything on how to write a bestselling book and market it on a shoestring budget. This spurred me on. I could see the need for a book in which both subjects were covered in detail by an author you could trust because they had walked the walk for many years.

You see, whilst writing a great book is important, if you want it to reach the bestsellers - and stay there - you'll need to do more work than that.

I've met many fiction and non-fiction authors when speaking at events. Browsing the pages of their books it's clear they have a real talent for writing and yet they're struggling to sell books beyond their circle of family and friends. Their Amazon sales are dismal. They have many five-star reviews but they're not selling books and they're baffled as to the reason why.

Sadly these authors are not marketing their book with a powerful, effective and sustained plan; one that starts from when they make the decision to write and that continues for several months after their book launch. If your goal is to have a bestselling book you have to know how to market your book effectively on a shoestring budget.

And that's what this book is all about.

As you delve further into these pages you'll find out how I have successfully marketed my three books—more often than not on a zero budget. The biggest investment was usually my time. The good news is that you can copy my approach. I realise that I have an unfair advantage over many authors because I've been a marketer since the age of 21, and so whilst marketing my books is second nature to me that might not be the case for you. Unless you have experience, it can be a challenge knowing how to market your book and when to start.

That's why more than half the content is dedicated to what you can do to effectively market your book. I've not stinted on the detail either because I consider that it's easier for an author to write a book than it is to promote it. I realise too that you may not be experienced at writing sales and marketing communications which is why I have included many of the templates I've used to market my books. Use my press releases, book launch invitations, speaker biographies, emails and more to help you when creating yours.

But let's go back for a moment to the beginning of this chapter and the ego-denting advice I was given. It's so important that you cultivate a positive attitude when writing and marketing your book and that you accept the road to achieving bestselling status is not easy. But with some effort you can most definitely achieve it. I know only too well that writing a book can be lonely and frustrating at times. The section you were so looking forward to writing turns out to be a struggle, needing more drafts than you'd planned. The time that you'd earmarked to write a chapter is unexpectedly snatched away because everyday life has to take priority. Or the person who said they'd support you doesn't pitch up when you need them the most.

In real life the plot both on and off the page doesn't always run smoothly. Sometimes you'll find it hard to write your book, let alone market it! You're not alone. Every successful author I've spoken to has faced these challenges but they've managed to overcome them and go on to write a great book. They remind themselves why they're writing and accept that challenges are part of their journey to bestselling success.

But how do you know when your book has become a bestseller?

I was asked this question by one of my readers when I was chatting to him about this book. This is more or less what I told him.

Before the book-selling giant Amazon came on the scene, most self published writers had little hope of claiming they were bestselling authors simply because it was hard to prove they had a bestseller on their hands. How could they measure this unless their book was, for example, a *Sunday Times* bestseller, in WH Smith's top 20 books, or further afield, on the *New York Times* list? It was easier for an author with a publishing deal because their publisher would confirm their bestselling status. (I was told by one publisher that the magical sales figure to reach is 5,000 books).

But now any author with a book on one or more of Amazon's sites can find out in seconds if their book is among the bestsellers. For example, my three marketing books are in Amazon's 'small business marketing books' category. Every hour, Amazon publishes a list of the top 100 bestselling books in each one of the thousands of categories their books are listed under. If my books are in the top 100 in their category, I am by Amazon's definition a bestselling author. If my books are in the top 10 bestselling titles in my category, which they regularly are, so much the better. Of course, you can be a bestselling author for just a few days simply because you encourage friends, family and fans to buy your book within the first week of it launching. But I'm guessing that you want your book to remain in its category's top 100 for many months. Being at the top of your category for a little while is definitely worth celebrating, but if your book sinks into obscurity afterwards you'll find it hard to maintain your credibility if you continue to promote it as a bestseller.

You can also find out on Amazon how your book is selling in relation to the 7 million+ titles they currently promote.

To illustrate this I want you to imagine that you have decided to look up my second book *The Ultimate Small Business Marketing Book* on Amazon. You will be taken to the page that holds all the information about it. At the top of the page you'll find the price of my book followed by the formats it is available in, the trade-in price and book description. There'll be a few adverts followed by the two or three books that are frequently bought together with my book and a section headed: '**Customers who bought this item also bought...**'

Now underneath all of this information (you'll have to scroll down the page) you access the information under the heading 'product details' which tells you in no uncertain terms how my book is faring in the bestselling ranks as follows:

Product details
The Ultimate Small Business Marketing Book
Paperback: 381 pages
Publisher: Filament Publishing (29 Jun 2011)
Language: English
ISBN-10: 1905493770
ISBN-13: 978-1905493777
Product Dimensions: 22.6 x 15.2 x 3 cm
Average Customer Review: 5.0 out of 5 stars
See all reviews (21 customer reviews)
Amazon Bestsellers Rank: 150 in Books (See Top 100 in Books)
#1 in Books > Business, Finance & Law > Small Business &
Entrepreneurship > **Sales & Marketing**

The Amazon Bestsellers Rank shows how my book is ranked compared
to every single book that Amazon sells across the board. You can see for
example that my book reached position 150 out of the 7,000,000+ titles
on their site (this is taken without alteration from my Amazon page
when my book reached that mind-boggling position). There was an awful
lot of celebrating going on that day I can tell you—especially as it stayed
in the top 3,000 of Amazon books across the board for a few years!

The number below this shows you where my book is ranking in the top
100 titles in the category it belongs to. As you can see it was at position
number one. If you were to click on 'Sales & Marketing', which is a link,
you would be taken to the page that shows my book at this position
followed by the other 99 books in that category in descending order (at a
rate of 20 books per page). If you were to also look at the right-hand side
of this page you would be able to see if my book was in the top three of
the 100 most wished for books and the top three of the 100 most gifted
books by clicking on the links on that page. Again you would be able to
see 20 books per page for each one of these categories.

When your book goes live you will be able to access this information in seconds. By the way if your book is not in the top 100 books in its category you will only see your Amazon Bestsellers Rank on your book page which is always shown. Get into the habit of checking your Amazon book page on a daily basis. It becomes addictive charting your book's success; its highs and lows. And when you're asked how your book is selling you can say in no uncertain terms that you are a bestselling author and even provide a screen shot to prove this is the case.

It's important that your book is placed in a category on Amazon and that you complete your author profile using Amazon's Author Central service. I cover this in more detail in chapter 14.

Writing a book that becomes a bestseller for several months or even years is not easy, but I imagine you know this already and are not in the least bit daunted by what lies ahead. I hope you believe in yourself and that you'll commit to marketing your book with no holds barred.

Chapter summary.

- Ignore your doubters and critics. There's a book inside of you!

- Self belief will carry you far. Make sure you tap into it regularly.

- Being a talented author does not on its own guarantee bestseller status.

- You must commit to marketing and to a marketing plan if your book is to become a bestseller.

- Motivate yourself to carry on writing even when the going gets tough and it's the last thing you want to do.

- Make sure your book is placed in the right category so that you can chart its progress on a daily basis.

CHAPTER 2

Why Your Book Needs a Big Idea

Have you procrastinated about writing a book because your subject matter has already been covered by accomplished and established authors? And so you're lacking in confidence, unsure of what you can bring to the table that's new and that will captivate readers.

If these thoughts have played a merry dance in your mind, you're not alone. They were also at the front of mine when I was contemplating writing my first marketing book, aimed at small businesses. A search on Amazon for 'marketing books for small businesses' yielded a whopping 2703 books. And a fair old number of these had been written by successful and respected authors. Once I'd got my head around the fact that I wanted to write a book on a very popular subject, I realised there was still room for me. I was determined to write a decent book that would draw on my decades of marketing experience with small businesses. On that basis alone I realised I could bring something new and valuable to a popular subject.

It really does not matter how many books have been written on your proposed subject. You can still sell thousands of books and take the number one spot from established authors just as I have done.

Here's why:

- Your experience is unique. It deserves to be shared so that readers can benefit from it.

- So is your expertise! Nobody on this planet has your expertise. You may have similar qualifications and training to other authors but your expertise is unique. It gives you different, fresh and new insights to offer readers.

- Your client or contact base differs from other authors covering a similar subject. This gives you additional opportunities to enhance your book with material and case studies that have not been shared in a book before.

- You have a unique writing style. Nobody in this world can write just like you.

- Many of your readers will be interested in buying your book because they have bought others on a similar theme and are keen to learn more. For many, their hunger will not be satisfied with just the one book. Do you buy just one book on a subject that interests you? Or do you explore other books within that genre too? I know from chatting to some of my readers that they don't have just one small business marketing book on their bookshelf. They have several. Many folk will be on the lookout for the next best book on the subject you're going to cover despite having one or indeed a shelf full of others.

Your book is going to bring something special and different to the table because you are passionate about your subject and have a unique author voice.

What's the big idea?

So what's your big idea? What's the central premise your book will hang on?

For me, the big idea for my three marketing books was simple enough. I wanted to share practical, effective marketing tips for small businesses, backed up by case studies with actual templates of work I had created for clients so that my readers could get results from their marketing fast.

Having browsed books online and spent many an afternoon in bookshops, it became clear to me that whilst there were many small business marketing books for sale I couldn't find one that encompassed my big idea. Many were light aeroplane reads—slender paperbacks with lots of gung ho talk but little by way of practical tips and templates. You could read one of these books on a plane or train in a few hours and forget most of the content afterwards. Some were complex books full of charts and diagrams with longwinded explanations on marketing theory. Books that I as a marketer might persevere with, but a small business owner would quickly become disenchanted with.

And so my big idea was to put my decades of marketing experience working with small businesses into a book. I wanted to demystify marketing for small businesses. I wanted to demonstrate that my tips were relevant for small businesses on a shoestring budget because they had been implemented many times before by the hundreds of small businesses I'd worked with over the past 31 years.

So, I would like you to write your big idea down when you've thought it through and are confident about it.

Don't be concerned if you find it hard to write. It may take a little time before all becomes clear! But once the seed has been sown in your mind, and you've mulled it over and written it down, you'll feel more confident about writing your book because you know you're heading in the right direction.

Lack of confidence affects so many authors and it can mean their book never sees the light of day. So I would like you to study the following list and put a tick by everything that applies to you. And please put your modesty to one side. It's time to boost your self-belief and faith in your ability as a writer!

My big idea is a winner because of:

- My expertise.

- My experience.

- My strong desire to share.

- The case studies and examples that will add credibility and interest to my book.

- My qualifications.

- My integrity, credibility and authenticity.

- The training I have had.

- My accreditations.

- My life experiences.

- My vocational experience.

- The results I have achieved with the businesses/individuals that I've worked with.

- My desire to share my knowledge and expertise for the benefit of others.

- My passion to write a book.

- My love of writing.

- My reputation.

- My willingness to learn new skills that will enhance my book.

- My strength of character: I don't give up when the going gets tough.

Hopefully this will make you realise that you are more than ready to write a book.

It's important too that you find a person with whom you can share your book writing journey, someone who will support you and act as a sounding board. My brother Andrew has been my biggest advocate and ally from the first day I spoke to him about my writing dream. I've shared all my big ideas with him and benefited immensely from his support. He's encouraged me to write and has always been there on the sidelines cheering me on. Find your ally and talk to them about your big idea.

When you are happy with your big idea it's time to move to the next stage which is that of summarising the purpose of your book and how your readers will benefit from reading it. Just a few hundred words will give you that extra vote of confidence that you can now move on to the next stage. As a guide here's what I wrote for my third book.

"I will empower, inspire and motivate readers by showing them in a series of easy to understand, easy to implement marketing masterclasses how to successfully bring marketing into the heart of their business so that sales increase, marketing mistakes reduce, they know what it takes to build or reinforce the foundations of a customer-driven brand and are able to do so on the smallest of marketing budgets. I am aware that some marketing books deliver what is best described as an aeroplane read - easy and enjoyable for the journey but lightweight on substance and bereft of examples and case studies; largely because the author does not have the experience as a businessperson to bring this pivotal dimension to their book.

In my book each masterclass will be presented with more than enough information on the subject under scrutiny to enable them to take action immediately. Based on the feedback from my current readers I know that a powerful combination of genuine small business case studies, real-life examples and practical tips underpinned by my 28 years experience as a marketer will really appeal to potential buyers."

The clearer you are about why you want to write a book and how your readers will benefit from it the better. Clarity of purpose is vital for any author. It saves so much time further down the line so don't move to the next stage until you have really thought through - and written down - your big idea and the purpose of your book.

Chapter summary.

- Don't be concerned that what you're planning on writing about has been written about many times before. It does not matter! There are thousands of books on how to write a book but you're reading mine right now!

- Remind yourself that you are bringing a unique perspective to your book; one that readers will appreciate.

- People usually buy more than one book on a subject that interests, inspires, educates, entertains and captivates them.

- Spend some time thinking about your big idea then write it down and refine it further until you're completely happy with it.

- Your big idea has success written all over it not least because of your integrity and passion for writing, your desire to share and your life experiences.

- Don't undersell yourself and what you are bringing to your book by way of your experience, expertise and passion to share.

- Find an ally you can share your big idea with plus the highs and lows of your writing journey.

- Once you've put your big idea to bed move on to summarising the purpose of your book.

CHAPTER 3

How to Plan the Content

Your big idea has taken shape. You're clear about the purpose of your book and you're pretty confident that you have a lot to offer to your readers.

What's next?

Should you head straight into writing chapters? No. Not yet. I can understand why you'd think this is the next logical step but, believe me, it isn't.

Instead I'd like you to do what I do for each one of my books and spend some time gathering the content that's going to shape your book into a bestseller. This means expanding further on your big idea. For example you could think about the case studies and all of the material that's going to give your book substance, depth and gravitas; material that will make it a compelling and captivating read. If you skip this crucial stage and head straight into writing chapters, you'll shortchange your book and your readers. Inspiration is fantastic and you need bags of it as an author but you need a solid platform on which to base your book and this can only come from planning your content.

At the content gathering stage you start thinking in detail about your book and exploring the options without putting the brakes on your thoughts and your ideas. Your best ideas are formulated when you're in this creative mode. You'll have days where ideas come thick and fast simply because you're allowing your mind to wander before capturing them on paper (which is crucial). At other times a conversation about your book will inspire a whole new chapter or a section you'd not considered until that very moment. Now you can't imagine your book without this new material or additional chapter.

There are other reasons why you shouldn't skip this process. This is the planning stage of your book and most successful books are the result of thorough and painstaking planning, stemming from one simple but well thought out big idea.

Gather your content.

I spent several weeks gathering the content for this book as follows:

1. I researched half a dozen books on this subject and made a note of the tips I thought were really helpful and that I should include. This included tips I wouldn't have thought about including even though I had more than enough experience to cover them. Sometimes you have to be inspired by other authors and, in my case, bloggers too, to dig deep into your experience and bring it to your book.

2. Over several weeks I wrote copious notes on the content I wanted to include with the reasons why I believed that established and budding authors would benefit from it.

3. I began to think about my guest contributors and the role they would each play in my book. I drafted their questions and then refined them as my thinking became clearer. You'll meet these special folk further on.

4. I sketched out the rough titles for my chapters, knowing I would change them further on but I needed a starting point.

5. I gathered the marketing articles, blogs, emails and tips I'd written in the last few years to promote my books. This was material I was keen to share in the marketing section.

6. I revisited the notes I had written for my previous books and extracted sections I thought my readers would benefit from in this book.

7. I gathered the communications I'd written to promote all of my books. For example, press releases promoting each book and invitations to my book launch. Some of these communications inspired me to include additional chapters, chapter 17 being an example.

How did I store this information so it was easy for me to access when I began the process of allocating it to the right chapters? I did what I've done with all my books. I bought a good quality pad with dividers and deep pockets for storing documents. I gained a real sense of satisfaction as the pad got thicker and the pages began to fill with my ideas. I could see real progress being made and this spurred me on. I would encourage you to do the same too so you can write your ideas down as and when they arise.

My friend Brad Burton who shares his tips in chapter 19 also dictates ideas into his iPhone when inspiration strikes on his travels so you may want to consider this too. Committing your ideas to paper eases you into the creative process of writing and the more you write the more those amazing ideas will tumble onto the page. Great ideas don't usually emerge the moment you pick up your pen so be patient and you will be rewarded.

How much time should I spend gathering my content?

You can spend so long on the content gathering stage of your book that when you've reached the end you've lost the will to write it.

Be disciplined.

Set a date by which you'll have completed this process. I can't tell you exactly how long it should take but, unless you firmly believe it needs to take longer, limit content gathering to three months. Make sure you get into the habit of capturing your ideas regularly during this time.

You can fall into the trap of thinking that you have to cover every single facet of your subject matter for your book to be perfect. Firstly, I would imagine it's nigh on impossible for you to do this. And secondly, even if you could cover everything there is to know about your subject matter, your book would resemble an encyclopaedia. Many readers would find a book that size disheartening.

You can write a bestselling book that's cherished and valued by your readers without giving them the complete A-Z of your subject matter.

What should I include in my book?

These questions will help you decide.

1. What is the content that I must share with my readers? Why?

2. What content can I include that's not essential but will add value to my core content? (You may want to include case studies and tips that will reinforce key points and make your book more enjoyable and easy to understand).

3. Would guest contributors enhance my book and if so what do I want them to share and why?

4. What am I not going to include in my book because it's outside of my skills, experience and expertise or because it's just not needed? I have more than enough great content anyway.

I find this stage of the book writing journey exciting and challenging. My third book, *The 15 Essential Marketing Masterclasses For Your Small Business*, started life at the planning stage as *The 20 Essential Marketing Masterclasses For Your Small Business*. While I was gathering the content in my ideas book I realised that it didn't need these five extra masterclasses and that by removing them I could share my marketing expertise in more detail on the 15 that had escaped the cull. Had I stuck with 20 marketing masterclasses I would have spread myself too thinly. Make sure you don't fall into this trap. Instead of one enormous first book there could be a second book in you - a sequel to the one you're planning on writing now.

By the way don't worry if you haven't decided on the title of your book at this stage. It usually takes at least three or four completed chapters before I start playing around with the title of my book, the only exception being when I was offered a publishing deal and had to offer up a title with my author submission. If you don't have such pressures, take your time and use my tips in chapter nine.

At this stage you must also be thinking about your readers; the people who are going to buy your book, love it, review it and recommend it. You are writing this book for them and I'm sure you'll have a good idea about who they are. You have to get inside their minds and look at your book through their eyes.

Chapter summary.

- Look upon the content gathering process as an enjoyable and important exercise.

- Invest in a lovely writing pad with plenty of pockets and dividers for adding copies of the documents and extracts that you want to include in your book.

- Allow your mind to wander and be prepared to capture ideas when they strike. A brilliant idea could occur when shopping so ensure you can jot it down.

- Think about the research you're going to do before you start writing your chapters.

- Dig into your personal and professional archives to locate the valuable resources that will make your book even more special and different.

- Think about the content you must share with your readers; the content that's not essential but will make your book even better and the content you don't have to include.

- Set a deadline for gathering the bulk of the content for your book.

- If you already have a title for your book, that's great. But don't worry if you haven't.

CHAPTER 4

Find Your Readers and Meet Their Needs!

If you want to reach the bestsellers and stay there you have to identify all the different groups of readers and understand why they're going to buy your book. Despite the importance of this, many authors struggle to provide a clear description of their readers because they've not given that much thought to them. That's often because they've become caught up in the romance of writing.

I don't just want to help you write a book, I want to help you write a bestselling one. And this entails identifying and getting under the skin of your potential readers because they're going to buy your book in their thousands. When you know who your readers are you can write inspiring content that captivates and entertains them—whatever your subject matter. And when you reach the marketing stage, you know exactly who you're going to target with your marketing on a shoestring plan - the very same people you were writing your book for in the first place.

To help you build a detailed picture of your readers here's what I submitted to Wiley, my publishers for *The 15 Essential Marketing Masterclasses For Your Small Business*. This was my response to the question in their author brief: 'Who will your book in the main be read by?'

This book will in the main be read by:

- People thinking of starting a business. They will buy it because it will be a jargon-free easy read packed with practical tips, case studies and examples. They can market their business successfully from the outset, avoiding costly mistakes.

- Existing small business owners at different stages of growth and success; in B2B and B2C. They will buy it because they know that, in the current economy especially, they have to be marketing savvy. They want an easy to digest book with real substance that they can identify with. My book will give them this in spades. Owners of businesses that are struggling to grow will buy it because it will provide a route map to marketing success, providing solutions to many of the marketing challenges they are currently facing. Successful small business owners will buy it to reinforce and improve their current marketing initiatives and lay the foundations for their future plans.

- Less experienced marketers employed by a business will buy it in the first instance because of my pedigree as an author, my marketing qualifications and trusted connections with The Chartered Institute of Marketing. With marketing budgets being cut, more is expected from junior marketers and whilst many of the academic-oriented marketing books play a part in achieving their qualifications, they lack the practical application, real-world small business case studies and easy-to-implement tips that my books are now renowned for.

- Business students will buy it because of my reputation as an author and the fact that in my experience (from working with Brighton University where my second book is on the syllabus for business and marketing students) course tutors are looking for integrity driven practical marketing books to balance out the usual fare of academic marketing content.

- My readers will be primarily small business owners. Geographically they can be based anywhere in the world because the tips and principles I am sharing have a universal application. Size wise, I anticipate they will range from start-up through to £8,000,000.

- Some of these business owners will have their own in-house marketer and they will give this book to them and ask them to study it. The other business owners will read it themselves.

- Some of my readers will be associated with The Chartered Institute of Marketing. They will comprise students, top-flight marketers reading out of interest and marketers pursuing professional qualifications. This will be on a worldwide basis.

- Business studies students in universities and colleges. Marketing will be either a dominant or small part of their studies. This will be on a worldwide basis.

It's your turn now!

Using my example as a guide and going into the same level of detail, have a go at answering the question *"Who will my book in the main be read by?"*

Go back to your ideas book to record your thoughts and answers so that you can keep on adding to them and refining them as your ideas take shape and your understanding of your readers grows. And don't herd your readers into one big group if, as in my example, it's clear you have different groups. Whilst they will be united in their enjoyment of your book and the appeal of its title, their needs, namely what they're looking to get from your book, could vary.

For example I was pretty certain that marketing students would use my book to assist with their marketing projects and that my content would give them a practical understanding of marketing. By contrast small business owners would use my book to plan their marketing campaigns on a small budget and would be more interested in how they could get results from my tips. They would be less interested in the science behind marketing campaigns.

If you take this book as an example, some of my readers will have already written a book and will therefore buy this one to help them to promote it, whereas other readers will be thinking of writing a book and will be more interested in the tips on how to get started. When you start marketing your book you'll find it easier to reach your different groups of readers and to motivate them to respond if you have segmented them into groups from the outset and are clear on how your book can help meet their different needs and expectations.

It took me three hours to answer that question! Be as disciplined as I was. This exercise will make it easier still to be even more critical about the content that is going to make it into your book and the content that will be left on the cutting room floor.

You have moved yet another step closer to writing a bestseller.

Chapter summary.

- The author of a bestseller is one who's written their book while holding their different groups of readers at the front of their mind.

- One of the benefits of understanding your different groups of readers is that you can then market to them. You've found the needles in the haystack!

- Answer the question: 'Who will my book in the main be read by?' Use your ideas book to record your responses.

- Don't herd your readers into one big group if in fact you have several different groups.

- Consider all the reasons why each group of readers will buy your book. What needs will your book satisfy?

CHAPTER 5

19 Tips to Motivate You *and* Keep You Writing

There's something magical and daunting when your planning is complete and it's time to start writing your book. This can often be the stage when your good work falters. Whilst you may not find it hard to start writing you could struggle to keep writing on a regular basis. Somehow you have to maintain your enthusiasm and motivation come rain or shine and this isn't always easy. Life can get in the way of writing especially if you hit a sticky patch and have to go back to the drawing board and rethink a section or, worse still, rewrite an entire chapter (this has happened to me on a few occasions).

So don't underestimate the importance of devising several strategies to keep you on track and writing, even when you would much rather be doing something else! I've had days when the last thing I've wanted to do is write but I know that I can't afford to let this sort of thinking take over. So here's what keeps me motivated to write from the first word to the last proof. There should be something in here for you too.

How to write your way from first word to last proof.

1. I block out time in my diary—usually a minimum of two hours (I often write for six hours with just the odd break if I'm honest). It's important I establish a writing routine that I can commit to for several months. Sometimes if the words are flowing I'll write for an entire day and evening with small breaks to recharge my batteries.

2. Before I start writing a new chapter I look at my ideas book and revisit its structure and summary. This helps me focus my mind on the task in hand. If I'm half way through writing a chapter I reread

what I've written so far so I can get my bearings and ensure it all makes sense.

3. I imagine my readers and how my books are going to help them grow their business and, in the case of this book, realise their dream of becoming a successful published author. This is what motivates me most of all; it's what keeps me writing, editing and refining a book.

4. I visualise what my book will look like when it's published and, in my mind at least, its position in the Amazon charts is always number one! This keeps me going when I am finding a chapter challenging to write or when I'm feeling sorry for myself because the sun is shining and I am writing without a break in sight.

5. I set a target for the number of words I will write in a session. This can range from 500 words if I'm tackling a challenging section to 2000 words or more. This is not pristine final copy because I will edit it several times before it goes to my editor for the final prune and polish.

6. I find a quiet environment where I will not be interrupted. This includes the guest bedroom, our bedroom and my favourite venue, the log cabin in our garden. I can't write in a noisy and distracting environment.

7. I ensure my mobile is switched off and unless it's an emergency, my family knows not to interrupt me. If they're bringing nice refreshments however... Cups of tea and mineral water are my fuel.

8. I don't always write my chapters in a logical order. Sometimes I will write the chapters I feel the most confident about. This motivates me in the early days when getting into my stride is so important. This is another reason why I am always relieved that

I took the time to summarise each one of my chapters and plan their structure.

9. I write even when I am not happy with the standard of my writing knowing I can return to a page, a paragraph or chapter and improve it later on. It's more important I get into my flow which is why I'm not too critical of my early efforts.

10. I ensure that after a writing session there's a reward in store. Treats include a walk with my husband, a coffee in town, catching up with friends, lounging in front of the television and reading a magazine. I am easy to satisfy!

11. I write at any time of the day or night. Sometimes I'm awake at dawn and raring to go. At other times, it's not possible to have an early start because I'm working so I will schedule an afternoon or evening writing session.

12. I will leave some parts of a chapter incomplete if they are particularly challenging or I'm waiting on some information. I make a note that I have to return to it at a later stage. By putting it to one side for the time being I don't lose momentum.

13. I ignore the ubiquitous writer's block. If I'm struggling to make headway with a chapter I will take a short break. A 10-minute walk, feeding our hens or catching up with what's happening in our business usually does the trick.

14. I share my progress on Twitter with my followers and am always heartened by their responses and questions.

15. Every week I set goals for the chapters I aim to write or edit and my To Do list is updated almost daily. I thrive on ticking off each goal and task as I accomplish them.

16. I write with a number of important dates at the front of my mind. For example the date I will pass the book to my editor; the date I will have the cover designed and approved; the launch date for Amazon; the date of my book launch. These dates motivate me to continue at the right pace.

17. I am my own best friend and so at the end of a writing session I will praise myself and reflect on what I have achieved.

18. I am a hard taskmaster. If I'm procrastinating or making excuses for not writing I will pull myself up short and re-establish my routine.

19. I remind myself why I am going to such extraordinary lengths when I see other authors producing their books in weeks. I'm aiming for the number one spot in my category and, most importantly of all, I don't want to disappoint my readers by producing a flimsy and lightweight book.

Accept that sometimes you will struggle to make any progress during a writing session. Some sessions won't turn out as you had planned. But if you can settle into a routine and chart your progress regularly, remembering to build in those little treats and to push yourself to even greater levels, you'll make amazing progress. And you won't run out of steam or enthusiasm.

Chapter summary.

- The life of an author is rarely smooth. You will encounter bumps in the road. Accept this and the fact that you will often have to motivate yourself to write.

- Find the strategies that will encourage you to write and put them to good use so they become habitual.

- Don't underestimate the importance of rewarding yourself with little treats.

- Commit to writing on a regular basis and block out writing and editing time in your diary.

- Find the perfect environment that will help you write without the risk of distractions.

- You may not have to write your chapters in a logical order.

- Your first few drafts of writing can be perfectly imperfect. It's more important to get into your flow.

- Setting goals helps keep you on track with your writing as does establishing important dates such as your book launch.

- Don't be despondent when you hit a sticky patch. Every successful author has their bleak and frustrating moments but they come out of them.

CHAPTER 6

How to Write Fantastic, Flowing and Easy-to-Read Chapters

Before you start writing your chapters in earnest it pays to consider and evaluate your style of writing. I say this because your book could miss the bestsellers not because your content was poor, but because it was hard to read.

By way of example I was recently approached by an author of a business book. He had spent a significant sum of money on having the book professionally presented. The title of each chapter was intriguing and well thought out. Had I been in need of his advice, I may well have bought his book based on the chapter headings alone. But his style of writing erred on the side of formal and corporate and there was too much unnecessary jargon. Had someone pointed him in the right direction, encouraging him to write in a more conversational tone and stripping out the jargon, I reckon that with a good marketing plan his book would have made the bestsellers. As it was, he was not selling any books on Amazon or in any bookshops.

When I was approached by Wiley for my third book, the commissioning editor told me that one of the reasons why I was being offered the deal was my friendly and conversational style of writing. Although I have always written like this, I am aided and abetted further still because I use Dragon Speech Recognition Software. It has a 'read back' facility which means my text can be played back to me. This helps me to identify and change sentences and paragraphs that sound stiff and formal. If your style is friendly, open and welcoming your book will be easy to read and you'll gain many fans because this is what most readers nowadays are looking for. They want a clear message that's engaging and easy to absorb. They don't want to have to concentrate so hard on understanding your book that reading it becomes hard work.

But how do you know if your writing style is friendly or formal?

Here's how you can put it to the test. Write a sample page for one of your chapters and when you've finished read it out loud. What does it sound like? Does it flow or falter? Is it easy to listen to or not? Are you planning on using complex phrases when a simpler description would suffice? Is the page full of references to 'you' and 'your', so your reader gets the sense they are having a private conversation with you? Or are you writing in a more formal manner?

Pass this sample page to a person you trust, ideally a target reader. Do they find it appealing and easy to read? Is your message clear and concise or complex and longwinded?

Don't be concerned if you realise there's room for improvement. It's better to identify your weaknesses before you start writing your chapters than it is to make radical changes to your style halfway through. For this reason I would advise you to get into the habit of reading your chapters out loud and evaluating each one along the following lines long before sending the manuscript to your editor.

Ask yourself:

- Is it free from unnecessary jargon?

- Is it full of 'you' and 'your'?

- Does it read as though I'm having a friendly informative conversation with each reader?

- Are my sentences and paragraphs easy to follow and easy to understand?

- Am I guilty of being inconsistent? Are some of my pages friendly and accessible while others are less so?

When a reader is browsing your book using the 'look inside' facility on Amazon for example, if it's clear in seconds that your style is easy on the eye they're more likely to buy it than if it's high on jargon and longwinded prose. So work on developing your friendly and welcoming style. It's inside of you. It's simply a matter of developing it.

What journey are you taking your readers on?

Having given some thought to your writing style it's time now to think about the journey that you are going to take your readers on. Most good books take their readers on an enjoyable journey. What's more the reader understands what they're getting at each stage of the book.

Perhaps your readers will have to read your book in chronological order to benefit from your message. Or is your book going to be a 'dip in and dip out' book that gives readers the option of reading it from cover to cover or selecting the chapters that appeal to them at that point in time? This format is very popular with business books and self help titles. My previous three books have been written in this way. For example with my third book, I created a series of masterclasses, presenting them in a modular format so that a reader could select the ones they needed without having to revert to any of the others for guidance.

Think about how you want your readers to read your book because this is going to influence how you write your chapters and the content of each one.

From general ideas to specific chapters.

It's now time to revisit your ideas book. You have gathered some amazing content and have many great ideas. You're confident of your writing style and you've thought through your reader's journey with your book. You now have to decide where the content you've gathered so painstakingly will be given a home - the chapters it will be allocated to.

This task will most likely take several hours over many sessions but I find it an enjoyable part of the process. It reminds me of when I was a child and my Dad bought me a really complex jigsaw. I was elated when the last piece was in place and this is how I feel after this exercise. I start a new section in my ideas book allocating several pages to each chapter and then I make a list of what is going into that chapter and what still needs to be added so I don't miss anything out.

Once you have completed this exercise it will really help you to review all of your planned chapters. Spend a little time summarising each chapter in your book; paint a picture of what it will cover. This can be a few lines or a few paragraphs. By doing this you can identify in seconds the chapters that are ready to write, the weaker ones that are in need of a little more planning, and perhaps some additional content you need to gather before you start writing.

To guide you here are four chapter summaries for *The 15 Essential Marketing Masterclasses For Your Small Business.*

1. **50 award winning copywriting tips.** I will share my very best tips which can be applied in all scenarios (online and off-line) and for all businesses. I will also share useful copywriting tools: AIDCA and COB. I will show readers how simple structures and techniques are at the heart of writing winning copy as opposed to the commonly held myth that you have to be a top-flight copywriter to get responses. I will share top tips on how to write letters and reproduce five extremely successful long, medium and short sales letters, taking them apart and explaining to the readers why they work and how they can emulate these techniques.

2. **How to write adverts that sell.** I will share top tips on how to write many different types of adverts (advertorial, selling off the page, two-stage adverts) and will include examples of adverts I have written that have won awards for generating the highest reader responses. This will include the overriding power of the special offer. I will share the relevance and importance of making offers; where they work best; timing; when not to and offers I have developed for clients that have worked extremely well. I will show the reader how they should present their offer so it enhances their brand.

3. **PR on a shoestring.** I will show readers the many different PR channels for promoting themselves and their business; how these channels can work independently and how they can work together. Most small businesses think of PR as gaining coverage in the nationals. They may think this is too much of a hill to climb, so they don't get started. Or they make a spectacularly inappropriate approach to a national editor which either gets the wrong coverage or none at all. I will take the reader through how to write news and press releases with contrasting poor examples, how to approach and communicate with journalists and editors; and the winning approach to get journalists to your exhibition stand. I will enlist the support of award winning PR guru Aneela Rose.

4. **Customer service.** How to convert a customer from a one-time purchaser into a raving fan and advocate. This will include sharing tips on customer service systems, teaching the Plus1 model I use when training clients, and the relationship versus transactional approach. It will also encompass the most common customer service mistakes made by businesses both large and small and how to avoid them.

You may be wondering why I am recommending you go to such lengths before unleashing your pen and embarking on writing your chapters.

The last thing you want is to start writing a chapter only to realise halfway through that you don't really have that much to say. You may end up having to abandon it because the content is weak or you may have to down tools and do some more research. What you don't want to do is to write a weak chapter and stick with it even though you know this is a bad move. Your readers deserve the same high levels of consistency throughout your book: each chapter should be as good, detailed and well-written as the previous one.

It's worth bearing in mind too that your readers will have their favourite chapters. Some will buy your book on the strength of the anticipated content in one chapter alone. I see this time and time again in some of my Amazon reviews when a reader describes the chapters that have really helped them. I'm always relieved when reading these reviews that I've spent an equal amount of time on planning each chapter and working through this final stage. What you don't want to see in those Amazon reviews are readers praising some chapters but criticising others because your heart was not in them and as a result they were poorly planned or they lacked in depth and meaning.

I'm often asked how long it takes before I am happy with the chapters I've written and at what stage I pass my book to my editor. So here's my process for writing chapters after I've completed my chapter planning and written the chapter summaries. It may seem longwinded but a bestselling book takes more than a couple of drafts and a quick edit. So if you were thinking you could get away with one draft of a chapter followed by some corrections this should persuade you to change your mind!

My 11 step approach to writing chapters.

1. I write each chapter by hand in ink on a lovely spiral bound pad with good quality paper (I use the Black n' Red pads or Pukka pads because the paper is super smooth). I have very peculiar shorthand which works for me but to anyone else it would make no sense at all.

2. I read through each handwritten chapter red pen in hand, crossing out words and highlighting the text that requires further explanation or that in the cold light of this review makes no sense at all. I regularly run out of red pens...

3. I dictate each chapter onto my laptop paying little attention to any of the small errors that creep in while I'm dictating. At this stage I am hell-bent on getting the chapter into print albeit in a rough and ready format.

4. I read each chapter at least four times on screen, making changes to it and correcting any mistakes.

5. I print each chapter off, re-read it, make edits and correct any punctuation and spelling mistakes. It's not possible for the human eye to pick up every error from a computer screen. I rephrase paragraphs and sentences and make a note of any points in need of further clarification. It's amazing the number of errors that I pick up on paper and yet I didn't spot them on screen.

6. I use the 'read back' facility on my speech recognition software so I can listen to the chapters. This is important because I want to ensure my style is friendly and clear throughout the book. I make more changes to the chapters after this exercise.

7. I read my chapters on screen again over several sessions looking for further mistakes and making more corrections. Even at this stage I might decide to merge a few chapters together or to add a whole new section to a chapter.

8. I print the chapters off yet again. At this stage I am looking for punctuation errors and not so obvious spelling mistakes. Whilst I try and ensure my headings and subheadings are consistent, there are no extra spaces between words, and bullet points and

numbered points are in a uniform format, I know that this is my weakness and it's what I rely on my editor to sort out!

9. I hand the book to my editor knowing my job is far from over. Within weeks I will be discussing further changes before it can be sent to my publisher.

10. I receive my editor's comments and corrections and after discussing these changes I work on the final draft of my book.

11. I read the entire book for the last time and then, happy but weary, I send it to my publisher.

I have to confess that being something of a free spirit, or to be more precise a writer who just likes to get on with writing (and to heck with the planning), that it took some time for me to realise the importance of following the detailed process I've shared in this chapter. My first book did not follow it and as a result it's nowhere near as good as my subsequent books. I hope therefore that I have encouraged you to follow this approach too. Your book will be all the better for it. You will stand head and shoulders above authors of similar books who have allowed their free spirit to have a field day at the expense of proper planning.

Chapter summary.

- Practice does make perfect! Make sure your style is flowing, friendly and welcoming. Readers don't want to wade through your book or find it a chore to read.

- Put your writing style to the test by writing a sample page, reading it out loud and then passing it to your ally for honest feedback.

- Think about the journey you're taking your readers on because this will influence the way you present and write your chapters.

- Allocate the ideas from your ideas book to their relevant chapters.

- Summarise each one of the chapters you are going to write. You don't have to go beyond writing one paragraph per chapter. Which chapters look the strongest and which ones are in need of more work?

- Be heartened by your preparatory work. Your readers will hold you in esteem for producing a book where each chapter was written to the same high standard.

- Establish a thorough process for writing, reviewing and critiquing each chapter. Don't be tempted to write a chapter and leave it at that bar a few hasty edits!

PART TWO

For Fiction and Non-Fiction Writers

CHAPTER 7

The Additional Pages
that Complete Your Book

You may think your writing days are behind you when you finish your chapters. But there are still a few more pages to write and they are important because they can increase your sales.

Adding the additional pages I suggest in this chapter will enhance the look and feel of your book, making it even more attractive to your readers. For example perceived wisdom is that the first page of your book should be the title page, but I'd like to suggest that this could be a missed opportunity. When people pick up your book and look inside it you have to work hard to convince them to buy it. The first few pages they flick through should act as an incentive; a real push to persuade them to part with their cash. And that's why you should consider the following before your title page:

- 'This book is for you if...'

- One or two pages of third-party reviews and testimonials.

Then, after these pages have worked their magic, you can have your title page. Backing on to this is the publisher's imprint page which contains:

The publisher's logo.

The publisher's registered address and contact details.

The ISBN of the book.

The © symbol, the author's name and the year of publication.

The paragraph: 'The right of the author to be identified as the author of this work has been asserted in accordance with the Copyright, Designs and Patents Act 1988.'

An 'All rights reserved' statement covering the protection of the book by international copyright.

A Limit of Liability/Disclaimer of Warranty statement.

The name of the printers.

The facing right-hand page after the imprint page is your dedication. This is followed by the table of contents on another right-hand page. Bear in mind that people will seek out this page as part of their evaluation of your book prior to purchase. Instead of just making it a list of your chapter headings, you can add a sentence or two (or more) about what each chapter contains just as I have done with this book.

Then there are a series of other pages that appear before your first chapter, each one on a right-hand page. These are:

- **About the author.**

- **The Foreword.** Please note the spelling—it's often misspelt!

- **An introduction** from the author.

Finally, at the back of your book consider adding:

- A conclusion page at the end of the last chapter.

- Details about other contributors.

- An acknowledgements page - the last page of your book unless you are having your book indexed in which case your index will round it off.

Before looking at these pages in more detail I want to share some useful advice from Suzanne Dibble, an award winning lawyer who knows her stuff on copyright.

Copyright for authors.

There are a number of "legal' things you need to think about when you're writing a book. The first that might spring to mind is 'how do I protect my content?'

That part is fairly easy.

If you have created an original work (i.e. you haven't copied it from anywhere), then in most jurisdictions you will automatically own the copyright.

All you really need to do is add the © symbol to your book, pop the year and your name next to it and you have asserted your copyright.

That effectively means that you can do what you want with your copyrighted content and if any third party infringes that right by for example reproducing some or all of it without your consent, you can sue them.

In some jurisdictions it may be sensible to use the services of a copyright registration agency in order to secure evidence of your original work, but generally this is not necessary.

The legal matters that are a little more complicated and take some time looking into are your use of images, quotes, extracts and any other content where the copyright in that content is owned by someone other than you.

If you are using images created by somebody else, then you need to be sure that either the image has been properly assigned to you or you are properly licensed to use it. If it is a stock photo, then be sure to read the terms of the license very carefully to ensure that the license permits you to include the image in a book for publication.

If you don't have the legal right to use the image, you could be sued for copyright infringement, which would not be a good start to your writing career....

If you want to include a quote or an extract of a copyrighted work for the purpose of review or criticism, then there will probably be specific 'fair use' or 'fair dealing' rules in your jurisdiction.

In the UK, our fair dealing rules, in summary, say that review or criticism is allowed as long as a sufficient acknowledgement is provided. That means identifying the copyright work by its title or other description and the author.

It can be a little more complicated than this with fair dealing so to be on the safe side, either get permission from the author (who will probably be delighted you are showing such an interest in his or her book) or consult a copyright expert.

Suzanne has produced a copyright factsheet which you can access at www.suzannedibble.com/copyrightprotection.

Now let's look at these additional pages in more detail.

'This book is for you if...'

My publisher Chris Day encouraged me to include this so that from the very first page I'm greeting the reader. It is a fantastic marketing tool. At book signings people flicking through your book may well be motivated to buy it on the strength of what you have to say on this page alone.

Here is the page from my second book:

This book is for you if...

1. You want to generate sales and plenty of them from your marketing.

2. You want to reduce the amount of money you're spending (or wasting) on marketing.

3. You want to unearth a treasure trove of powerful, effective and proven 'insider' marketing tips and techniques.

4. You want to reduce your marketing mistakes and increase your marketing successes.

5. You want access to page after page of easy to absorb, expert marketing commonsense, not textbook theory.

6. You want to learn and be inspired by real business case studies.

7. You don't have all the money in the world to spend on marketing but you are willing to invest some time.

8. You've read marketing books before that have either baffled you or left you unimpressed.

9.   You want to grow your business consistently through delighting your customers and turning them into raving fans.

10. You just don't 'get' marketing. You need to be convinced as to its real value in growing your business.

I've also included a 'this book is for you if...' page with this book which is naturally different in content to the one above, although it's similar in its layout and style. Add one to your book even if you're writing fiction. Instead of a series of numbered points which may look out of place in a fiction book, you could write a paragraph of text instead.

Testimonials.

In Chapter 10 I discuss the subject of your book cover and why testimonials on the front and back covers can boost sales. But I'm aware that some authors like to include testimonials within their book too. A word of warning: pages of eulogies about you and your book is overkill and it can backfire as it gives the impression that you've got an inflated ego. So, if you'd like to include them within your book, have one page of genuine and powerful testimonials, two at an absolute push.
Steer away from gushing testimonials along the lines of: *"Joe is a wonderful person. I love his books and this is no exception, blah blah blah."* They say nothing of value. Be ruthless too. If two testimonials are similar, pick the one you think your readers will most enjoy reading. If you're aiming for testimonials from influential folk to add more gravitas to your book, approach them and explain how much it would mean if they could endorse your book in this way. If they're happy to help, give them a few edited chapters and your list of proposed chapters. They don't have to read your entire book to provide a positive testimonial and it could be worth its weight in gold given their reputation. I've been asked to endorse books in this way.

Your dedication.

It's rare indeed to find a book that doesn't include a dedication. There's something poignant and special about dedicating your book to a person who has inspired or helped you. You may want to make your dedication a short one, simply sharing the name of the person or people with a few extra words or, you may want to write something a little more substantial.

About the author.

This is your mini biography, an opportunity to share your experience and your credentials on the subject matter of your book. It answers a typical reader question: "Can you tell me about yourself?" Many of the people considering buying your book won't have heard about you before discovering you online or in a bookshop. It makes sense therefore to share some interesting things about you that will encourage them to buy your book. But don't go overboard on this. Readers don't want to wade through several pages of your accomplishments and expertise. I was advised by my publisher, Wiley, not to exceed 175 words.

To help you create your page, look at the page in this book.

Accompany your mini-biography with an image of you smiling to reinforce further still that you are a warm and friendly person.

The foreword.

Your foreword adds another layer to the perception of you as a credible author. It should be written by a person of standing who can praise you and your book, and shed light on your credentials. Look upon it as the text that sets the scene.

For my third book, I asked Andy Fernandez, Manager of The Chartered Institute of Marketing bookshop, to write my foreword. There was a connection between me as a CIM Fellow and an author of marketing books promoted by CIM and Andy who manages the organisation's bookshop.

Your foreword underpins your author credentials and sheds further light on the subject matter of your book. Think carefully about who you are going to ask so they can do it justice. I asked Jeff Scott to write the foreword for this book. Jeff is a renowned and respected PR guru and also a successful author who specialises in helping well-known and new authors secure PR coverage for their books. I worked with Jeff when I was writing my third book and during this time he got to know me as a marketer and an author.

Introduction.

This is a personal message from you. It gives you the opportunity to share with your readers:

- **Why you have written your book.** Hopefully to address your readers' deep underlying needs and bring a fresh and insightful perspective on the subject matter.

- **How you have written your book.** You can explain the structure and layout; why you've included any special sections and images and any reader tasks.

- **What you hope your audience will gain from reading your book.**

If you need some inspiration in creating your introduction, look at the one in this book. Your introduction is an important communication so spend a few hours planning what you want to say before writing it. It took me three hours and three drafts before I was happy with mine.

The conclusion.

I made a mistake with my first book (one of several if truth be told). Instead of ending it with a nice, upbeat message for my readers, a conclusion page, they were greeted instead with a few blank pages sandwiched between the last chapter and the back cover. It appeared as though I had abruptly ended my book (unwittingly I had). Don't miss out on creating your conclusion page. Make it positive and upbeat and if your readers can take advantage of additional resources on your website, or anywhere else for that matter, which will enhance their enjoyment of your book tell them. Again use the conclusion in this book to help you create yours.

You may also want to signpost your readers to any additional free resources on your website in your conclusion and, if you have not done so elsewhere, provide your contact details. You want as many of your readers as possible to get in touch.

About your contributors.

Including expert contributors could bring another valuable dimension to your book. The likelihood is that if you're planning on featuring experts the ones you have in mind will be busy and in demand. If this is your first book, they may need persuading to take time out of their schedule to write for you. Make it worthwhile for them to contribute by including a section in which you single them out for thanks and promotion just as I have done in this book. You'll also find your experts keener to promote your book to their contacts if they are given this star billing.

Acknowledgements.

Your acknowledgements page gives you the opportunity to thank the people who have helped you write your book. It's usually located at the back of the book, after your conclusion. I'll wager most of your readers will read it so make it interesting and be generous in your praise. How long should it be? I've read books where it comprised page after page of tributes. Aim for 600-800 words and you'll maintain your reader's interest and should still be able to thank everyone. Cut the waffle!

I hope you've found these tips useful and can see how your book will be enhanced with some or all of these additional pages. I've always found them a breath of fresh air to write after the much tougher task of writing chapters.

Chapter summary.

- Writing these extra pages won't take too much time. They will complete your book and you'll be paid back with increased book sales.

- A This book is for you page delivers a really powerful message to potential readers, one that on its own could encourage them to buy your book.

- Additional testimonials add more credibility to your book but don't go overboard on them. A couple of pages at the most!

- A Dedication is always a nice touch for you, your readers and the person receiving it.

- An About the author page gives you an opportunity to showcase your credentials while answering the question: "tell us a little about yourself."

- Your Introduction gives you an opportunity to share why you wrote your book, how it's written, and what you want readers to gain from reading it.

- Don't end your chapters with blank pages. A conclusion allows you to share a warm message with your readers and signpost them to other resources on offer.

- If your book has benefited from the additional wisdom of expert contributors, be sure to thank them.

- Your Acknowledgements page enables you to thank the special people that have helped you write such a brilliant book.

CHAPTER 8

Behind Every Bestselling Book is an Editor

I remember my husband's face as he walked up the garden to the log cabin where I was writing. In his hands was a printed copy of the first masterclass of my third book. I had delayed writing this masterclass to the end because I knew it would be a challenge. My husband, Malcolm, had just finished editing it, or so I hoped. In my eyes it was then just a hop, a skip and a jump to performing the final checks on the entire book and sending it to my publishers.

But I knew from Malcolm's face that all was not well.

As he settled himself in the armchair, he delivered his verdict. It went something along these lines:

"I don't think this masterclass is anywhere near the standard of the previous ones you've written. In some parts you're assuming your reader knows about marketing plans when they won't. The structure isn't there yet and in some pages it's obvious you were tired because you've skipped over some important points. It doesn't have your usual flow. I'm sorry - but I think you are going to have to rewrite it."

After protesting for all of five minutes to no avail I realised he was right. And so with a somewhat heavy heart it was back to the drawing board, spending as much time on the rewrite as I did on the initial drafts. And guess what? Many readers have commented on Amazon and on Twitter just how useful they've found this masterclass. I shudder to think what would have happened had I not subjected this and the other 14 masterclasses to Malcolm's ruthless, laser-honed and objective editing. I hasten to add that this was the only masterclass I had to rewrite, thankfully!

So please do not skimp on the services of an editor if you're aiming to write a bestseller rather than a book that is little more than an extension of your ego.

Self publishing enables authors to share their words with the world when this would not have been possible years ago. But this new freedom has resulted in thousands of poorly written books. I've been given several books from self published authors; with the odd exception they have not been edited and it shows. Many are littered with careless mistakes an editor would have picked up on immediately ('you're' when 'your' was meant,' 'it's' instead of 'its', 'their' when it should have been 'there' being some of the biggest culprits). All have included errors that were obvious on first sight to me as a reader but clearly weren't to the author.

The inescapable fact is that it's nigh on impossible to edit your book to the required standard if it is to become an enduring bestseller.

As authors we become too protective of our work, unable to see the imperfections an editor will spot in seconds. An editor will approach your book with a fresh and experienced pair of eyes. They have been trained to edit! What you or I may think is eloquent and descriptive, an editor may deem longwinded and lacking in clarity.

A great editor will hone in on:

- Sloppy and incorrect grammar.

- Poor and inaccurate punctuation.

- Spelling mistakes.

- Text where you're contradicting yourself.

- Or you're repeating yourself.

- Places where it's clear you've strayed from the point.

- Text that will confuse your readers.

- Poorly written sections.

- Text that should be removed because it adds nothing of value to your book and may even detract from it.

- Any words and phrases you're overusing.

A good editor will not tell you that your book is perfect. They'll tell you what you have to hear for your book to be as close to perfect as you can get it.

That said, although I firmly believe that behind every great book is a great editor, I am not for a moment suggesting that you accept everything your editor says without challenging them if you really don't agree with something. But be prepared to listen to their comments and embrace their suggestions if it's simply your ego that's getting in the way of making these changes. Look upon your editor as the reader you don't want to come up against when your book is published. You may have to accept that some of your chapters will need more reworking than others. And that's okay. The time you spend on this stage is time well spent.

When the first copy of your lovely new book is in your hands you'll not begrudge the time spent on editing it and the quality of your book will be reflected in your five-star reviews and your rising book sales. Of course the opposite can happen too. I was reading the reviews of a book on Amazon recently. Several reviewers had commented on the book's many irritating spelling errors. The author responded defensively saying these mistakes did not detract from the quality of the content he was sharing. I believe that as authors we should set a high standard and not expect our readers to pick up on our mistakes.

Here's what Jane Mallin, the very talented editor of this book, has to say about editing and how you can review and edit your copy before sending it to your editor.

Advice from the professional.

There are several stages to the editing process, just as there are various types of edit: editing a novel, for example, is very different to editing a work of non-fiction. The final edit though is the same whether you've written non-fiction or a novel. This is where you look at the surface details because the deep structure has already been sorted.

If you skimp during this phase, you're not only doing yourself a disservice but your readers too. Think of your reaction to errors in books or magazines. Don't they spoil your enjoyment of the story or article? Or if it was a non-fiction work, didn't they tarnish the credibility of the author a little? Maybe not. It could be that you're not so exacting - but some of your readers will be.

So let's assume you're ready to put the final polish on your prose. Where do you begin?

1. Take a break.

Yes, that's right, start by taking a break and disentangling yourself from the book. There's a very good reason for this: you need to take a more objective stance when you're editing your own work. Ideas that are crystal clear to you as the writer may not make logical sense to someone who is coming to the book for the first time. So taking a break and changing your mindset is essential. And, while you're about it, take off the rose-tinted specs and dig out a magnifying glass. It's time to look at *all* the details.

How much of a break do you need? At least one day, ideally longer if your schedule allows.

2. Take your copy out for a coffee.

Reading a hard copy is much easier than reading on screen. The light emitted by a computer screen strains your eyes so, as Dee has advised, always print out your chapters and review them on paper. Before printing, double space the paragraphs and maybe increase the point size too so you can read your text with ease.

Then find a place where you can read undisturbed such as a local café or library or even another room in your home. I'm not sure why changing places aids concentration... Maybe it's because it helps you shrug off the role of author and assume that of the critic. Although I don't know why this works, it definitely does. Try it and see for yourself.

3. Read right to the end.

Read your book all the way through first: does the writing flow? Do the sentences make sense or are there any howlers - clumsy, clunky phrases - that need tightening? As Dee said earlier, it also helps to read out loud and highlight any parts that don't make sense straightaway. Clarity is key. If a sentence doesn't make sense the first time you read it, then change it.

4. Easy does it.

If editing and proofreading was a dance, it would be a slow one. Slow is the way to go when you're editing as the mind is very good at seeing what it expects to see. Read actively, asking questions as you go. Is that the right word? Could I put this more simply? Should that comma be there? Every time you have a query, make sure to highlight the relevant part of the copy.

5. Simplify.

- **"Never use a long word where a short one will do."** *George Orwell.* Cut the jargon and the 'ten dollar words' as Hemingway called them.

- **Jargon is sometimes necessary** but, on the whole, the world and its readers can live happily without it. Used indiscriminately, jargon alienates the reader and makes the content difficult to understand.

- **Cut redundant words.** For example 'this will help you in the development of new skills'. How about 'this will help you develop new skills' instead?

- **Cut some more.** The pruning process happens in stages. With each read-through, you'll invariably find something else to cut or re-work; extraneous sentences, woolly ideas, and repeated or over-used words and phrases.

6. Be precise.

- **Have you used the right word?** Find the right word to express your thoughts clearly. A good thesaurus is essential.

- **Is the meaning unclear?** Then change it until it is clear. Imprecise writing usually means muddled thinking and, as you are trying to present your ideas in a compelling way, it's wise to rethink and rewrite until the sentence or paragraph makes sense.

  If you get stuck, try this exercise. Take out a notebook and write: 'What I really want to say is...' Then write it down. Don't think about spellings or punctuation at this point. Just focus on crystallising your core idea.

- **Throw out unnecessary adverbs.** For example, "Pauline screamed loudly." Screams are loud, that's the point of them. But if Pauline screamed silently then you'd need to use the adverb. Or, even better, ramp up the action taking place so you don't need the adverb at all.

- **Spellings.** Use a spell-check first as this will weed out all the obvious errors. Don't rely on spell-check alone though; you also need to read and re-read for yourself. This is especially true if your book includes foreign or unusual names and words.

- **Punctuation.** I find punctuation makes more sense when I read aloud. Look at where you naturally pause as you read the text. Listen as you read and ask yourself what sounds right.

- **A note on numbers.** Numbers from one to nine are usually spelled out. Numbers from 10 upwards are typed in numerals—unless they come at the beginning of a sentence or quote. I was taught this rule in my very first job as a sub-editor. It's the one that all reputable newspapers and magazines adhere to so why not use it in your work too?

  One exception is when numbers are used in headings, for example, '13 mistakes every author must avoid'. It's a simple way to attract attention so, although the purist in me recoils, I guess those numbers have to stay!

- **Check your corrections.** After each edit, read through the text to make sure you've included them all and that the corrections themselves are correct. Beware! All kinds of errors can creep in during the editing phase.

- **Use the active voice.** One sure-fire way to improve your writing is to change verbs from passive to active. Instead of saying: 'costs must be controlled by you', say 'you must control costs'. The problem with the passive voice is that it tends to sound pompous rather than professional. Active writing is far more engaging.

- **Check headings**, sub-heads, lists and so on. For example, what style do you use for lists? Bullet points or numbers? If you use numbers, are they all there and in the right order? I know that sounds silly, but you'd be surprised at how often these sorts of mistakes get through.

- **Spacing**. On your last read-through, turn on Word's 'show formatting marks' function (or the formatting tool for whichever software package you're using) and check for extra spaces between words and at the beginning of each paragraph.

7. Know when to let go...

In one conversation about this book, Dee commented on how she'd found herself making little changes that weren't really adding to the content just before she sent it to me. And in some cases those changes even detracted from it. If you find yourself tinkering with tiny details then it is time to pass your book on to your editor.

Why you must cast an eagle eye over the publisher's proof.

You may be thinking that your editing days are behind you when you take your book from being a pristine document incorporating your editor's comments to the next stage—the first proof. But at the proof checking stage there is still important checking and reading to be done!

I remember sending my second book to Chris Day for typesetting; confident it had been edited so meticulously and read through so many times that there couldn't possibly be any errors. But when the proof came back and we checked it against the manuscript sent to Chris we still found a few spelling mistakes.

Don't stint on the proofreading stage because you will find errors that have somehow escaped your radar and your editor's. What's more some of the mistakes on your proofs aren't always down to you. It's entirely possible for diagrams to suddenly appear on the wrong pages and for a whole paragraph, a few sentences, a few words, and even entire pages to be missing from your proofs. Typesetters make mistakes too. I have not yet proofread a book that has not had some serious typesetting errors.

And don't proofread on your own. It takes two people to proofread: one to read the manuscript that was sent for typesetting out loud, the other to check the proof against it word for word to ensure nothing has been missed out and it has been reproduced accurately in its entirety. There's no doubt about it, this is a painstaking process; two people sitting together checking each word, every page, every chapter, every image and every diagram until the last page has been reached.

But it has to be done.

As you can imagine proofreading requires concentration so I would recommend you don't do it for more than two or three hours at a time. Drink plenty of water and work in a nice environment, but not so nice and relaxing that you can nod off. Proofread in natural daylight and when you're feeling mentally alert. Checking proofs in artificial light at the end of a long day when you're tired will result in small errors going unnoticed.

But take heart; if you can proofread with this degree of commitment, consistency and enthusiasm, you should be able to send your book to print after just two sets of proofs.

So please don't spare the horses when it comes to finding an editor. There's one behind every great author! Check out the Society for Editors and Proofreaders website (www.sfep.org.uk) if you don't already have an editor in mind.

Chapter summary.

- Don't let your ego get in the way of the fact that you need an editor if you want a bestselling book. You don't want your readers to assume this role.

- Behind every bestselling author you'll usually find an editor sitting in the wings, red pen and thesaurus to hand.

- A good editor will pick up on the flaws in your manuscript that are invisible to you; including sloppy grammar, spelling mistakes, poor punctuation, and repetitive, contradictory and longwinded text.

- Before you pass your manuscript to your editor, put your editor's glasses on and critique your book objectively. You're no longer the creative writer at this stage.

- Print your book off and then edit each chapter, making amendments as you work through each one. Cut out the jargon and don't be afraid to shorten sentences and paragraphs.

- At the final stage, read through your book making small tweaks before sending it on.

- You don't have to accept every single correction your editor suggests but you should be willing to accept most of them.

- It takes two people to proofread. Create the right environment so you can proofread effectively.

- Typesetters make mistakes so don't assume your proofs will be flawless. There will also be mistakes that have escaped the attention of you and your editor. Check each page with a fine tooth comb.

CHAPTER 9

How to Create a Great Book Title

Whilst you may already have ideas for the title of your book you should be prepared for it to undergo some revisions when you start writing. This is to be expected and it's part and parcel of the creative process. For example this book started out as: *How to write and market a bestselling book*. When I was planning the content, the title *The ultimate guide to writing and marketing a bestselling book* with the strapline *'on a shoestring budget'* was in my eyes and my publisher's, a much better description of the book. But I needed a starting point and so do you.

If you're struggling to think of a great title I hope these tips help you.

- Study the titles of books that fall into your category. You may come up with a title from this exercise alone. Are there any particular words that jump out at you and that describe the impact you want your book to have? Make a list of the words you're considering and play around with phrases. Have them pinned up so you can consider them long after the first flush of inspiration.

- Do you want your title to be self-explanatory so that your readers will grasp its purpose in seconds and identify they have a need for it? The title of this book is an example of this as indeed are the titles of my other books. I am not a fan of quirky titles that don't give any clue as to what the book is about. I prefer self-explanatory titles that will pop up in an online search when a person is looking for books on how to market their small business or how to write a book.

- You are not me of course and you may be rather taken with the idea of a quirky title - and it could be perfect for your book. Bear in mind however that your readers may struggle to understand what your book is about even though your title means something to you. So if you're going down this road make sure that your book cover includes additional text; a few lines or phrases that explain what your book is about so that readers can grasp its purpose in seconds.

For example you could add a strapline underneath your quirky title or beside it. Of course famous authors don't have to conform to these guidelines. They can get away with titles like *Purple Cow* (by Seth Godin) simply because they have an army of loyal readers eagerly awaiting their next book. The title of their book comes second to the weight and influence carried by their own name. Most of us don't have this luxury. Many of your potential readers will not be looking for you by name. They'll come across you when searching online and your book may well be recommended to them by virtue of the books they've bought in the past. If your title is so unusual that it means absolutely nothing to them they may well skip over your book and buy one from a competitor who has chosen a clear title that explains what their book is about.

- Make sure the title you're planning on using has not already been taken. You can make subtle tweaks if you find it's too close for comfort to another book in your category. Changing a few words can create a new title that still retains the spirit of what you want to convey. Put the title of your book into a search engine and on Amazon to make sure that it hasn't already been taken.

- If you're writing a business book or a self help one why not experiment with the following phrases and words to get those creative juices flowing?

Check 'Strange Tales into Dales' Isn't published already

- How to...

- The (7, 10, 15, or 20) secrets of...

- Make money from...

- Free up your...

- The successful/healthy/ wealthy/person's guide to...

- The simple way to...

- (100, 200, 300) top tips on...

- The secrets of successful...

- How you can...

- Because choosing a title is such an important task, don't worry if yours takes a while to materialise. Sometimes you have to write the whole book before inspiration strikes. It may be that one chapter alone inspires you or you have to wait until your chapters have been edited before you find the right title. Sow that seed of intent in your mind confident that a great title will manifest itself and have a pen and pad close to hand so you can record your thoughts whenever they arise.

- Should you have a strapline or not? There are no hard and fast rules but, as mentioned earlier, I'd encourage you to have one, especially if your title is off the wall. For my third book, the strapline was *Powerful Promotion on a Shoestring*. This was added at the suggestion of the commissioning editor who said it described my approach to marketing and that it would appeal to readers. I added one to this book too, retaining the shoestring theme. A strapline can be very useful if it reinforces your book's title and conveys an important benefit that will encourage readers to buy. And of course it explains what your book is about if your title leaves readers none the wiser.

If you have several titles on the go and are unsure which one works best, ask a handful of potential readers to vote for their favourite. But don't be too hasty in seeking their feedback. Allow yourself time to ease into the creative process. You will come up with a great title!

Chapter summary.

- Your title will materialise even if it takes more time than you'd envisaged.

- Research the titles of other books in your category. You can be inspired by what's already out there.

- Will your title be self-explanatory? If it is it will appear more frequently in online searches. Readers will be able to access it - which is what you want.

- If your title is going to be quirky be aware that whilst it means something to you, it could mean absolutely nothing to your readers.

- Consider adding a strapline whether your book title is quirky or not.

- Search online to ensure your title has not already been taken. If it has can you change a few words whilst still retaining its purpose and meaning?

- Be prepared for your title to change whilst writing your book. You need a starting point but this does not have to be set in stone if you come up with an even better one.

CHAPTER 10

The Secrets of a Successful Book Cover

Your book cover is in effect your shop window. At book signings I'm always fascinated by the people examining my book. Most will browse the front cover for a few seconds before turning it over to read the back, spending more time on this because there's usually more to read. Satisfied, they will then dip into the book itself. When a person is evaluating your book online, it has to stand out in a beauty parade of other books that have been recommended or that are in the top 100 best category sellers.

And yet I see so many examples of covers failing at the first hurdle because:

- **They look drab and amateurish.** Dull colours, hard-to-read text and poor quality images. They have not been designed by a professional designer and it shows. To be honest the cover of my first book belonged in this category. It was unremarkable and instantly forgettable. Thankfully I had learnt my lesson by the time it came to my second book!

- **They are lacking in any supportive, persuasive text.** All that's on offer is the title, nothing more to entice readers to look inside or explain what the book is about.

- **The author has embarked on an ego trip.** Most of the space is filled with them grinning like a Cheshire cat or attempting to look moody and mysterious. What a waste of valuable space that could have been put to better use!

- **There's too much text** crammed into a small space making it impossible to read.

- **The design is so complex** you can barely read the title let alone any supportive text. The designer has had a field day and been allowed to flex their creative muscles without a clear brief to guide them or rein them in.

- **The cover is a classic example of a tick box exercise.** It's a hurriedly assembled, lacklustre and charmless affair. The author has given no thought to it because they've not realised its importance in generating interest and sales. They have been happy to settle for a mediocre design. Again my first book cover stands accused of this.

Don't let this happen to you!

Grab your readers' attention right from the start.

Make sure your book stands out from the crowd, shouting 'buy me now!' Here's how...

- Visit your local bookshop to study the book covers in a few categories making notes on why some appeal to you and why others don't. Do the same online too because you'll get a very different impression there. Here you're initially looking at a tiny image, so a book cover that grabs your attention for the right reasons is one worth taking note of. Can you read the book title and its strapline clearly?

- Study the book covers in your category. You don't want to copy them but there's nothing to stop you from being inspired by them or steering away from a particular look because it doesn't work.

- Don't design your book cover unless you're a designer. Find a local freelance graphic designer so you're not paying over the odds. Before commissioning them look at examples of book covers they've already designed. If you're happy, ask for their fee in writing. How many changes will you be permitted to make to their designs before incurring additional charges? Your designer should present you with three designs and an accompanying explanation of what inspired them for each one. You should be allowed to make at least one set of changes to your preferred design without incurring an extra fee. Make sure this is all covered in their quotation.

- Don't just tell your designer to 'get on with it'. Brief them thoroughly with a written document that includes:

  - Details about your target audience. Revisit the work you did in chapter four and condense this into a thorough target audience brief. Your designer has to know who they're designing the book cover for - because it is not for you.

  - The 'trim size' of the book (the height and width of the page), the number of pages, and type of paper to be used so they can calculate the spine width. They will also require the barcode for your ISBN, and any QR codes that will link people to your website or blog.

  - The additional text that will be on the front and back of your book cover.

Let them have three images of book covers you like and three you don't and explain your reasons why. If there's a particular style of design that you really don't like (for example cartoon images) include this in your brief. They can't read your mind so the more information you provide the better.

An attractive book cover will usually contain these elements:

- An easy-to-read title. *Top - Front* *And Spine*

- Your name. *Bottom* *Front*

- Some powerful testimonial about your book. *Back*

- Some succinct and persuasive text about you as an author. *Back*

- A concise but appealing summary of the contents of your book. *Back*

- The price of your book, the bar code and ISBN. *Back*

Designer Louise Lucas explains how she designed this cover.

"I have worked as Dee's principal graphic designer for a few years now, so when she approached me to design her latest book cover I was thrilled at the opportunity and keen to create a really striking, contemporary look.

"Dee is already an established author, keynote speaker and Chartered Marketer with a number of retained clients, so I had to make sure this cover was in keeping with the design style already established on her website and her current brand image.

"The front cover had to contain a fair amount of information, so I wanted to break it down into bite size, easy-to-read segments that would lead your eyes down the page. The top of the page had to show 'Dee Blick' the author's name quite clearly, so I used a dark blue bar that spans the front and the back of the cover with Dee's name in bright yellow to create a degree of separation from the rest of the page. The sans serif typeface I used is called 'Bliss'. I chose it because it's modern, fresh and legible. I used this typeface in both upper and lower case and in different sizes on the front cover and the back.

"The next line down is an important quote about Dee's selling power as an author. The text: *"No.1 bestselling author of The 15 Essential Marketing Masterclasses For Your Small Business & The Ultimate Small Business Marketing Book"*, is a long sentence but, by styling it into two lines in the same 'Bliss' font as before (but smaller), it still creates an impact and it balances perfectly.

"This leads on to the main title of the book *The ULTIMATE GUIDE to WRITING & MARKETING A BESTSELLING BOOK on a shoestring budget.* This is another long title to say the least! So I broke it up into three distinctive sections with a mixture of type sizes and the same key colours as used previously, all in upper case to make it stand out which is so important when the book is being viewed online. The final line 'on a shoestring budget' was added in the style of a friendly handwritten font.

"Looking at Dee's previous books and her current website, she has a strong colour scheme of bright cyan blues and yellows. I therefore wanted to continue using them while adding in some additional complementary colours. To give the book a strong visual impact I compiled a graphic montage of arrows in different shapes and sizes. By crossing them diagonally they lead directly towards the title of the book. This draws the reader to the title yet again. I also introduced the circular decal in a complementary magenta colour to spotlight an important message that would otherwise have got lost. This little decal leads the reader to a different area of the page. The bottom of the page is finished with a contrasting yellow bar. I wanted to create a vibrant, positive and interesting looking front cover that would make a reader stop in their tracks and explore what the book has to offer without confusing them because of the amount of text there is to absorb.

"The back cover is more text heavy as back covers tend to be. Again I wanted to make it easy for the reader to take everything in which is why I have created clearly segmented areas. I set the back cover over an opaque contrasting blue with the arrow pattern knocked back behind it. As the colours on the back cover are vibrant and bold, I felt that the image of Dee worked best in black and white. This contrast between the colours was also duplicated at the bottom of the page with the perfect positioning for the bar code.

"I wanted the testimonial from Andy Fernandez to really 'pop', which is why I set it in yellow against the graduated shade of blue. This leads onto the text in which Dee summarises some of the key benefits about the book. I broke this text up using bullet points for quick and easy viewing.

"I hope you like the cover too and that my explanation helps when you're briefing your designer."

Chapter summary.

- Your book cover is an important space that plays a key part in persuading a reader to buy it online, at a bookshop or at a book signing.

- Many book covers fail to have any impact because they are drab, poorly designed and with either too much unreadable text or not enough text...

- Don't just fill the space with your face! Make sure you allow plenty of space for testimonials, a summary of your book, a few compelling reader benefits and so on.

- If you need a starting point for inspiration study the book covers that you like and the ones you don't; in your category and in general.

- Hand the task of designing your book cover to a designer. Ask to see samples of their work, get a fixed fee in writing and be aware of how many changes you can make before incurring additional costs.

- Give your designer a decent brief. They have to know your target audiences, your preferred colours and colours you really don't like. They also need specifics such the size of your book, page count and so on.

- Make sure your designer has the text for the front and back of your book because they have to incorporate this into their design.

- A book cover that sells will usually include a powerful testimonial, text about you, and a summary of what's inside the book in addition to your name and book title and strapline.

CHAPTER 11

Don't Neglect Your Layout

When I attended a literary supper a few years ago, one of the authors, a well-known journalist, showed me her latest book. She had broken away from her publisher to self publish a collection of charming stories and poems. Alas, I couldn't read a single thing because the font was so tiny. To make matters worse, each page was a solid block of text; no paragraphs or breaks to make it easier to read and absorb. It was page after page of miniscule eye-straining text. On that day I realised that commonsense is not always in common supply even for the most gifted of authors.

Undoubtedly setting out the interior of your book before it is printed is nowhere near as interesting as writing it, but it is one of the most important parts of the publishing process. You can become so wrapped up in planning and writing your book that you don't give much thought to the layout. Don't be tempted to skimp on layout if you want it to contribute to your readers' overall positive experience of the book.

Of course how your book is laid out will vary depending on its purpose. A novel will not have the same layout as a business book; a cookery book will have a very different layout from a self help title. But please embrace my general message and scrutinise your layout. Don't publish your book until you're happy with it.

Start the evaluation of your planned layout by standing in your reader's shoes. Is the text so cramped that a magnifying glass is required? Have you opted for tiny text in a bid to keep your page count down? Is your chosen typeface so harsh or wacky that it's tough to read?

Simple tips for a lovely layout.

- **Consider including a summary of each chapter to enhance your reader's understanding of what they've read.** Readers have told me they find the summaries in my books helpful. If your chapters are substantial, a summary at the end of each one should enable readers to grasp the key points in seconds. Study the chapter summaries in this book to help you create yours.

- **Ensure that every right-hand page has the chapter title as a heading and the left-hand page has your book's title.** Readers will be able to flick through your book and locate the chapter they're looking for without having to refer to the contents page.

- **If you're using graphics or images, caption them** and explain their purpose in the accompanying text. Only include them if they help explain a point you're making or if they enhance your readers' appreciation of a page or chapter.

- **Break your text up with headings and make them stand out from the accompanying text** by emboldening them. You may want two or three sets of headings in different sizes. For example:

Your main heading	20pt.
A section heading	18pt.
A subheading	14pt.

A main heading tells your reader when they're about to embark on a brand-new section whereas smaller headings can be used to start a related subject within a chapter or to share a paragraph of really important text. Be consistent throughout your book sticking to the same format for your headings and the same point size.

- **Break up your text with paragraphs** even when you're still presenting the same facts, the same story or the same train of thought.

When a person is flicking through your book or using the 'look inside' feature online, unbroken slabs of text can be a real turn off. How long should a paragraph be? There are no hard and fast rules. I suggest you review each page and determine how you can break it into paragraphs so it's easier to read. You can also end a paragraph with a question to encourage your readers to read the next line and you can follow a long paragraph with a single line.

Why should you do this?

Well, as you can see, it breaks the page up nicely even when you have been generous in your use of paragraphs. And it makes an important sentence or question stand out without the need to embolden or enlarge it.

- **Use bullet points because they are useful for:**
  - Emphasising key points.
  - Breaking up the text nicely.

But...

  - Ensure you don't break up a group of bullet points so that you have 'orphans'; a bullet point on its own straggling at the bottom of one page or at the top of another. This is another important reason to proofread your proofs.

  - Be consistent when presenting your text in bullet points. You don't have to start each bullet point with a capital letter and you don't have to finish each one with a full stop but if you decide to do this, make sure that every set of bullet points follows the same format.

- **Opt for black text on white paper unless you must have colour in your book.** This keeps your printing costs down and for readability you can't beat black text on white paper.

- **Choose an attractive typeface for your book and an easy-to-read point size.** If you want your text to be easy on the eye select a typeface from the serifs family. Serifs are the little tails at the end of each letter. They make it easier to read individual letters and lines of text.

Garamond is an example of a serif typeface as is Century, which takes up more space than Garamond. Times New Roman was once very popular but it's out of vogue now because it has been done to death.

The main typeface for this book is Caslon Pro.

You may want to have a serif typeface for your book with the exception of the headings and subheadings. Why not make them stand out in a sans serif typeface? These fonts have no little tails just strong verticals so your eyes are drawn down each line.

Like this typeface, Arial or...

This one Trebuchet or...

This typeface, Calibri or...

This typeface, Verdana.

Incidentally these four typefaces have been produced in point size 12 and yet Calibri looks smaller doesn't it?

What size should your typeface be? This book has been produced in point size 11.5 with the chapter titles at size 24pt (they're in Bliss). The subheadings throughout each chapter are at size 14pt and also in Bliss.

If you're unsure about the typefaces and point size for your book I would encourage you to experiment by producing one of your chapters in a range of fonts and point sizes using these tips to guide you. Read each chapter in natural and artificial light. If you're squinting, go back to the drawing board!

The next time you're in a bookshop, make a point of looking at the layout of several books, especially the ones that are in the same category as yours. Even a book published by a mainstream publishing house can fall foul of these simple tips so make yours stand out as a shining example.

Chapter summary.

- Startling but true, many authors do not consider the layout of their book and yet it is so important.

- The most compelling content can be spoiled if it is presented as a block of tiny typeface.

- The layout of your book should ultimately enhance your reader's enjoyment of it.

- Consider summarising your chapters.

- Make sure that any images or graphics are captioned or explained in the text.

- Break your text up with headings and subheadings but be consistent throughout your book.

- Paragraphs are useful for making any page easy to read.

- Bullet points are useful when you want to emphasise key points.

- Spend some time experimenting with different typefaces. Should your body copy be in a serif font and your headlines in a sans serif font?

- Put your typeface and point size to the test. Print a chapter in different fonts and different point sizes. Always write and test the manuscript with your readers in mind.

CHAPTER 12

So Many Choices! How to Publish Your Book

Nowadays you can publish your book in so many different ways. Gone are the days when your only hope was securing a deal from a publishing house. You can now publish a book under your own steam and secure its space on Amazon, in bookshops, and globally in paperback, eBook and audio format. It's exciting stuff.

In this chapter I explain how each one of my four books was published in the hope that my experience will help you too. But I realise that my publishing knowledge can only take you so far which is why I've enlisted the support of Chris Day, the MD of Filament Publishing and founder of Authorcraft, a nationwide networking group for authors of all genres. Chris has helped hundreds of authors realise their dream of publishing a book - including me. A little further on in this chapter you can read my interview with Chris.

After that, I'll introduce you to two respected authors, Richard White and Janice B Gordon because they self published their books on a shoestring using CreateSpace, Kindle Direct Publishing and Smashwords. Jeff Scott then shares his fascinating self publishing story using Lightning Source and we conclude this journey of your publishing options with useful advice from literary agent, Susan Mears.

But first, here's my publishing journey, book by book.

My first book: *Powerful Marketing on a Shoestring Budget For Small Businesses.*

I knew back in 2008 when I was considering writing my first book that I was about as likely to secure a publishing deal as I was to be struck by lightning. I was not a safe bet for any mainstream publisher because I was not an established author with a track record of selling books. This didn't bother me. I rather liked the idea of being able to write a book and call the shots without being told what to do and when to do it by a publisher. I looked upon my first book as a positive experiment that I was in charge of.

After researching my publishing options online I found Authorhouse, an organisation from America with a base in the United Kingdom. Back then they seemed to offer the best of both worlds. I could take as much or as little of their publishing services as I wanted but I could hand over the proofing, printing and fulfilment of my book to them. I had neither the time nor the inclination to research suitable printers and find space in my home for storing books. I didn't want to have to learn how to liaise with book distributors and sellers, including Amazon. For less than £1,000 my book was published in paperback and Kindle. And to this day Authorhouse stocks and distributes this book.

Would I change anything with the benefit of my experience? I would've taken responsibility for the design of the book cover and used my own designer. The cover of this book is underwhelming to say the least and it proved difficult trying to make changes to it. I would also have read the fine print in my contract. It was a shock when I received an invoice for the corrections that I'd made to my first proof. I had naïvely assumed I wouldn't be charged for these. If I was starting out with my first book today and had to choose between Authorhouse and CreateSpace, I'd opt for the latter because there is little difference between the free services provided by CreateSpace and the paid-for service I received from Authorhouse. But it was my first book and I was pleased to get it in print.

My second book: *The Ultimate Small Business Marketing Book.*

With my second book I decided to look for another 'partnership publishing' arrangement in the UK and found Filament Publishing. This time I knew what I wanted from the partnership. As before I would take care of the editing, layout and marketing, and I would use my designer to design the cover. I wanted Filament to organise the typesetting of my book and proofs, to arrange the printing; to hold stock; to distribute it via the mainstream UK distributors; to arrange the 'look inside' facility on Amazon and to ensure my book was placed in the right category (small business marketing books).

I also wanted to benefit from the plentiful advice that was on offer at no extra charge because I had my sights set on overseas sales. It proved to be a winning partnership. When I was offered a publishing deal in China for *The Ultimate Small Business Marketing Book*, Filament Publishing played a key role in liaising with CITIC Publishing in Beijing before the contract was finalised and the advance paid. Had I self published this book under my own steam CITIC would not have considered it. (I was told this by Glacier Ding, CITIC's Rights Manager). And so with my sights set on international sales for this book, I returned to Filament Publishing.

I negotiated the royalty fee I would be paid for each book in paperback and Kindle before signing any contracts with Authorhouse or Filament Publishing. When you opt to work with a partnership publisher you will earn a smaller royalty per book compared to self publishing using, for example, CreateSpace and Kindle Direct Publishing. Your partnership publisher is not going to distribute your book to bookshops and online out of the goodness of their own heart. But if, like me, you want a more involved, proactive relationship with your publisher it's worth settling for a slightly lower royalty.

Indeed whilst I was writing this book, Chris Day contacted me with the exciting news that he had negotiated a publishing deal that will see it translated into Arabic. These incredible opportunities would not have come my way had I opted to self publish these two books.

My third book: *The 15 Essential Marketing Masterclasses For Your Small Business.*

For my third book, I was offered an international publishing deal with Capstone, a division of Wiley, the world's biggest publisher of business books. Although I was still responsible for writing my book and my husband was yet again my zealous editor, this time I was surrounded by a team who took care of everything from the cover design, layout and proofreading to the PR and securing bulk orders from overseas resellers. Naturally my royalties per book from Wiley were lower than my previous two books, but it didn't cost me anything to publish and I received an advance payment. Working with the team at Wiley has been an amazing experience. For many years I'd dreamt of being spotted by a publishing house and getting a deal. It took me two books to realise this ambition. But of course by this stage I was a known quantity - a successful author with a track record of selling thousands of books. The publishing team knew I could write and that my books sold.

How to evaluate a partnership publisher before signing up.

If you're considering a partnership publishing arrangement whereby you pay a publisher to produce your book and take care of its distribution, here are my top tips to help you find the right one.

1. Do your homework on every publisher, even looking them up at Companies House. The last thing you want is to have a bestseller and your publisher goes out of business or is financially unstable and so cannot guarantee to hold stock of your book.

2. Be clear about what you want your partnership publisher to do and what you are willing to do. You will be charged for every service you use or you may be quoted a fee that includes services you'd rather take care of yourself. A good partnership publisher should offer the full range of services including editing, design, layout, illustrations, distribution - even marketing and PR to launch your book. Don't buy more than you need. And don't sign up to a marketing or PR package until you've studied the tips in this book. You should hopefully arrive at the conclusion that you don't need any further support.

3. Find out how they promote their authors' books to publishing houses and book distributors in other countries. As I mentioned earlier, I wouldn't have secured a publishing deal in China for *The Ultimate Small Business Marketing Book* without Chris Day's experience in negotiating overseas contracts. Your book could have international potential but, for this to happen, you may need a partnership publisher with the right experience and the right contacts plus an understanding of how to deal with overseas publishers. Some overseas publishers will not deal with you as the author especially if they want to translate your book.

   Does your partnership publisher attend the major book fairs and if so will they promote your book there? They should, and what's more, this should be part of their basic offering.

4. Speak to at least three of their authors. Ask to see their books. Find out what they paid, the services they used and their satisfaction or otherwise with the relationship. How many books are they selling and where are their books being sold? You will gain a good insight into a partnership publisher's experience and credibility from this exercise alone.

5. Negotiate your royalties per book upfront (paperback, Kindle, audio and other electronic book formats) and ensure these figures are included in the subsequent contract should you decide to go ahead. Find out how frequently you'll receive royalty payments. I receive an annual payment from Wiley and quarterly payments from Filament Publishing and Authorhouse.

6. What will your partnership publisher charge you per book when you're buying books direct from them? You should be able to make a decent profit on each book when you sell from your own stock. Ask for the courier costs per box of books too and the minimum quantity of books you must order to benefit from this price.

7. Ask to see a draft contract and study the fine print. For example, will you be expected to pay for stock even though your publisher is distributing your book? (I have not had to do this). Will you be expected to pay for proofs and for corrections to proofs? How long is the contract valid for? It pays to know the minimum period of time that your publisher will be willing to stock and distribute your book. Don't assume your relationship will last forever.

8. How will your book be distributed? A good partnership publisher will have access to all the major distributors in the UK, such as Gardners, which can give you a route to bookshop sales. They should be able to promote your book on Amazon in the UK and overseas and to overseas publishing houses. This should be part of their service. But I know from talking to some authors that some partnership publishers only offer a very basic service that is not worth paying for. You can do the basics yourself at a lower price or even for free.

9. Make sure they can publish your book across all platforms including Kindle, paperback, limited edition hardback, eBooks and audio books. You may not want to take advantage of all these options now but this could change in the future.

10. Don't settle for the first publisher you find. Speak to three ensuring that you have face-to-face meetings with each one. Get like-for-like quotes in writing, with each service itemised together with the terms and conditions you have to comply with. Divide their fees by the number of books you'll have to sell in order to cover this sum. Are they reasonable?

11. Trust your instincts. It's in the interests of your partnership publisher to make your relationship a success. For every book you sell, they will earn a fee too. But you're going to be working with this person or team for a long time so it's important that you get on with them and that you like and trust them. If they are not enthusiastic about publishing your book and their track record leaves you in doubt, I would give them a miss.

An interview with publishing guru Chris Day.

This is what Chris Day had to say to the questions I wish I'd asked before I embarked on writing my first book. He certainly doesn't pull any punches!

Q. The publishing world has changed. What impact has this had on authors?

A. The world of publishing is frantically trying to reinvent itself to accommodate the new dynamics of online and the changing habits of the book buying public in much the same way that the music publishing business did some years ago. Whilst we are buying more books, the difference is that we're now buying them in many more formats and from different places. Far from this being a bad thing it has created more opportunities for authors to be found. But at the same time it has redefined what it means to be a successful author.

In the past there was only one definition. To be a successful author you had to send your book proposal to enough publishers, build up an impressive collection of rejection slips until you hit the jackpot and your manuscript was accepted. This process usually excluded the author from any further input on the basis that 'the publisher knows best' in everything. It also meant that the author wasn't required to become involved with any marketing or PR because the publisher assumed control of this. Generations of authors have grown up without the skills or the need to promote themselves and their books.

For many, the traditional way of getting published is the only way to get published and anything else is 'Vanity Publishing' and in some way inferior. But is this fair? Does it reflect the new dynamics of the marketplace and the fact that instead of the vast majority of books being sold through bookshops, most are now sold in the accessible online world?

Q. But it's harder than ever to get a publishing deal nowadays isn't it?

A. Yes. For many traditional publishers cost-cutting is king with the once mighty marketing and PR departments but shadows of their former selves. The business model that has underpinned publishing for many years is now broken.

When every high street had a bookshop, a publisher could rely on minimum orders of multiple thousands for every new title. These books would be distributed to the shops though the big book distributors like Gardners Books in Eastbourne. Each shop would have an account with their distributor and would even have an ordering terminal in the shop directly connected to them. Books could be ordered and dispatched overnight and the supply chain worked like a well-oiled machine. But now that the bookshops have shrunk to a fraction of their original numbers, publishers can no longer count on the huge minimum order quantities on which royalty cheques were based.

Life is much more uncertain, which is why they're becoming cautious in their selection of new titles.

Publishers are now looking for authors who've built a following on social media, raised their profile in the press, know how to market themselves and their books and are not afraid of public speaking. But even if an author ticks these boxes they're still not guaranteed a publishing deal. The industry has become risk averse and unless a publisher can confidently predict a significant demand for an author's book on the day of publication, they're not going to invest in it. This is the harsh reality and the reason why so many authors are now taking things into their own hands opting for the equally less-certain self publishing route.

Q. What does self publishing and vanity publishing mean?

A. Apparently, not what you would think! Instead of an author taking personal responsibility for all aspects of the publishing as the name implies, many are going to a variety of publishing houses that will - for a price - take everything off their hands and do it for them. So 'self publishing' doesn't mean doing it all by yourself.

But publishing a book under your own steam has never been easier. With all sorts of online tools, templates and options to choose from, all you have to do is upload your manuscript, send a payment and hey presto, you are now a published author. For those authors writing a book to show to their friends and with no desire or knowledge of how to make a commercial success of their book, this may be fine.

The new definition of self publishing has become 'when the author pays to be published' - but to many publishing diehards, this still means 'vanity publishing'.

For me the definition of vanity publishing hinges not on the amount of money an author has paid a publisher to publish their book but whether their book has a viable business model. Many vanity publishers will charge a significant sum of money to authors for the privilege of seeing their work in print. There's a simple acid test. If you were to sell all the books that now fill your garage at full price and the money you receive is significantly less than what it cost to produce them, and you have made a loss then there is something very seriously wrong with that business model! Every book has to be a start-up business and generate a return on investment. If it is not designed to do that and it is just an expensive hobby - that is vanity.

Q. Do you see a difference in the quality of self published books when compared to books produced by the traditional publishing houses?

A. Definitely. Because it is so easy to publish a book the internet is full to bursting with books that should not have been allowed to see the light of day. They have not been thought out and are full of spelling mistakes and grammatical errors. Self publishing without the checks and balances of editing and proofreading has created a tolerance for self published books with a low expectation of quality.

You don't have to be an expert to spot a self published book! Often a really good book is let down by a few simple things that can be so easily avoided. The bottom line is that authors are rarely graphic artists, nor are they typesetters and editors. The secret to creating a professional looking book is to use professionals when you know in your heart they can do a much better job than you can.

There are no prizes for doing it all yourself. Know your strengths and have the commonsense to outsource everything else. For a self published book to become a bestseller it has to be written to a high standard, edited to a high standard and be well laid out and designed. The author has to know their stuff inside out too. There is a world of difference between writing a book and creating a bestseller.

Q. So how can you make a proper business out of your book?

A. It will always be the case that the books an author sells direct to their readers will make them the most money, which can be up to 70% of the cover price. By contrast, books sold through other platforms and through the book trade with a discount of up to 60% will generate a very low return.

It is not enough to get your book up on Amazon where it will sit with thousands of other books. If nobody knows it's there because you haven't created a demand it will not achieve its full potential. It's the savvy authors taking charge of their book and using all routes to market that are now making the most money. Unless you look at your new book as a business and invest time in marketing it, it will never generate the return on your time and effort that you richly deserve.

The choices you make at the beginning of your project will determine your ultimate success. Authors have far more choice than they realise. In order to evaluate the many options for origination, production, publishing and marketing, you must be clear on your strategy - what you want to achieve and what your business model looks like. It is pointless to choose a way to get published that does not take into account your main routes to market, how people will be discovering you and where you expect be selling the majority of your books.

For example, if you are planning on selling your books through the book trade - that's bricks and mortar shops and online - I recommend your book is printed by short run digital and distributed by a national distributor (like Gardners in Eastbourne) to make it viable. It's worth checking with the partnership publishers you're looking at that they have these routes to market.

If however your main route to market is via your website, email marketing, speaking engagements, joint ventures or strategic partnerships, then you have a greater margin to play with from your sales. Print on demand becomes viable. If you can commit to even a few hundred books and use short run digital, the unit price will come down dramatically. It's all about margin.

If you are producing a full colour book, then digital is not the answer, you will need to use full colour litho in order to get the unit price down below the magic 20% figure discussed in Chapter 13 of this book. You may well need to commit to a run of at least 2,000 to get the optimum unit price and you'll have to pay for this upfront. Unless you can do this, colour might not be the best option.

Q. Should all authors publish an eBook?

A. This is a question I'm often asked. The building blocks of all books are your words, but words can be repurposed and purchased in a variety of different media. Nowadays people will purchase a book in the format they prefer. For example, some people will travel to work by car and will only purchase a book if they can get it as an audio CD to listen to as they drive. Others might travel on public transport and their preferred format might be a downloadable MP3 to listen to on their iPod. Today you will see people reading a book from their Kindle, Nook, iPad, Android tablet or Smartphone. These are all in different electronic formats. Kindle is a proprietary platform used by Amazon (although you can download a Kindle viewer) but you also have EPUB, MOBI and PDF.

The internet is afloat with PDF downloads of varying sizes and quality. No matter how they are dressed up, everyone knows they started life as hastily written Word documents that have delusions of adequacy because they're now being described as a book. Many are poorly written, full of spelling and grammatical mistakes and do no justice to the author whatsoever.

A poorly written eBook can do more harm than good to an author. It is a case of 'publish and be panned!' Whilst eBooks do have their place, and in their various forms are some people's preferred form of receiving information, because of the lack of any third-party quality control and the endorsement that a publisher gives to an eBook, they rarely do much for an author's reputation or standing in the marketplace. They are seen as more of a throw-away business card with no real value. Make sure that if you're writing an eBook that it is written, edited and produced to the highest standard possible.

Q. How do I create an eBook?

A. There is an open source programme called Calibre which is a free download. It works on Windows, OSX and Linux. There are plenty of videos on YouTube that will show you how to use it.

Bear in mind that an eBook is a flowing text format. This means that the amount of text you can view on the screen of your device will change depending on the text size you have selected and the size of your screen. Out of the window go your page numbers. The Table of Contents becomes a table of links to jump to the start of a new chapter.

You are also restricted in the amount of text formatting you can do. Italics and bold in your text are fine, but that's about all. Don't mark out your paragraphs with tabs and don't use multiple paragraph marks for anything. Paragraph indents with multiple spaces should also be avoided. You can use a paragraph style with a first line indent instead. You can set this when you create your document using the Styles Menu. Use Reveal Formatting to see what your layout looks like.

Sometimes Calibre files can be rejected by Amazon for technical reasons. Amazon has now created a Kindle creation programme, KindleGen, which is free to use.

Q. How easy is it to become your own publisher?

A. Most people agree that self publishing is a bit of an obstacle course. Some people make it and others fall at one of the hurdles. It has not been in the interests of publishers to give away their trade secrets and few authors realise all of the steps involved. But despite what publishers would have you believe, there is nothing to stop anyone becoming their own publisher. There's no smoke and mirrors. A publisher is in effect just a project manager with specialist knowledge and contacts plus a flair for marketing and publicity. There is no reason why any author prepared to learn these skills should not succeed. In response to this need we have created a writers group called AuthorCraft. The purpose of this group is not to show authors how to write but to show them how they can bring their books safely and successfully to market by teaching them at a detailed level what a publisher actually does.

Being equipped with this knowledge enables an author to understand the tasks they are best suited to take on and the ones they can delegate with authority—rather than abdicating everything to somebody and paying a hefty sum for the privilege, as so often happens nowadays.

Q. What's the best way to print your book?

A. Authors are spoiled for choice when it comes to printing their book. There are many big businesses offering their services online that talk a good talk and can also print a good book. However many of the best known internet book printers are offering 'consumer' facing services not a 'trade' service - which is why they are not used by the big publishing houses. You'll pay a premium for short runs, and may also be restricted by choices of size, finish and quality.

If you are only distributing through your own routes to market, then you may well only need a few copies at a time. You'll always pay more for short runs. However, if you're a serious author and plan to make a proper business out of your book, then it will cost you much less to go to a trade printer. You may need to commit to a few hundred books at a time rather than a handful, but you will find you're getting better quality for less. Don't compromise.

Q. Please explain Partnership Publishing.

A. Putting ego and the 19th Century publishing model to one side if you were looking to bring any other product than a book to market, you would not hesitate to engage and pay for whatever creative services, production facilities, marketing, publicity and distribution services that were needed to bring your product to market. This is how business works. You invest your money to get a return and a profit. Why should knowledge products such as books be any different?

These days, when an author can be found by anyone in the world in three clicks using a search engine, why get so hung up about treating their book as a business - rather than hoping that some publisher will ride out of the sunset on a white charger brandishing a cheque and taking over? It actually makes little business sense when authors can directly engage with their potential customers and earn vastly more than any publisher would be prepared to pay them. It is ego, not commonsense, that gets in the way.

The reality is that whilst most authors know most of the things a publisher does, few know everything. There are those essential missing links in the supply chain they don't know about. This is not helped by the fact that some organisations look down on humble authors, while others seem to go out of their way to discourage them from taking things into their own hands. There are many who would like to keep the world as it was.

Authors who see the wisdom of being in charge of their business also see the need for a safe pair of hands to work with; a safe pair of hands that can steer them through the hidden crevices of the publishing industry so that they can emerge triumphant with a successful book. To meet this need, there are a growing number of experienced publishers, like Filament, prepared to offer holistic support by working with authors in partnership, rather than reverting to type and going for a land grab of rights. True partnership publishing is just that. The author is in charge with the publisher mentoring as required and handling those tasks that the author chooses to outsource.

A good partnership publisher will have existing relationships with editors, proofreaders, graphic artists, illustrators, printers and distributors and will speed up the process of getting to market. They will also understand the importance of getting as full an entry as possible in all book databases to ensure the title is easily discovered.

Q. What is an ISBN?

A. An ISBN (International Standard Book Number) is used by the book trade to find out the publisher and distributor of a title. The ISBN database in the UK is administered by Nielsen Bookdata (http://www.nielsenbookdata.co.uk/).

If your book is being distributed through the book trade, you will need an ISBN. If you are distributing through your own routes to market only, you don't.

If your book has an ISBN and can be sourced by the book trade, then it can be sold by them at a discount. The book trade will then be your competitor if you want to sell your book at full price from your website. If you want to have price integrity and not be undercut, then don't have an ISBN. But in making that decision, you will restrict your channels to market.

An ISBN on its own is like a car with a registration number that the DVLA doesn't know about. Unless you submit a full and comprehensive entry about your book on to the ISBN database, then it will not be easily found. Always complete all the fields when registering your book ISBN including the author biography, short form and long form book description, table of contents and reviews, plus the technical information about the book dimensions, price, and distributor. A partnership publisher should arrange your ISBN and complete these fields for you.

Q. How can you get your book stocked in a bookshop?

A. As a local author you have a special status with bookshops in your area because you can bypass their normal centralised purchasing procedures. You can approach them direct and they will usually agree to deal directly with you and buy stock at a discount of 40% to 50%. Independent bookshops even further afield can be approached by you in the same way.

To help any book shop make a quick decision in your favour you should produce an 'AIS' or Advanced Information Sheet. This is a one pager that contains:

- Publisher's logo.
- Name of author(s), editor, illustrator, as appropriate.
- Title and strapline, and series title where relevant.
- Cover illustration.
- Publication date.
- Suggested retail price.
- ISBN.
- Number of pages and illustrations.
- Format and binding(s).
- Language.
- Two or three key selling points.
- Brief summary of contents, indicating localities where relevant.
- Brief details of the author(s) or editor: including where they are from and where they live.
- Intended readership.
- Promotional details: serialisation, press, TV and radio features, launches, etc.
- Reviews and recommendations: brief quotations from respected, named sources.

- Author photograph or other appropriate image.
- Publisher's contact details.
- Distributors' contact details.

Remember - one page only!

Q. How can you get your book stocked by the big book distributors?

A. All the book chains centralise their book purchasing which can prove a nightmare for authors. It has to be said they don't readily publicise the names of the category buyers to the public, and that doesn't help either. However, all the bookshops will have an account with Gardners Books in Eastbourne. They have a massive warehouse which seems to cover many acres on multiple floors full of people running around with trolleys. So huge is their stock that Amazon has a dispatch point. If your book is in stock with Gardners it should be in stock with Amazon.

Authors can approach Gardners to set up an account in order to sell their book to the book trade. As a distributor, Gardners will require a discount which covers their margin plus that of their end customer, the retailer. This can be as much as 60% but you can try negotiating! Send Gardners a copy of your AIS which they will make available to the trade. They also produce a monthly Gardners Gazette that is sent to all bookshops with information about new titles.

The buyers at Gardners would place an order with you to hold an amount of stock in their warehouse on a consignment basis. You also need to make sure that Gardners are shown as the distributor on the ISBN database held by Neilson. If you have chosen to work with a partnership publisher they should ensure your book is stocked by Gardners.

Q. What category should you put your book in?

A. Choose more specific categories instead of general categories. Readers looking for very specific topics will find your book more easily. There is an online tool you can use to research your perfect category (http://www. bic.org.uk). Put yourself in the mindset of 'what is my perfect reader searching for?' and 'where are they likely to be looking?'

Q. What common mistakes can authors avoid?

A. When it comes to publishing a book, speed is your enemy. If you rush things, or impose impossible deadlines, mistakes will creep in. It's sensible to get your manuscript read by a professional editor and to obtain a reader's report from them. They will also suggest how you can make your manuscript even better. A reader's report can cost up to £250. Well worth the investment. And always involve a professional proofreader. They see things us ordinary mortals miss. Don't forget that once printed and published your book is going to be around for a while. There is nothing worse than having to apologise for every copy!

Useful websites.

www.gardners.com
www.isbn.nielsenbook.co.uk
www.authorcraft.co.uk
http://calibre-ebook.com/
www.filamentpublishing.com

Case Study No.1:
Self publishing on a shoestring - using CreateSpace and Kindle Direct Publishing.

Author Richard White has published his second book *Consultative Selling for Professional Services* using Amazon CreateSpace and Kindle Direct Publishing, selecting their free services only. This is what he told me about his experience of self publishing using these DIY platforms.

"I used CreateSpace because I was frustrated that my 'paid-for' partnership publishing was not working. I wanted to take control of the process. I had written my book and paid an advance to a publisher but they were taking far too long so I walked away. I looked at a number of self publishing options online but CreateSpace appealed to me because it's free—provided you only use it to upload your manuscript and cover.

"The other services offered by CreateSpace such as typesetting, cover design and editing seemed expensive, which is why I found a professional freelancer on Elance with experience of publishing via Kindle and CreateSpace. She ensured my book was submitted using the right format and layout. Using her, my costs were minimal. I had already done most of the editing, but a final polish including proofreading edits, typesetting and designing my cover, cost just £350 in total.

"I used Kindle Direct Publishing which is owned by Amazon because uploading my text was free and my royalties are paid monthly.

"Because I used the free service I was worried about the quality of my book. Would the paper be too thin? Would it look like a self published book? I ordered printed proofs and a proof book for just £4 and was reassured by the quality, which was excellent.

"The whole process from uploading my book to selling it on Amazon was completed in four weeks.

"Because my books are printed digitally, the cost per book is very low even though they're printed in America. My paperback book retails at £14 on Amazon and £6 for the Kindle version. Even with shipping costs and a two-day delivery I am paying less than £3 per copy.

"With regard to my royalty payments, for the paperback version I get the list price minus the cost of my book and the usual sales channel discount which is 60% for Amazon sales.

"I can change my book at any time by uploading the changes without incurring any additional costs - although if I increase the number of pages for the paperback version the production cost of my book will increase.

"The only downside of using CreateSpace is that I sometimes get charged duty which is a hassle to sort out. There are no downsides to using Kindle Direct Publishing."

Useful websites.

www.elance.com
www.CreateSpace.com
https://kdp.amazon.com/

Case Study No.2:
Self publishing using CreateSpace and Smashwords.

Author Janice B Gordon published her first book *Business Evolution: Creating growth in a rapidly changing world* using Amazon CreateSpace and Smashwords. In this candid interview she shares her self publishing experience.

Q. Why did you use CreateSpace?

A. CreateSpace is not the only print on demand self publishing option but it appears to be the most popular. In my book I discuss the importance of making life easy for your customer. CreateSpace, which is owned by Amazon, makes it easy for authors to publish their book and access their audience through paperback books and Kindle on the Amazon platform only. This is my first book and I worked with a coach who had used CreateSpace to publish her books. She guided me through the many intricacies of the book writing and publishing process. It was absolutely the right decision. I wanted to concentrate on the quality of the content rather than worry about other important elements such as layout and weight of paper. Many self published books look as though they have been printed in a shed in the back garden. I didn't want mine to suffer the same fate and I believe you should play to your strengths. Having gone through the process I now feel confident that if I did it again I wouldn't need further guidance.

Q. How does CreateSpace work?

A. You upload a PDF file of your manuscript and within minutes you can view the digital proof. You can also order a proof copy of your book. Mine arrived from America within five days. Within 24 hours of approving your book it can be selling on Amazon. It's that easy. CreateSpace has a really useful online dashboard system which tells you when your order is complete, incomplete, awaiting action or in process and whether you are at the setup, review or distribute stage of publishing.

CreateSpace has an author community too. Authors can post and answer questions and there are useful FAQs.

Q. What services did you use on CreateSpace?

A. I used the free services on CreateSpace namely setup, review, print, distribution and fulfilment. I used my own cover designer to maintain consistency with my business brand. I had a team of readers and my coach edited my book.

Q. Does CreateSpace sort out the more technical stuff such as your ISBN number, copyright wording and so on?

A. You retain the copyright and yes CreateSpace can assist with the copyright wording and it offers the ISBN free of charge. It is best to purchase and use your own ISBN number though which you can then use on Amazon and through other distribution channels. So if you want to expand your distribution to libraries and bookstores in the UK through Gardners, for example, you don't need another ISBN number. If you have two ISBN numbers your sales will be split between the two numbers which will affect your sales ranking.

Q. How easy was it to get your ISBN number?

A. Self published authors can download an application form at the UK ISBN Agency's website (http://www.isbn.nielsenbook.co.uk/controller. php?page=123). Click on 'services for new publishers' where you can download the application and apply for 10 ISBN numbers at a cost of £132 including VAT.

Q. How did you arrange the 'look inside' facility on Amazon?

A. Books published through CreateSpace automatically become eligible for the free 'look inside' on Amazon.com and Amazon Europe; however you don't get to choose the pages that are shown.

Q. How are the royalty payments worked out?

A. A royalty is calculated on the list price you set for the location where your book is printed. Amazon takes a percentage of the list price for each sales channel. There is a useful tool on CreateSpace called the royalty calculator. You can work out the royalty for your chosen list price based on the trim size and the number of pages in your book.

Q. How easy was it for you to get your book on to Kindle with CreateSpace?

A. You are offered the option of converting your file into Kindle format for free when publishing your book through CreateSpace. A word of warning though. When I received the Kindle version of my book it had many mistakes that my proofreader picked up on including missing words and mixed up sentences.

Q. Have you used other channels to promote your book electronically?

A. Yes. My coach introduced me to Smashwords which is the world's largest distributor of indie eBooks. With one click your book is on Kindle, iTunes and many more platforms. Smashwords offers the fastest and easiest option for distributing an eBook to the world's largest eBook retailers. I did not realise there were so many eBook retailers. I have sold more eBooks through them than through Kindle. The royalties vary.

Q. Are there any downsides to using CreateSpace?

A. CreateSpace is based in America so I have to plan ahead to allow delivery time and balance the cost of postage. For priority shipping it's best to allow up to 10 days; for expedited shipping up to three weeks and standard shipping up to six weeks. Because the CreateSpace paperback version of my book is only sold through Amazon sites I am now looking at extended distribution in the UK and I'm considering Lulu.com, Lightning Source, Berforts and Gardners.

Q. What postage costs do you incur using CreateSpace?

A. For sending one, 30 and 100 printed books they are currently:

		One book	30 books	100 books
Standard	(Six weeks)	$4.88	$48	$112
Expedited	(15 days)	$7.99	$58	$131
Priority	(Seven days)	$14.38	$78	$146

Useful websites.

www.smashwords.com
www.berforts.co.uk

Case Study No.3:
Lightning Source

Jeff Scott is a highly acclaimed and hugely respected PR book publicist and a successful author of several titles. Here's his experience of using Lightning Source.

"The holy grails of self publishing are lots of publicity, critical acclaim and sales. If we have to choose only one then: sales. That said, profitable self publishing is founded upon the business fundamentals of keeping inventory costs low, while achieving ease of availability for the punters and effective distribution. As self publishers, sadly, we don't have the muscle, reputation, systems or deep pockets of commercial publishers. Nevertheless it is still possible to punch above our weight on these fundamentals by using print on demand (PoD) aka print to order publishing services. My recommendation would be to use the services of Lightning Source (LS).*

In a nutshell, if you sign up as a publisher at LS and then upload your book(s), they will always appear as in stock and will immediately be available at Amazon as well as with their 38,000+ other suppliers - namely the booksellers, distributors, libraries and resellers in 220 countries and territories throughout the world who are part of their robust LS/Ingram distribution network.

After you've uploaded your book on LS (and had it accepted), if/when your book is then ordered from Amazon - or by anyone else in their 38,000+ vendor distribution network - LS will immediately print the book to order.

Your book is usually printed and ready for shipment within 12 hours. LS is, in fact, a business unit of the media giant Ingram. It specialises in PoD publishing and distribution. It was an early entrant into PoD book publishing. The story then was that its out of stock frustrations - with publishers who slowly/rarely reprinted their books - were compounded by the significant levels of lost revenues from sales for orders it already had on hand at Ingram. Unprepared to lose these revenues (mostly from single copy orders), initially LS explored PoD to satisfy its own customer demand but, pretty soon, acquired the expertise and product qualities to build such a good market leading mousetrap that it was able to sell its services to big, small, independent and self publishers (as well as authors) alike. Since it entered the PoD space, LS has expanded its product offerings (it now offers PoD colour), extended its geographical reach, expanded its customer base and also enhanced the quality of its product offerings (to the point where, unlike some PoD suppliers, you almost cannot tell a LS book from a traditionally offset printed book).

Unless prone to optimism, people rarely write a book - let alone get it published! If you self publish, you are chief cook and bottle washer but - even if you're extremely careful - it's easy to overestimate potential demand for our own bon mots and, therefore, print too many books. Apart from the storage and distribution issues this immediately creates, if we decide to use a traditional offset book printer then their minimum print is in the region of 500 copies. Whatever the quantity of our offset print run, almost inevitably printing our book is immediately far and away our largest cost expenditure (and a potentially disastrous one at that!) Worse still, we have no guarantees that the stock will actually sell! Amazingly, though it doesn't encourage it and would prefer to work with recognised publishers, you could quickly set yourself up as a publisher with LS and get your books listed as in stock and available on Amazon for a minimum of £50! I'd suggest you spend more money (with Nielsen) to really maximise your impact as a publisher but we'll come to that in due course.

First off, as a self publisher/author, LS gives you exceptional 24/7 control over your book (printing, pricing, discounts, market restrictions), analysis of your book (sales reporting) and, of course, most important of all regular payments for your sales. Another complete joy of the situation is that you never have to hold or store actual print copies of your book (unless you want to do so)! Its minimum print number is ONE copy and there is no maximum print run (bulk stock order discounts automatically apply plus it has promotions and you can even negotiate for larger orders). It provides excellent guidance to using its services remotely (user-friendly interface, step-by-step simple instructions and FAQs), easily available customer service (online, email and phone) for all manner of queries about their processes, publishing protocols, publishing philosophical questions (there are many!) as well as payments.

I have used LS's services for many of my own self published books including my first book *Showered in Shale*. It is surprisingly easy to set up your titles and then sell them (well, obviously, as Dee so helpfully and thoroughly explains in this book, you also do need to create awareness of and demand for your book). Let's briefly consider the case study of my first book with LS to establish the process. I'll look at the charges and revenues as well as suggest possible tips and tricks.

On the website, LS says to new customers, "How do I enter my titles into the Lightning Source system?" It replies with confidence, "In a word, easily." LS continues, "Submit your titles and we do everything else. Titles can be submitted as electronic files or as hard copy to be digitized. You pay only a minimal set-up charge but the benefits are enormous…We handle all aspects of order management including receipt of payment, printing, fulfilment, and paying you for your books that have been purchased each month. There has never been an easier way to profit from your catalogue."

When it comes to producing books, speed is not the only strength at LS. It works fast but also pays close attention to the craftsmanship and also note that it conducts 10 quality control checks on each book before it is shipped. It keeps your book specification options wide open so you can choose from all the most popular book types (black and white or colour), bindings (including hardback and paperback), and trim sizes. LS claims (justifiably) its sharp graphics and crisp text make it virtually impossible to distinguish its on-demand books from the offset copies produced by traditional book printers.

The first stage on the process of working effectively with LS is to - obviously enough - register as a customer. In an ideal world, you will already have a publisher (brand) name and I would recommend that this is how you present yourself to the world (and LS) rather than just as an individual author. I called my publishing company Methanol Press. Though it is not essential (and ignoring that LS always assigns its own ISBN number to any book it prints to order), I would recommend that you have your own ISBNs [International Standard Book Number] from Nielsen (these cost £132 including VAT for 10 ISBNs). This enables you to have complete control over your bibliographic data but also because you can then take advantage of what Nielsen terms its "Enhanced Service". If you have the budget, it is worth investing the £180 required for one year initially before then deciding about any future investment. These sorts of prices are a scandal but that is the Nielsen monopoly (I have had completely shockingly unprofessional customer services experiences with Nielsen but also reasonable ones).

It is worth noting that LS can produce a facsimile of an already existing book as well as working from text files but, for the best more professional looking product, you should use a bespoke pdf. Like all printers, LS has quite specific but straightforward requirements that you must adhere to. It will also need to know a number of other key pieces of information: binding (paperback is best with LS); page extent (number of pages of the book); book format (my recommendation is to choose the formats you like most but, at the same time, remember that LS charges per page printed so if you choose a larger format you require fewer pages); price (in £, $ and €); discount (this determines the wholesale price; I'd recommend 35% as a standard discount—the lower you go the more money you keep but, equally, the less incentive there is for any supplier to promote your book(s) if their earnings per book sold are low); credit card details (to pay for any bulk orders of your books); and bank account details (so they can pay you).

LS has an unavoidable one-off title set-up fee for each and every book of (at the time of writing in July 2014) under £50. That said, LS periodically offers promotions where it waives the title set-up fee if you place an order of a certain quantity - say, 50 books or similar. Whether or not you go down this route to save on set-up costs should be looked at on a case-by-case basis. LS also suggests - but don't mandatorily require - that you "approve" its version of the final copy of your book before it certifies it for sale on its system. This (currently) costs £35 and should be an important part of your own quality control but, if you are confident your pdf is already perfect, you can skip this stage of the process and save this fee. However, if you subsequently require corrections (due to your own errors) this is a false economy since, then, LS treats the new pdf as a new book and again charges the one-off set-up fee. There are shipping charges if you ship books to yourself but you aren't charged shipping fees if wholesalers purchase your books.

To print to order a single copy of any book, in the UK LS charges 1p per page plus a fixed charge of £1.25 per book (this fee applies to all books irrespective of page extent). My book Showered in Shale is 512-pages long so LS charges per unit £6.39—this is calculated as £5.14 (cover adds two pages) + £1.25. My price is £20, my discount 35% so my wholesale price is £13.00—£6.39 giving me £6.61 per copy sold. LS reports sales monthly and pays three months in arrears (i.e. it pays December sales in March). Clearly certain variables could potentially increase my revenue per title—notably, lower page count, higher price, lower discount. Some of these variations are practicable, others not.

Overall, I'd heartily recommend LS as a flexible, cost-effective, quality assured and efficient way to sell your books (especially via Amazon). * Caveat, I have no business connection with this company other than as a contented and successful self publishing user.

Useful website.

www.lightningsource.com

An interview with literary agent Susan Mears.

I have always wondered what a literary agent does and how they can help you get your book accepted by a publishing house. So when I was given the opportunity to interview Susan Mears, a literary agent of some esteem, I jumped at it. This is what Susan told me.

"Before founding my literary agency in 1993, I was a commissioning editor at Century Hutchinson, which later became amalgamated with Random House. I then moved to Piatkus Books (now part of the Little Brown Group) as managing editor for fiction and non-fiction, finally becoming the senior managing editor at Element Books. Throughout this time I was at the receiving end of presentations and proposals from many literary agents and aspiring authors via posted submissions and at the book fairs. I had strict criteria of what I wanted them to provide me with for their title to be taken seriously. As a commissioning editor, I had to have my finger on the pulse of the market on behalf of my publisher and select manuscripts that would sell in all markets around the world. Publishing is a highly commercial business. It can only survive if customers buy books. Then, as now, commissioning editors are under intense pressure to select the right titles. Over the past few years with the publishing industry continuing to go through fundamental change, publishers are more risk averse than ever before with fewer books making the grade. But the rewards are still there for authors who can tick all the boxes.

"And so when I set up my own literary agency, I knew what worked and what commissioning editors were looking for. This enabled me to match authors and their manuscripts to publishers, particularly in the UK and the USA, and to represent them in the way I knew was most effective; now sitting on the other side of the desk.

"I also knew that the big publishing houses were cutting back on running costs and that the 'slush pile editors', who evaluate new manuscripts, were being made redundant. As a result, publishers were becoming even more reliant on literary agents to do the reading and filtering of new manuscripts.

"When a publisher works with a literary agent they expect the agent to have undertaken a thorough evaluation of a manuscript; to believe it has real potential and that it matches the genres they are looking for. A literary agent will not command the ongoing respect of any publisher if they are seen to be wasting their time.

"Every day I receive at least half a dozen unsolicited approaches from authors all over the world. Some are keen to find out if their idea is worth developing. Others will send their completed manuscript and expect me to read it and provide detailed comments. Very few present their book proposal in the form that I require and so fall at the first hurdle.

"So what can you do to give your manuscript the best possible chance of going forward?

"In the same way that publishers increasingly rely upon agents to sift through and find the best manuscripts on their behalf, in turn I rely on experienced readers and editors to read manuscripts and produce a reader's report. A credible third-party endorsement of a manuscript from a professional whose job it is to know what 'good' looks like makes my job much easier. Those authors that use an editor to produce a reader's report give themselves the best possible chance of being accepted. In addition, an independent reader's report often highlights things the author has missed which could make a big difference to the final manuscript. This report should be accompanied by some sample chapters.

If I am then happy to represent the author they will be under contract to the agency and I will include them in my portfolio.

"Most of my meetings with commissioning editors take place at the big book fairs around the world. In the UK the London Book Fair takes place in April every year. I also travel to the Frankfurt Book Fair, the Emirates Literary Festival and other big events in the USA.

"Many authors don't understand these are trade events and so turn up at them clutching their manuscript, hoping to be signed up. Whilst all the big publishing houses have stands, they are staffed by sales people whose job it is to sell books, not commissioning editors. Many don't know who the commissioning editors are within their company, let along be able to broker an introduction to them! The editors are tucked away in the Agents Hall which is only accessible by appointment. It's here where the literary agents and the editors do business and weave their magic.

"At a book fair, I will have a portfolio of one-page proposals that I use as the basis of my presentation to an editor. I will have found out from an editor the genres they are looking for and will spend a couple of minutes highlighting the main points of the proposals that match their criteria. At this point, all that's required is a well written one-page synopsis highlighting the author's track record, their success at media, PR and marketing, their previous publishing history and sales figures. There isn't time for anything more. The editor will identify the books they are interested in, and after the fair I will follow up with a more substantial document. This all takes place via email.

"To help me to represent any author I need the following:

- A well crafted 'one-pager' - a tightly written summary of what the book is about.

- The gap in the market that the book will fill.

- A few facts about the author and their background, including previous titles.

- Recent media activity.

- The following the author has in their sector.

"Whilst I know that any author worth their salt could easily write 10,000 words on this all I need is one page.

"If this does the trick and an editor wants to find out more I will require the following from the author:

- A synopsis of each chapter.

- A 'long form' description of the book.

- A more extensive author biography.

- A minimum of four well proofed consecutive chapters.

"At the last London Book Fair there was interest in every proposal in my portfolio which is wonderful but this initial interest has to be whittled down to firm offers.

"Once a publisher has expressed an interest, and we have followed up with a full submission it's quite normal for a few months to elapse before I hear back from them. Authors expect to hear something the following week which is unlikely unless they have a track record of selling millions of books.

"It's most definitely a waiting game and first-time authors particularly have to understand this. If you're lucky enough to be made an offer, it can take a while to negotiate any advance payments and sadly many books do not sell in sufficient quantities to earn out their advance.

"However, new authors don't have to wait for a commitment and a deal from a publisher before starting to receive an income from their manuscript. Commissioning editors are increasingly influenced by the success an author has had with their own edition. For those authors who self publish, achieve good reviews and positive media coverage, a book deal is more likely because any risk to the publisher is minimised."

As you can see, when it comes to publishing your book you have many choices. I encourage you to use this chapter as a springboard for researching the publishing options that interest you in more detail before making your final choice.

Chapter summary.

- It pays to explore your publishing options in detail. Weigh up the costs and benefits of self publishing, partnership publishing and using a literary agent.

- If you're considering a partnership publisher do your homework. Look at their financial standing, the services on offer, how much you'll pay and how they'll promote your book beyond online placement.

- Don't sign up to a partnership publisher until you have spoken to some of their authors and are confident they can provide you with more than just a bog standard book production service that you could do yourself.

- A good partnership publisher should be able to promote your book in other countries and open doors that you can't.

- If you decide to self publish your book, don't cut corners. You want it to look and feel as good as any book from a mainstream publishing house.

- Whilst it's easy to become your own publisher, you may want to outsource some parts of the publishing process.

- You need to weigh up the merits of digital printing and print on demand.

- A bestselling book should be a profit-making book.

- If you want your book to be stocked in a bookshop, prepare a concise Advanced Information Sheet.

- If you want your books to be stocked by Gardners or other distributors you can approach them to set up an account - but they will ask for as much as a 60% discount on your cover price.

- Make sure that your book is placed in a category. When it reaches the top 100 bestselling books in its category you can legitimately say you are a bestselling author!

- A literary agent has strong bonds with mainstream publishers. But make sure you present your pitch appropriately if you decide to contact one.

- If you're using online resources such as CreateSpace and Kindle Direct Publishing be aware of the services that are free and the services you have to pay for. Would you benefit from a little extra help?

CHAPTER 13

How to Price Your Book and Avoid the Mistakes Many Authors Make

Tempting though it may be, you can't just pluck a figure out of thin air for the cover price of your book for either the paperback or hardback version. There are a number of factors that will influence its cover price. A big factor is the cost of producing your book which will be based on the following:

- **The number of pages.** Your final page count is dependent on many factors including your total word count, any additional pages you're planning on using for diagrams and images and your font and point size. As a rough guide, divide the number of words in your manuscript by 300 (words per page) to give you an approximate page count - excluding pictures, diagrams and your additional pages such as the foreword, acknowledgements and conclusion.

  Of course, you can cram more than 300 words onto a page by using a smaller point size and adjusting the line spacing, but this won't make your book attractive and it won't make it easy to read. Don't be tempted to shoehorn text in to save on the expense of adding a few more pages.

- **The quality of the cover.** If you're keen to have special printed finishes on your cover and extras such as pull out flaps or special pockets, these will increase your unit cost. However a nice gloss laminate or matt laminate cover finish is fairly standard these days and should not add noticeably to the unit cost.

- **If you're keeping costs down** opt for black-and-white printing inside your book rather than using colour. Digital colour is expensive right now. It can add around six pence per page to the cost of printing. If you're relying on the book being printed to order around the world, you may find that some platforms don't allow for adding colour pages. On most systems the book is either in full colour or in black and white. If colour is going to feature heavily in your book, you might have to look at full colour litho printing, which has the downside of requiring a significant run (1000-2000) to make it viable.

- **The quality of the paper.** There are a number of different finishes and paper weights to choose from. The heavier the paper the more you pay. The paper weight of this book is 100gsm. Be aware too that whilst a luxurious paper might look very attractive, the extra weight will also push up your postage costs.

- **How your book is going to be published.** Short run digital publishing is much cheaper than print on demand as Chris Day explains further on.

So whilst I would encourage you to steer away from an obviously cheap and cheerful approach to your book's look and feel (it won't make it popular with readers), you can keep production costs down by opting for an attractive, professionally designed cover without any embellishments, fancy flaps or special finishes. Select a nice quality paper for the inside of your book that feels smooth to the touch and that's not transparent when held up to the light; a small gesture that won't bump up the price of your book. You can get carried away and create a book that's far too expensive to produce. By doing this you won't be able to fund the additional costs and the discounts demanded from resellers - costs that have to be funded from within the cover price of your book.

It's wise to research the options for printing your book whether you are self publishing, using an online publisher such as CreateSpace, or working with a partnership publisher. For my books I have always opted for good quality basics with a full colour cover but 100% black and white inside, no frills. This means I still get a decent royalty per book and my books sell globally on different publishing platforms.

The book resellers want their cut too.

Another factor that must influence the cover price of your book is the discount that online resellers such as Amazon will take - an eye watering 60% discount on the cover price, with bookshops taking around 40%.

Online resellers such as Amazon offer you the potential of a global reach on a huge platform. They can get your book out there in the big wide world. I have benefited tremendously from Amazon, selling thousands of books, but at a cost. This is why you have to keep your book production costs low and your book sales high. These discounts have to be found from within the cover price of your book!

Bear in mind too that if you're working with a partnership publisher you will have to deduct their fee per book from the cover price. This should ideally be no more than 10% of the cover price of your book.

Let's look at how this works.

A book with a cover price of £14.99.

- Trade discount at the maximum 60% = £8.99. This leaves you with £6.

- Out of the £6 comes printing and distribution costs, say £3 (20% of the cover price).

- This leaves £3 left to share between you and your publisher.

A book with a cover price of £16.00.

- Trade discount at the maximum 60% = £9.60. This leaves you with £6.40.

- Out of the £6.40 comes printing and distribution costs, say £3 (19% of the cover price).

- This leaves £3.40 left to share between you and your publisher.

You can see how important it is to keep your costs as low as possible. And you can't afford to overlook the cost of any extras that could make it impossible to make money when you market your book through book resellers. It's entirely possible to end up with a book that is producing a loss no matter how many copies you sell simply because you have made it so expensive to produce. By the time the resellers have taken their cut, there's nothing left over for you or, even worse, you're making a loss on each book.

You want to sell books from your own stock and make money.

If you're bulk selling from your own stock, for example when you're speaking at an event and the organisers want to bulk-buy copies, you'll be expected to offer a discount of around 30% on the cover price. If you don't, you run the risk of them buying online instead because your price can't compete with the online discounted price; another reason to keep your unit costs down. You should be able to offer a generous discount and still make a healthy profit margin from your own stock.

Find out the prices being charged for similar books.

Another factor that will influence what you can charge for your book rather than what you would like to charge for it is the cover price currently being charged for similar books within your category.

For example, many paperback fiction books are priced between £4.99 and £9.99. If you're planning on charging £15.99 for yours, you run the very real risk that readers won't give it a second glance because it's not within the market price range they are accustomed to paying. There is however more flexibility on the price that can be charged for a non-fiction book.

I have seen business books comprising a measly 120 pages with an eye-watering cover price of £14.99 on Amazon. They're not selling however. Bear in mind that the readers you are aiming at will be weighing up the price of your book with others that fall in the same category. If yours is the most expensive by a mile it could cost you in sales (unless readers can grasp in seconds that your book is offering something that far exceeds similar books). So, instead of being tempted to increase your cover price to accommodate the production costs of your book and the discounts demanded by the resellers, consider how you can make some nips and tucks to the finish and feel of it instead.

Wise words from Chris Day, an experienced publisher...

"It's not easy to get the retail price of a book right. Some authors will want to overprice it which means they won't sell many, and other will underprice it and make a loss on each copy. Do your research and see what similar books are being priced at. I say 'priced' rather than 'sold' because the book trade will discount a book from its cover price in order to tempt the customer to buy from them. There is currently a very unhealthy culture of over-discounting with some online retailers which is damaging bookshops.

"Whilst you can set the cover price, you have no control on what others will sell it at. As Dee says, if your book is going to be sold through the book trade, it will be supplied to them at a discount of up to 60% which means that you only get 40% of the cover price to pay for the printing - and to put bread on your table.

"That is why the rule of thumb when pricing a book is that the single copy print price has to be less than 20% of the cover price.

"If this doesn't work, that is if by multiplying the single copy price by five, the book is too expensive, then you will need to print more copies in order to bring the price down to that magic 20%. The formula from books printed by print on demand makes achieving this percentage difficult because it typically costs 1p per page plus around £1 to print and bind. This puts the cost of printing a 200 page book at £3. If it was selling at £10 that'd make the single copy price 30%, leaving the author with just 10% of a margin after a 60% trade discount. Short run digital printing provides a lower print cost and is the reason why we as publishers now choose this option."

"Before making the final decision on what you want your book to look and feel like and how it will be printed, make sure that you get prices in writing for every option you are considering including the shipping costs of your book if you are using a self publishing platform such as CreateSpace. You will have to consider your production costs and how much they will eat into the cover price of your book. The last thing you want is to produce a book that looks beautiful but doesn't make money or, worse still, makes a loss on each book. If you can focus on producing a very well written and laid out book and you're selling it at a fair price, you shouldn't need costly additional touches to generate book sales."

Chapter summary.

- There is a formula for pricing your book. It's not simply a matter of deciding what you want to charge for it.

- The cover price of your book has to be based on the cost of producing it and this should encompass: the number of pages, finish of the cover, and whether it is printed in full colour, part colour or black and white only.

- The cost of producing your book should not exceed 20% of its cover price.

- You can keep production costs down by opting for a book that will be 'brilliant at the basics' - no fancy frills to bump up the cost.

- Book resellers will take their cut too - typically 40% to 60% of the cover price of your book.

- You can make money selling books from your own stock but be prepared to offer up to a 30% discount on the cover price so you can be competitive with online resellers such as Amazon.

- Before arriving at your final price compare it with the prices charged for similar books. You can underprice your book and overprice it.

CHAPTER 14

How to Market Your Book to Bestselling Success

If you read the following chapters and formulate your marketing plan before you've finished writing your book, so much the better. By the time it's published you will have built up a full head of steam. There's much you can do to get the upper hand when it comes to marketing your book as will become evident in these chapters.

But please do not despair if you've bought my book because your book is nearing publication or it's already been published and you're struggling with the whole concept of marketing it.

You can make up for lost time if you put these tips into practice and refuse to allow excuses to get in the way of marketing your book.

As I've mentioned before, a good book can become a bestseller if its great content is teamed with an equally great marketing plan. By the same token a good book can sink into obscurity through a lack of marketing. Marketing isn't difficult once you've decided what you're going to do to promote your book and you don't need previous marketing experience if you follow my tips closely.

The biggest commitment you have to make is that of your time. You'll need to promote your book consistently and not just when you're in the mood. You'll also have to harness your writing talent to create enticing press releases, interesting articles and attention-grabbing news.

The paybacks are fantastic. If you can build a marketing momentum over several months your book sales will steadily climb. You'll get more five-star reviews on Amazon which will lead to more sales. And you'll be offered all manner of exciting opportunities that will increase your profile as a successful author.

Sooner rather than later you will reach the number one spot in your category on Amazon, which is cause for celebration indeed. But this is just the start of your journey as a bestselling author. A surge of interest can mean that you stay at the number one spot for hours, maybe even days, but eventually your book will move down the ranks, possibly even out of the top 100 books in its category. And that's why your marketing has to be ongoing and consistent. You're aiming for book sales that increase over a period of time so that you stay in the top 100. You should be aiming for book sales every day, which is why I recommend that your marketing begins when you start writing your book and that it continues in earnest for 12 months after your book has been published. I'm not suggesting that you abandon marketing after 12 months but, by this time, you will have generated enough sales for your book to feature in searches and, by regularly reaching the number one slot in your category, Amazon should be promoting it to its database. This is most certainly my experience.

So, I hope you're excited at the prospect of marketing your book.

Where do you start?

To give you an idea of the many low cost and no cost ways there are to promote your book, here's how I have successfully promoted mine on a shoestring budget.

Make a note of what appeals to you but only after answering this question: "Will this help me reach potential readers and people of influence who could endorse or recommend my book?"

1. Social media: Twitter, Facebook, LinkedIn.

2. Blogging on my own website.

3. Guest blogging on other sites that are popular with my target audience.

4. Responding to questions on forums as a helpful and expert voice.

5. Public speaking: 10 minute talks at local business networking groups; being a seminar speaker at exhibitions and local interest groups; being a keynote speaker at national conferences and company conventions.

6. Email marketing to my database and to third-party databases.

7. Business networking at regular events organised by national networking organisations such as 4Networking and BNI plus local networking events and special interest networking groups.

8. PR: editorial, author features, book reviews, top tips, news, serialisation of my book in printed magazines and newspapers and in online publications.

9. Radio: community radio, regional and national stations.

10. Seminars and masterclasses: combining book signings with informative presentations.

11. Video: creating videos for my website, for my readers in China; working in partnership with organisations such as the Institute of Directors and The Chartered Institute of Marketing and creating videos sharing marketing tips with their audience.

12. Podcasts: being interviewed by experts with a following of small business owners.

13. Skype interviews with university students studying marketing.

14. Book signings: at bookshops, at events I've been invited to speak at, and exhibitions I've attended as an exhibitor.

15. Book promotions/book of the month initiatives with influential groups: working with membership organisations, trade associations, and other groups with a membership base of my target audiences, offering my book at a special price or with an added value extra such as a free webinar or a one-to-one marketing session with me.

16. Book launches for all of my books.

17. Exhibitions: exhibiting at local events, selling books on my stand plus keynote talks and book signings.

18. Giving away copies of my books to key people of influence; folk I am hopeful will review my books in glowing terms/promote them on their blog/in their magazine/recommend them to their subscribers/readers/members.

19. Swapping books with other business authors for mutually beneficial promotion.

20. Giving copies of books away at exhibitions as competition prizes in exchange for publicity in the pre-event communications.

21. Being a guest author in other authors' books; writing the foreword or sharing marketing tips in exchange for promoting my latest book.

22. Being a guest contributor in one of my clients' newsletters.

23. Asking readers who contact me if they will write a review on Amazon.

24. Asking attendees at my book launch if they will recommend my book to their contacts.

25. Creating pages on my website to sell my books.

I would encourage you to commit to at least six to eight marketing channels. Most of your time will be spent on these but it also pays to be open to opportunities that have not made it to your shortlist. I've spent most of my time on:

1. Twitter.

2. Public speaking.

3. PR in printed and online publications.

4. My book launch, other book launches and book signings.

5. Blogging on websites popular with small businesses.

6. Book promotions through membership organisations.

7. Exhibitions.

8. Business networking.

Ideally your choices should complement one another. For example if you're exhibiting at an event you can try and secure a speaker slot and can promote the event using social media.

Blogging, PR and Twitter are complementary. You can promote a blog post via Twitter and in any articles or columns you write for magazines, other blogs and newspapers. So spend a little time thinking about how your chosen marketing activities can join up to intensify their impact.

Make sure to keep an eye on other marketing opportunities that are not on your shortlist but are still worth considering.

I would recommend you take full advantage of social media (especially Twitter) to promote your book - unless you have good reasons not to. Many readers will find you via social media and will want to message you on Twitter. And of course with social media it's easy for you to ask a happy reader if they will pop a review on Amazon.

Creating your 'marketing on a shoestring' plan.

Your book promotion marketing plan should ideally be divided into four stages so it's easy for you to know what you have to do and why, when you are going to do it and how you will do it. As I mentioned at the start of this chapter, if you have already written your book you can still follow this process. It's just the timescales that will be different.

Stage one: Starting out (when you're in the planning phase of your book).

Stage two: One to three months before publication (when you've finished writing your book and it's in the proofing/production phase).

Stage three: Launch date (when your printed book is in your hands).

Stage four: Post launch (the 12-month period after your book has been released).

Here are some tips based on my approach to help you build a powerful, easy-to-implement marketing on a shoestring plan.

Stage one: researching opportunities.

This is the time when you are researching the potential opportunities for promoting your book. Look upon this stage as laying the foundations for the three that follow it.

Depending on your choice of marketing activities you'll want to find out more about:

- The magazines, newspapers, newsletters, blogs and forums that are popular with your target audiences.

- The opportunities that exist for you to speak locally for example at your Rotary club, special interest groups, business groups, business networking groups, your local Toastmasters group.

- The exhibitions and events aimed at your target audience that are taking place locally, regionally and nationally. You may be interested in exhibiting and speaking at one or more of these depending on the timing, the costs and the visitors they are targeting.

- Local and community radio stations that are hungry for news and interesting stories.

- The membership organisations and groups that could be interested in promoting your book to their members, followers or visitors.

- The key people of influence who could promote and endorse your book to their 'tribes'.

Hopefully you get my gist which is to spend this time on researching how you can promote your book using your preferred six to eight marketing channels.

When you've completed your research you can create a marketing shortlist of the potential opportunities you're going to pursue in the subsequent stages.

Amazon Author Central.

At this stage I would strongly encourage you to familiarise yourself with all of the free services at Author Central; a free resource that has been created for authors so they can promote their books for free on Amazon. You can create your biography, add photos and upload your book cover. You can also enrol your book in their Associates programme and arrange the 'look inside' tool. These are simple things you can do to promote your book. To access Author Central your book has to be listed on Amazon. You can use your existing customer account to get started or you can create a new one. I have always found Amazon really helpful in providing advice by email, phone or live chat so if you're unsure how to use Author Central just get in touch with them as I did.

If you hover over the name of an author on their book page it will provide a link to Author Central and from there you can contact Amazon. They will tell you how you can get your book listed. Or you can access Author Central immediately if your book is already listed. If you are working with a partnership publisher they should arrange your book's listing, loading your cover and 'look inside'. They should also ensure your book is placed in the right category.

Alas, Authorhouse placed my book in the wrong category. I only discovered the category it should have been in when browsing another author's marketing book. When it was placed in the category of small business marketing books it went straight into the top five bestsellers. Your book could be a bestseller, but it has to be placed in a relevant category for you to claim this. You can find the right category for your book simply by looking at the categories that similar books are listed in.

Research pays off: a case study.

What sort of information should you be gathering at this early stage so you can effectively pitch your book when the time is right? Let me answer this by sharing my approach.

The Federation of Small Businesses (FSB) is a membership organisation I was interested in targeting. After researching the FSB online and attending some of their events I knew they warranted being on my marketing shortlist because their small business members were the ideal target audience for my book. I was therefore keen for my book to be reviewed in the FSB magazine which I discovered was distributed to 180,000 members who were mostly small business owners. I got a copy of their magazine and read it thoroughly, paying attention to the book review page and the style of the reviewer. I then contacted the FSB HQ and asked for the reviewer's full contact details because I wanted to contact him at stage three when my book would be available for him to review.

When my book was published I composed a handwritten letter for the reviewer outlining my appreciation of his reviewing style with a few facts about my book and why I believed it would be a valuable resource for FSB members. I enclosed a copy of my book in the hope it would persuade him to review it. I followed up by telephone a week later. He subsequently reviewed it in glowing terms. This resulted in my book reaching the number one spot in the small business marketing category on Amazon and remaining there for several days. Because I'd done my homework in the early stages of planning my book, I knew who I had to target within the FSB and how to communicate with the reviewer. I had asked for his address when contacting the FSB helpline knowing it would be hard for him to ignore my personal approach of a letter and copy of my book.

But this review was not the end of the story.

Reinforcing the point I made earlier about the importance of choosing marketing activities that complement one another, as soon as the review was published in the FSB magazine, I targeted the local FSB business networking groups with a copy of it. I offered my services as a speaker and suggested a book signing. As a result I was invited to speak to several groups. My talks and book signings were then promoted in the local FSB newsletters and I was subsequently invited to exhibit at a regional FSB exhibition free of charge. I was given a keynote speaker slot too.

These opportunities stemmed from me identifying the FSB as an organisation I wanted to target and doing my homework on it. It's an approach I've adopted when targeting, for example, The Forum of Private Businesses, Royal Mail, The Business Show and The Financial Mail. It definitely works. Start as I do by researching the opportunity, building a profile of the people you want to target and ensuring your messages are charming and relevant. And don't wait for busy people to get back to you.

What else can you do at stage one?

If you haven't already done so, set yourself up on Twitter. Share your writing progress with a daily tweet. By the time you've reached stage three your followers will be eagerly awaiting the launch of your book. If you're already on Twitter share a daily tweet charting your book writing progress.

Stage two: one to three months before publication.

By now the finishing post is in sight so you can make firm plans confident that production delays won't scupper them. The last thing you want is to agree on a whole load of promotional activities only to cancel them because your book has been held up in production.

I have seen this happen before and it can be frustrating to build great momentum and then have to slam on the brakes. That's not to say you can't approach journalists, editors and bloggers, for example, before this stage. But it's best to sound them out and tentatively talk dates rather than agreeing to inflexible copy deadlines for submitting articles when you're still planning your book. That would just put you under unnecessary pressure.

At stage two you should be thinking about:

- Confirming the date for your book launch. You can compose your guest list and ensure every person is aware of the date before you send out formal invites.

- Pitching your ideas to editors, journalists and bloggers, and agreeing to their copy deadlines and the dates you will be sending copies of your book for review.

- Approaching the radio stations you'd like to interview you and suggesting dates when you can pop in with your brand-new book in your hands.

- Approaching the membership organisations and trade associations you've shortlisted for your pitch; the reasons why they should promote your book to their members and how they can benefit from being associated with it.

- Emailing your database so they know when your book is being launched and when it's available to pre-order.

- Visiting local networking groups so you can talk about your book; what it's about, why it's going to be a bestseller, and how people can get hold of a copy.

- Approaching your local bookshops and pitching the idea of a book signing in the first few days or weeks after your launch.

- Creating videos to promote your book.

- Intensifying your activity on social media. For example you could offer a free chapter to your fans and followers, share your book cover, drip feed some of the content, and ask for introductions to journalists, editors, bloggers, and event organisers.

- Writing the sales literature that will promote you and your book.

- Pitching your speaking and book signing services to event organisers so you can fill your diary with speaking engagements.

- Creating the web pages that are going to promote your book.

- Enlisting the support of the key people you've earmarked for reading and reviewing your book within the first few weeks before it is launched. This should kick-start your Amazon reviews.

- Letting everyone within earshot know the launch date of your book with a countdown two weeks before that glorious day.

And more of course depending on your chosen marketing activities! If stage one is all about researching opportunities, stage two is about turning those opportunities into action.

However I don't want you to think that you can't commit to a marketing activity before this one-to-three month window. You may well be offered opportunities to promote your book at stage one and declining them would be foolish. For example when I was writing the chapters of this book I was offered a public speaking engagement, a book signing and the opportunity to attend a conference. It would have been madness to turn any of these down simply because my book was not at the final stage of production. In fact, being offered these opportunities so early helped keep me on track and focused on my deadlines.

The reason why I suggest you start making commitments in the three months before your book is launched is because you're not only on fairly safe ground but getting the marketing momentum going a few months before it's published will help your book reach the bestsellers sooner rather than later. You can then build on this positive beginning with more targeted promotions. I have seen too many authors leave the promotion of their book until after their book has launched.

Stage three: launch.

That wonderful day arrives when you're holding the book in your hands. Now it's time for your marketing to really kick off. So book time out from your usual routine to focus on your launch marketing.

At this stage I would encourage you to:

- Send copies of your book to the influential people, journalists, editors, and reviewers who made it onto your shortlist.

- Chase up the Amazon reviews you were promised from the people you sent your final manuscript to.

- Email your database with the good news that your book is now available. Include an extract from it and the first positive comments from readers.

- Post regular messages on social media about the availability of your book interspersed with positive comments from your early reviewers.

- Deliver the articles, top tips, blogs, and book serialisations you promised to those journalists, editors and bloggers. This should be an ongoing exercise.

- Promote your videos as a footnote on every email you send, on your blogs, in all printed communications, and on social media.

- Research more opportunities to promote your book keeping your targeted audiences at the forefront of your mind when doing so.

- Put the final touches to your book launch, reminding your guests what's in store.

- Visit as many networking events as possible - morning, lunch and evening events - with plenty of copies of your book.

- Visit the special interest groups and associations that are popular with your target audiences.

- Create new press releases to include positive comments from reviewers.

- Build on your growing community of readers on social media by responding to their messages promptly.

And more of course! This is an exciting time - one where you are rewarded for the hard work you put in at stages one and two. But if you're aiming for an enduring bestseller, your marketing should not grind to a halt within a month or so of your book being available. It's time for the next stage...

Stage four: ongoing marketing.

At the time of writing this book I have reached stage four of promoting my third book and I am moving into stage two of promoting this book (effectively juggling two books at different stages of their promotional journey!) I thought you might find it useful if I shared what I am currently doing and what I've done recently to promote my third book which is, as I write, number one in its category of small business sales and marketing books.

- Nearly every day I post messages on Twitter sharing tips from the book, giving updates on its Amazon position and respond to messages from readers, retweeting their photographs of my book and their lovely messages.

Here are two tweets I've posted in the past 24 hours promoting my book:

"The 74th review just been added for http://www.amazon.co.uk/product-reviews from the eminent Wiley business networking author @NoRedBraces."

"In need of a powerful marketing plan + hundreds of proven tips? My latest book's rocking the bestsellers at #1 http://www.amazon.co.uk/gp/bestsellers/books…"

And here are tweets from two readers that I retweeted to my followers:

"I just bought: The 15 Essential Marketing Masterclasses For Your Small Business by @DeeBlick via @AmazonUK http://www.amazon.co.uk…"

"Just finished reading @deeblick marketing book for small businesses. What a helpful book! Thanks Dee."

- I am writing regular columns for several magazines and blogs.

- I am continuing to build relationships with readers, reviewers and influential folk who have been kind enough to promote my book. I keep in touch by phone, email and Twitter. Only today, one of my readers contacted me and told me that she recommends my marketing books to anyone within earshot.

- I have speaking engagements booked 12 months ahead and have negotiated a book signing at each event with promotion of me and my book within the organiser's marketing communications.

- I give away three copies of my book at every exhibition I speak at in exchange for some publicity on Twitter and on the exhibitor's website.

- I approached BBC Radio Sussex and Surrey a few weeks ago and suggested they interview me as a successful local businesswoman/author. This paid off handsomely and I was invited to take part in a live 20 minute interview at their HQ. (If you don't ask you don't get!) You can read more about this interview and how you can shine on the radio in Chapter 17.

- After being told my book had been awarded *Talk Business Magazine's* 'Best business book of 2013', I approached the editor on Twitter and offered to write a marketing article. This paid off and I was given a full page and offered an additional 200 words to promote me and my book.

- I ask every reader who contacts me if they will post a review on Amazon. When the review has been posted, I tweet about it and use the growing number of great reviews to persuade organisations to consider recommending my book to their members. I also ask publications to consider reviewing it.

- I am always on the lookout for opportunities to speak, to exhibit and do book signings. My book promotion radar is permanently switched on. In the past few weeks I have been a keynote speaker at a couple of conferences organised by The Chartered Institute of Marketing, at a local exhibition and at The Business Show in London. I have been able to promote my book at each event.

- Every month I take stock of the coverage of my book, identifying where my sales are coming from and using this information to decide where I should focus my time and energy in the next few months. This is important. I have a full-time business to run and, as an established author, I am sometimes offered opportunities to promote my book that would take too much effort for too little a return. Make sure that you keep tabs on what is working and what isn't so you can improve, change and jettison!

How to get your book on the first page of related Amazon searches.

In this chapter we have been looking at what you can do to promote your book at its various stages. And, as I mentioned earlier, it pays to take advantage of the free services provided by Amazon Central. But this doesn't guarantee that your book will appear even when a person searches for you on Amazon by author name or book title. Similarly, when a person is searching for books in your category, there is no guarantee that the details of your book will appear on the first few pages that the Amazon search engine delivers, let alone the first page, which is what you should be aiming for.

The most likely reason behind this lack of visibility is that your book has not yet sold enough for it to rank highly when any relevant search terms are used. As it grows in popularity it is more likely to feature with other popular books but you may still find that it's buried several pages in. Sadly few people are willing to scroll through several pages of books before they find yours. They are more likely to buy a book that is on the first page.

But all is not lost. There are a few simple things you can do to rectify this situation so that your book features on the first page of any relevant search even before it has become a bestseller. I learned what I am about to share with you by trial and error with my second book and this is the first time I've ever shared it. This is what I do:

- I use the search bar on Amazon and, one by one, type in phrases that are linked to 'small business marketing books', the category my books are listed under. For example, I'll type 'marketing books for small businesses' and 'small business marketing books' and other similar phrases.

- Next I click on the link which will bring up many pages of marketing books.

- I find the page my books are on. (In the early days it would take some time to find them whereas now they are on the first page for the search phrase 'small business marketing books').

- I click on the link that takes me to the buying page of my book. I exit the page and start the process again using other relevant search terms.

- I repeat this entire process three to four times every day. Yes, every day!

What is the benefit of doing this? My books eventually reach the front page for some of the most popular search terms. What this means is that when a person is searching for small business marketing books using one of these terms or a similar one, my books are the first ones they see and more often than not they appear at positions one and three. It's much more likely that if a person is genuinely interested in buying a book about small business marketing they will buy mine because they are the first two books to greet them.

This simple little exercise takes no more than five to ten minutes every day. The payback is well worth it because you want to be on the front page and as high up as possible for relevant searches. When your book has reached the bestsellers the likelihood is that it will remain in its coveted spot on the front page but, to ensure it stays there, repeat this process every day. That's why it is important that your book is placed in the right category too because this will increase the likelihood further still of a person finding your book when they are searching online.

I would encourage you to spend some time playing around with the search terms that will locate the books in your category before your book is listed on Amazon. Then when your book is listed, start this process and stick with it. Very few authors know about this so let me know how you get on!

I'm hoping that if you believed before reading this chapter that marketing your book would be an uphill struggle, you can now see that with effort, planning and time you can do it!

Chapter summary.

- Behind every bestselling book you'll usually find an author committed to marketing it through thick and thin.

- Marketing experience is not necessary to effectively market your book but you will have to devote time on a regular basis.

- Initially marketing might seem strange or unfamiliar especially as you move from being the writer of your book to its marketer, but stick with it. In no time the tables will turn and you will become sought-after.

- Choose six to eight marketing activities to promote your book on the basis that these chosen tactics will enable you to communicate with your different groups of target readers.

- The first stage of your marketing is all about researching opportunities. At the second stage you're confirming, pitching and creating.

- Stage three is about delivering on your promises and at stage four you're maintaining the marketing momentum.

- Search and click on Amazon every day to get your book on the front page for relevant searches.

- Is your marketing plan working? Evaluate it on a regular basis.

- Be on the lookout for new opportunities to promote your book but bear in mind that you don't have to agree to every one of them.

CHAPTER 15

Use PR and Sell
Thousands of Books!

Over the past 31 years I have worked with many journalists and editors from a wide range of publications and so have built an understanding of what they're looking for when approached by a person keen to secure coverage in their publication.

The day I cottoned on to the power of PR for generating book sales was when my book was reviewed in the FSB Magazine (as outlined in the previous chapter). The combination of 150 words, a hearty endorsement from the reviewer and an image of my book propelled it to the number one spot in its category on Amazon where it stayed for several days. From that moment on I have committed time and effort to getting PR for my books and have benefited immensely from this ongoing exposure.

I'm confident that if you can use the tips in this chapter which focus on how to approach the media and how to write good quality targeted content, that you will benefit from generous media exposure too.

Whilst this chapter covers how you can get PR for your book from printed publications, the same principles apply to getting coverage in online publications too. I don't really distinguish between pixels and print although I often find it easier to get coverage in an online publication as opposed to a printed one.

By printed publications I'm referring to all manner of titles from your local newspaper to the daily tabloids and broadsheets, trade magazines, special interest titles and glossy magazines.

What I can say is that regardless of the type of publication you'd like your book to be featured in, the way in which you identify interesting ideas and news about your book and then communicate these to a journalist, are the same. That said it's much easier to get PR coverage in a special interest magazine read by your target audience than the daily broadsheets or tabloid newspapers. This is because they have a never-ending supply of newsworthy stories that are fed to them by PR agencies. It's not impossible to get coverage in a daily newspaper and if your subject matter is topical at the time of publishing it might be easy. But by and large securing national exposure takes an awful lot of persistence and charm for what can amount to a mere smattering of coverage.

Thankfully sitting beneath these in-demand dailies are magazines, journals and newspapers crying out for good quality news, articles, reviews, columns and press releases about your book. I would therefore encourage you to focus your efforts and your precious time on these. Your target audiences will read publications that appeal to their interests and it's these publications you should be focusing on. I've gained full page and double page features of my books in many trade and business titles that you may not have come across - but they reach my target readers and they are the people I want to appeal to. I've also written a monthly news column for the past three years for our local newspaper, *The District Post*, which has a thriving business column and is very popular in the Horsham area. Because of our relationship, the editor is always happy to publish my press releases. There could be many similar PR opportunities in front of your nose right now.

Although my books have been featured in *The Daily Mail*, *The Sun* and *The Financial Times*, the coverage in each paper comprised little more than a small reference to my book. I reckon I've sold more books by promoting this coverage on social media, at networking events and when public speaking than I have from the papers' readers buying a copy of my book. So whilst I am not discouraging you from aiming for national coverage, I'd advise you to focus your time on publications that are much easier to access and that offer the potential for substantial exposure because you're able to build a relationship with the journalist. A regular column in a publication read by your potential readers will give you more sales in the long run than a one-off mention in a national newspaper.

It's worth noting too that sometimes a journalist will turn your pitch down but will give you the green light to be featured in their online publication because online content has to be replenished on a more regular basis. Don't turn your nose up at this. What starts out as an online relationship could result in coverage in their printed pages a little further down the line. It may simply be a matter of showing your media contact that you're reliable and that you can submit good quality content on time every time.

Therefore, I would urge you to put PR on your marketing activities list because it will work in promoting your book regardless of its subject matter. Establish a momentum by setting goals for the amount of coverage you'd like to secure every month. Aiming for between one and three good quality features a month (which could include your press releases, a column, an article, top tips and a book review) may seem challenging at the moment but with a little planning and commitment it's possible.

PR: a few of the benefits.

- **A rapid increase in book sales.** Just one article in a publication promoting or reviewing your book can propel it to the top of its category. Multiply this several times and you can see how it's not that difficult for it to remain in the bestsellers.

- **A notable increase in the opportunities that come your way.** These will include invitations to speak at prestigious events, judge competitions and attend awards ceremonies. This shines even more light on you and your book and helps build your reputation as a successful author with a book that's well worth reading.

- **Competitive advantage.** Positive and ongoing PR exposure elevates you above other authors. As the momentum builds you're less likely to find yourself competing for the attention of readers with other authors from your category.

- **The cumulative effect of the positive exposure** you've worked so hard for results in the media looking for you. That wonderful day arrives when you are contacted by an editor, a journalist, a television presenter, or a radio researcher, keen for you to share your thoughts or insights on a subject that's connected to your book. Or perhaps they want to interview you to review your book. Or they offer a generous amount of space for sharing extracts from it. Why have they approached you? Because they've read good things about you or you've been highly recommended by someone they trust. But it was you who started the ball rolling.

PR mistakes to avoid.

Finding the details of media contacts is not a challenge in today's online world with so many journalists and their respective publications on social media. It's easy enough to send news releases and articles to them, but getting your material published is far from easy. There are many reasons why an author will find their press releases, news or tips consigned to the recycling bin. Here are the common ones:

- **The quality of the submission was poor.** A journalist won't thank you for sending a communication with glaring or even subtle spelling mistakes and grammatical errors. They have neither the time nor the inclination to correct your work and will have many good quality submissions to choose from. Make sure your email and accompanying attachment is well-written, accurate and clear.

- **The news you sent was not suitable for the publication.** Later in the chapter we look at the importance of spending time reading a publication so you can be certain that what you have to share will be relevant to it and its readers.

- **Your news came too late in the day.** It pays to find out copy deadlines and any features schedules in advance so that you know when to submit your news.

- **You were one of many authors vying for attention.** You have to stand out from your peers for the right reasons. Building a relationship with your media contacts and securing their agreement beforehand to publish your news, features or articles gives you a big advantage over authors who don't share your commitment, charm or know-how.

- **Some publications will not accept press releases or features** because their content is written in-house. All is not lost! By finding this out beforehand you can pitch your ideas instead.

- **A publication believes they have commissioned an exclusive article about your book** or a number of extracts only for the same coverage to appear in a rival publication. If you're given a decent amount of space to showcase your book or share your expertise, make sure your contact knows that you will not be offering the same content to a rival. It's not that hard to rework an article or a press release so that a large proportion of it (I would suggest 70%) is new material. You can then release this to a rival publication without alienating anybody.

- **Dear editor/Dear journalist...** Don't send a press release or story with this salutation in your email. It's guaranteed to offend any editor or journalist before they've even got off the starting blocks. Find out their name beforehand.

Powerful PR: how to get PR coverage for you and your book.

Instead of approaching the different publications that are read by your target audiences on an adhoc basis I advise you to create a media list in advance using the internet and social media sites such as Twitter to search for them. Browse the racks in your local supermarket for publications too and buy the ones you'd like to feature in.

Don't lose sight of the aim of this exercise which is to discover what your different reader groups are already reading so that you can begin the process of identifying news and stories that will appeal to them. Your media list should include printed publications and online ones. And don't dismiss your local community magazines and newspapers. They should be on your list because they are always on the lookout for interesting stories about local people. A book review and some nice coverage of you will stimulate interest. You may also find that talking to local journalists builds your confidence for targeting bigger publications.

The devil is in the detail you gather.

For each publication that's worthy of inclusion on your list, include the contact details and social media addresses of the editorial teams as well as a concise description about the publication and the reason why you're keen to secure some coverage. How does the editorial team like to be communicated with? Whilst most media folk nowadays prefer to be contacted by email, some still prefer a telephone call. Creating this list should take a few hours.

So, list to hand, what's the next task?

Contact the publications and ask for their latest copy, their rate card and, if they have one, their features schedule. They may have planned features that will coincide nicely with the ideas you have for promoting your book. The rate card provides useful information on circulation and readership as well as advertising rates. If you have to telephone for a copy, don't disclose you're interested in editorial coverage. If asked to expand on your reason for calling express a general interest as a potential advertiser - that way you're more likely to receive a copy.

For each publication on your list you must now consider:

- Who reads it? The rate card will answer this question and tell you how the publication is distributed. Does this back up your initial research that it's ideal for reaching your book's potential readers?

- Its structure. Does it include regular features and columns, guest writers and contributions from readers? Can you see a potential opening for you to write a column or some top tips? Could you share some extracts of your book or perhaps become a guest writer?

- Does it include competitions and giveaways? Can you see the potential of offering a competition or a giveaway of some signed books?

- How much editorial is included in the publication such as informative articles, features and tips that have not been supplied by an advertiser paying for the privilege? Do you think you could provide useful editorial on the subject matter of your book?

- Does the editorial outweigh the adverts, or vice versa? If the publication is full of adverts with a token amount of editorial you'll struggle to get any PR unless you're willing to pay for it. But if the publication is packed with editorial you are in with a good chance.

- The tone of the publication? Is it friendly and easy to read with interesting articles or is it full of heavyweight technical submissions? What's the synergy between the tone of the publication and your book? Can you see a connection?

- What is your gut feeling about this publication? It's going to take some time for you to create original and interesting material that will appeal to readers and that's written in the style of the publication. Is it worth your time and effort? Don't be afraid to dismiss a publication if you no longer think it's suitable.

Research done, it's no longer about you.

Having completed your detailed research on each publication you'll probably refine your media list further still, excluding the publications that don't measure up. Then it's time to switch your focus.

It's not all about you any longer. Now it's time to focus squarely on the publications' interests and needs. There are many reasons why you want your book to feature in these publications, but a journalist is unlikely to share your enthusiasm. They're used to being targeted by authors keen for coverage and are accustomed to rejecting most of them.

So here's the $64,000 question. How can you gain free, high quality PR coverage of your book?

These are the questions you must answer for each publication in as much detail as possible. Take notes so that when you send your first email or pick up the telephone what you have to say will strike a chord with the journalist.

- Why would a journalist from this publication be interested in featuring me and my book rather than another author?
  For example:

  - What can I bring to the table that's different, interesting and relevant?
  - What's in it for the editorial team?
  - Where can I add real value to the publication for both the editorial team and the readers?
  - How can I demonstrate I am a safe and reliable pair of hands?

- What should my initial approach consist of? Could I...

  - Sponsor a competition prize with some free books?
  - Write an articulate letter for the letters page in response to an article or feature?
  - Compose a release about the launch of my book, what inspired me to write it, and why it has bestseller written all over it?
  - Create a press release about the challenges I've successfully overcome to write my book?
  - Create a press release on why my book is so topical?
  - Offer a series of extracts from my book?
  - Propose they interview me?
  - Suggest they review my book or that one of their readers does?
  - Offer to contribute a top tips article or a Q+A column based on the subject matter of my book?
  - Complement any forthcoming features?
  - Offer myself as a trusted voice, someone a journalist can approach for an insightful comment?

I have done all of these things for each one of my books. For example in the past year I have...

- Had four 500 word extracts of my book published at the rate of one a month in the business section of our local newspaper and in two business magazines.

- Had my books reviewed in the biggest local community magazine which is distributed through 20,000 letter boxes.

- Given away copies of my books in trade magazines I have an existing relationship with and magazines and blogs that I don't.

- Had my books reviewed by several business publications and blogs after sending a copy for them to review - but only after building a relationship with each editor and blogger. Sue Magee's tips in chapter 24 are invaluable. Please study them before approaching a professional reviewer.

- As mentioned earlier, written a monthly column for our local newspaper's business section.

- Contributed top tips based on my book's content and the readership of the publication. For example in *Family Business Magazine*, I was given a double page feature of 1,200 words after the editor contacted me via Twitter and we subsequently met up. I shared marketing tips that would appeal to family-owned businesses.

- Written press releases when my books have launched and press releases when I've had something interesting to share such as securing my publishing deal in China and being invited as a keynote speaker at events such as The Business Show. (I have included some of these press releases at the end of this chapter).

- Had a Q+A column in a popular trade magazine and promoted my book within the column with an image of the cover and some details about it.

- Been interviewed for business blogs and business magazines.

Pitch time!

After asking the previous questions and considering my suggestions, you should now formulate two really good ideas for pitching to the journalist or editor from each publication you're going to approach. Scope these ideas out so you don't become tongue-tied because you haven't given them enough thought. Then, when you're happy with your ideas, talk them through out loud before picking up the phone or sending an email. Use my approach to help you.

Email pitching.

When emailing, it pays to present your idea in 300 words at the most with the most compelling reasons why the journalist should bite your hand off in the first paragraph. Don't be afraid to use bullet points after this paragraph and before your concluding few lines. A journalist will be able to grasp your message in seconds. They are on the receiving end of many pitch emails. A long and rambling email about your ideas or an equally long and rambling press release is overkill. Your fantastic idea may be dismissed just because you didn't present it in a concise manner. Your email should cover:

- Who you are. You need some credentials about you and your book that will impress them. Be sure to mention any awards your book has won and any positive critic reviews.

- Why you're writing to the journalist. You have studied their great publication and are confident that what you are proposing will appeal to their readers.

- What your interesting proposition is. For example a book review or a book giveaway, a competition or top tips article.

- Why their readers will appreciate your proposition. Be sure to refer to any existing coverage you've secured that will support what you are proposing.

- A reassurance that you will not offer this to a rival publication.

- That you can be contacted daytime or evening. Provide all your contact details.

Spend some time creating this email and go through it with a fine toothcomb before sending it. Read it out loud to ensure it is pacy and interesting. You are sending this to a super-critical journalist who won't appreciate longwinded sentences, spelling mistakes and grammatical errors. You may well get the coverage on the strength of sending such a charming and well-written email!

Telephone pitching.

This is how I introduce myself to an editor or journalist I've not spoken to before.

"Hi, my name is Dee Blick. I'm a Fellow of The Chartered Institute of Marketing and the UK's number one bestselling small business marketing author. Can I briefly present an idea for an editorial feature that I believe, having read your fantastic magazine, your readers would really enjoy? If you like the sound of it I would not offer it to any other publication."

If the answer is yes, that's a good start. But sometimes I get a no simply because the editor or journalist has more pressing things to attend to. When confronted with this I offer to send an email summarising my idea and arrange a call-back at a more convenient time. If I'm greeted by an answer phone, I won't leave a message but will keep on trying until I eventually get to speak to them. Persistence pays off!

Be aware, too, that although an editor or journalist may be receptive to your idea they may not want to follow it to the letter. You may be thinking of a book review or a press release about your launch, they may be thinking of an interview or a competition. Be flexible. You may end up with more coverage than you'd initially bargained for simply because you presented your original idea and its relevance to their readers in a friendly and concise manner.

Please steer clear of the following after being given the thumbs up...

I had lunch with a journalist a few weeks ago. Knowing I was writing this chapter I asked if he would look over the following list. He nodded emphatically at each point. So for the record here's what frustrates or irritates an editor or journalist when they have agreed to feature you in their publication only for you to let them down by...

- **Being unavailable.** If an editor or journalist has agreed to interview you make sure you're available when you said you would be and that they have your undivided attention. Better still be available in the hour before and after the interview so they can adjust the timings if required. Ensure they have all your contact details including your mobile and your social media addresses. They may decide to contact you out of hours or at the weekend. Be accommodating.

- **Ignoring their brief on how your feature should be presented.** Follow editorial instructions to the letter including the word count for your submission. If I'm asked to write 500 words I write exactly 500 words. This earns me bonus points because I am competing with people who either exceed the word count or provide a fraction of what was requested. Writing too much or too little gives a journalist a headache because they will have allotted a space for your article based on an exact word count.

- **Using the space you have been given to sell your book.** There is a clear distinction between editorial and advertising. You have been given an opportunity to provide high value editorial. The simple fact that you are in the publication will help your book sales.

- **Providing an article or press release that needs a good edit.** Spell check is not enough so read chapter eight before sending your submission.

- **Sending blurry images** of you and your book that won't cut it in print. They will be discarded and the space that was earmarked for images will have to be filled with something else.

- **Missing the copy deadline date.** This is the cardinal sin and yet it happens so often. Don't be on time, be early! If you're late submitting your copy the publication will have to fill the space earmarked for you at the last minute.

Small touches make a big difference.

Don't take the coverage you have been given for granted. Instead make sure that you say thank you to every journalist and editor who's been good enough to promote you and your books. Believe it or not, very few receive a personal message of thanks, a lovely tweet or an enthusiastic phone call. Here are some of the things I have done to go beyond a simple thank you:

- Giving cupcakes and Easter eggs to the team at my local newspaper.

- Sending a signed book when a journalist has shown a keen interest in reading it.

- Sending a lovely card with a handwritten message of thanks.

- Sending organic vegan chocolates to an editor who was vegan.

- Taking an editor out to lunch at a really swish venue.

- Taking an editor out for coffee and cakes.

It usually pays to go the extra mile...

How to write great press releases.

Press releases are still popular formats for sending out news about your book and exciting developments about you as an author to the local and national media. I don't ever send a press release without picking up the telephone and promoting it to the journalist or editor beforehand or sending an email if I can't get hold of them by telephone. You can of course take your chances and just send a release and you may get some coverage. Sometimes I will change my release after talking to a journalist so that it reflects our conversation. As mentioned earlier I rarely send the same release to different publications but instead create several versions, all pretty much saying the same thing but sufficiently distinctive so that I can truthfully tell a journalist I've written this release for their publication only. Before sending a release I will ask a journalist how they would like to receive it - embedded in my email or as a separate attachment. Most now prefer to have the email and release within the one communication.

Here's my advice on writing great press releases and getting them published, followed by some examples that show these tips in action.

- **Identify the reach of your story.** Is your news of potential interest on a local, national or even a global scale? For example your book launch will be of interest to the journalist covering business news in your local newspaper but it's unlikely to have national interest. However if you've secured a publishing deal in another country, your release will have local and national interest and it will be of interest in the country your book is being published in.

- **Find your 'reader relevant' hook.** Every great press release has an interesting angle. Whether you're communicating a message about your book that's topical within your sector, you've secured a big book signing, a membership organisation has agreed to promote your book or you've won an award, you have to ask: *"Why would this news be interesting to the readers of this publication?"* Your press release should answer this. Local publications are usually interested in success stories of local people so you have a good way in there.

- **Write a memorable headline.** Your headline should have an impact and tell the story of what follows. It can be half a dozen words or a few sentences but it must be relevant, so avoid a gimmicky headline. Read the news headlines in the publications you're aiming for coverage in. There may be a style you can emulate. Study the business headlines in the broadsheet and tabloid newspapers and look at mine.

- **Make the layout appealing and easy to read.** Look at the layout of my press releases. They were printed exactly as I wrote them and follow a standard approach that's acceptable to journalists and editors. Don't send your news in a solid block of text.

- **Have a strong opening paragraph.** If your opening paragraph lacks bite and there's no immediate connection with your headline, your press release will be in danger of being deleted. Establish the two or three compelling messages that your press release will focus on in the first paragraph.

It usually takes me as long to write the introductory paragraph as it does the remaining text. Imagine an editor or journalist is going to crop your release after your first paragraph, which can happen if they're short on space. In the opening lines, you must answer: Who? What? Where? How? Why? Remain objective and stick to the facts. Look at your story from the journalist's perspective and what the readers will find interesting and relevant. If you can reinforce a point you're making in the opening paragraph with a fact or a statistic then do so. For example in my press release: 'Horsham Author Secures Chinese Publishing Deal' I delivered the key points in the first paragraph knowing that if the rest of the release was cut I still had a powerful message.

- **Journalists and editors like quotes.** They are interesting (or they should be!) so include at least two in yours. Sometimes a journalist or editor will be so taken with your quotes that they will embolden them in the final published piece. Are yours interesting? Read them out loud to ensure they are. Opinionated quotes or ones that include facts and figures tend to be popular.

- **Keep your press release concise. Don't go beyond the equivalent of one side of A4.** Before anyone actually reads your press release, they're likely to scroll over it. If it looks too long they may not go any further. My releases tend to be 350-500 words. I always look at the news and features in a publication beforehand so that my press release is at the right word count.

- **Use bold text and italics** when you want to reinforce an important point or highlight an interesting quotation, but don't overdo it or the impact will be lost. And resist the temptation to pepper your press release with SHOUTY CAPITAL LETTERS, quirky typefaces and varying point sizes. Don't put distractions in the way of a good message. Stick to one typeface and one point size for the body copy and make your headline larger so it stands out.

- **Don't rely on spell check alone.** One spelling mistake is enough to rile a journalist so comb through your release word by word. Then read it out loud to reveal further mistakes. You'll know in minutes if your release is flowing and interesting or longwinded and repetitive. Editors love press releases they can read and drop straight into their publication without any need for any editing.

- **Include your contact details at the foot of your press release.** Give your full name, your mobile number so you can be contacted out of hours, your website address, and email and social media addresses. Make it easy for a journalist or editor to contact you. If your book has won any awards mention this too.

- **Make your accompanying email a mini press release.** It should summarise the conversation where the journalist agreed to include your press release. Remember to thank them for the coverage.

- **Make sure any accompanying images of you and your book are of a high resolution print quality** and explain their connection to your release. For example: "The attached image shows me speaking at The Business Show at Excel a few weeks ago." "I have attached the front and back cover images of my book as discussed." A journalist doesn't have the time to contact you for to get an explanation about your images. They are important because they bring your story to life. A nice image of you and your book in a publication alongside your press release is worth its weight in gold.

To illustrate these tips in action, here is a selection of press releases I have written for newspapers and magazines. Each one was published without editing so they should act as useful templates for yours. I tend not to send press releases to trade publications or national newspapers and national magazines, preferring instead to offer my services as a marketer, sharing marketing tips in exchange for promoting my book in the mini-biography accompanying each article. This approach seems to be more effective in securing ongoing exposure. This may not be the case for you though, so stay open-minded.

Press Release For Immediate Release February 2014 Horsham Author Secures Chinese Publishing Deal

For one Horsham-based author the dream of being offered an international publishing deal has materialised. Dee Blick, author of *Powerful Marketing on a Shoestring Budget For Small Businesses, The Ultimate Small Business Marketing Book* and *The 15 Essential Marketing Masterclasses For Your Small Business* has accepted a publishing deal with CITIC, one of China's top 10 publishers and the only publisher in China with a chain of retail outlets. It's a deal that will see *The Ultimate Small Business Marketing Book* translated into Mandarin and sold in bookstores throughout China and online too on dangdang.com, the Chinese equivalent of Amazon.

Explaining how this happened, Dee said: "Twelve months ago I was contacted by Glacier Ding, the Rights Manager at CITIC. Glacier had found my book on Amazon and emailed me to say how much she liked my style of writing and that the content was perfect for start-up businesses in China. Ten months later and my book is now at the final edit stage. I'm hoping to visit China later in the year and have already been approached by Professor Kevin Li of the MBA Start-up School in Beijing. For any author, having your books recognised at an international level is incredible so I'm thrilled with this."

Glacier Ding said, "We knew from the very beginning this is a leading title on marketing and particularly suitable for small businesses. Many readers have benefited from the wisdom and rich experience of Dee Blick and so this is a title that will not be missed by Chinese readers. CITIC is a leading commercial publishing house in China, with its parent company CITIC Group a state-owned company founded by Rong Yiren, a famous entrepreneur in Chinese history. With decades of development, CITIC Press has published many bestsellers and grown into a publishing group, with more than 100 airport bookstores and its own eBook publishing platform. We are delighted to see this book published in China. Dee's book is a precious gift for the relationship between the UK and China."

Chris Day, Managing Director of Filament Publishing, the UK publishers of *The Ultimate Small Business Marketing Book* said: "Dee is our star author and it's no surprise her books have taken off internationally. She communicates in a practical, down to earth manner sharing proven marketing tips that any small business can apply irrespective of where they are based. Given we have recently confirmed bulk orders of Dee's book with the University of Texas where it is now required syllabus reading for their marketing students, I'm sure China will not be the only country to fall under her spell."

"To think that small business owners as far afield as China will be reading my book in their own language and putting my tips in to practice is a dream come true," concluded Dee.

Ends

Editor Notes

For media interviews please contact Chris Day, Filament Publishing Ltd on: 020 8688 2598
Mobile 07802 211587
chris@filamentpublishing.com

Contact Dee on: 07845 439332, dee@themarketingggym.org
@deeblick (Twitter)

Dee Blick Running 2 Marketing and PR Masterclasses at Microbiz

Amazon Number 1 bestselling business author and Chartered Marketer Dee Blick is running 2 free 40 minute marketing masterclasses at Horsham Microbiz, Drill Hall, Denne Road on Saturday 8th March. Dee will be sharing dozens of powerful and practical tips honed over her 31-year career in marketing. Her first seminar 'How to Build your Small Business into a Brilliant Brand' starts at 10.05am, and her second seminar 'Powerful PR For You And Your Business' starts at 1.20pm. Dee will also be signing copies of her latest bestseller *The 15 Essential Marketing Masterclasses For Your Small Business* afterwards and answering your marketing questions. Dee's seminars are very popular so booking online at www.horshammicrobiz.co.uk is advisable.

Ends

Dee Blick speaking at Business Startup Show Olympia

Bestselling author Dee Blick will be speaking at the iconic Business Startup Show, Olympia on Thursday 28th November and Friday 29th November, sharing tips from her latest bestseller *The 15 Essential Marketing Masterclasses For Your Small Business.* Dee is speaking at 2pm on 28th November on 'How to get PR for your business' and at 2pm on 29th November on 'The 7 Marketing Secrets for Small Business Success' - both talks in Hall 17. After each talk Dee will be signing copies of her new book. Dee has also been invited as a marketing contributor on the Forum of Private Business expert panel at 10am on both days. If you want to see Dee in action and find out more about her talks visit http://www.bstartup.com/ Tickets are free and you will receive a copy of the show magazine.

Ends

Local businesswoman shares marketing know-how with The Institute of Directors

Horsham-based businesswoman Dee Blick has recently been filming with the Institute of Directors based at Pall Mall in London sharing marketing tips from her soon-to-be-released third book *The 15 Essential Marketing Masterclasses For Your Small Business*.

Dee said: "Last week I spent the morning with the video production team at the Institute of Directors, filming a series of short marketing tips videos for the benefit of members. It was lovely to be approached to share my marketing expertise in this way and it's increasingly likely I will be going back to deliver a series of longer videos."

This news comes on top of Dee being invited to be a keynote speaker at the iconic Startup Show at Olympia in November followed by a book signing. In the past month she has also contributed to a Microsoft eBook - *Key Metrics for Business Success,* sharing tips on social media. "I am excited about the imminent launch of my third book and looking forward to embarking on a mini book signing tour, culminating in speaking at the Startup Show," said Dee.

Dee's book is now available to pre-order on Amazon, with a release date of September 6th.

Ends

Press Release January 2013
International book deal for District Post Columnist Dee Blick

District Post columnist and Chartered Marketer Dee Blick has landed an international publishing deal for her third book *The 15 Essential Marketing Masterclasses For Your Small Business* which will be released worldwide in September. Dee was approached by global publishers Wiley after her professional body, The Chartered Institute of Marketing, recommended they offer her a book deal. Dee's second book *The Ultimate Small Business Marketing Book* was the number one bestselling marketing book in 2012 for the CIM bookshop in addition to being the number one bestselling small business marketing book throughout 2012 on Amazon UK.

Jonathan Shipley, Chief Commissioning Editor at Capstone, the business book division of Wiley said: "We're delighted to be publishing Dee because she's a terrific marketer and a great author. She's passionate about making marketing work for small businesses and that level of enthusiasm comes over in her writing, alongside hard-earned, practical knowledge which can only be acquired through experience and savvy. You can tell from talking to Dee for five minutes that you'd want her doing your marketing. That's why we want her writing for us on the subject, and the hundreds of positive reviews of her work to date suggest that plenty of others stand to benefit from her straight-forward, clear and impactful advice."

In an exclusive, Dee told Benjamin Coren, business reporter at The District Post: "I am very excited to be working with Capstone. The publishing team are incredibly enthusiastic about this book and its potential to sell globally as well as in the UK. It differs from my others in that I am taking 15 subjects that I know small businesses are in need of expert marketing commonsense advice on and creating 15 masterclasses instead of chapters. I won't be short changing my readers. This book is as big as my previous one so it will be a meaty read! So expect to see masterclasses covering public speaking, telephone cold calling, Twitter, LinkedIn, how to write great web copy, e-marketing, advertising, PR and more! I am now putting the final touches to each masterclass and thankfully am ahead of schedule! As usual my many and varied clients have been very supportive in allowing me to include them as practical case studies. I know from the feedback I get from the thousands of readers who take the time to contact me that these case studies are really appreciated."

Ends

Why your articles and tips need a short biography.

Of course, not every submission you send to a publication will be a press release. You may be writing articles, top tips and expert columns. Because you're not selling your services or your book in any of these submissions you will usually be allowed to promote yourself and your book via a short biography that appears at the foot of your piece. If it's being posted online ask the publication if they will include a link to your Amazon page, your website, or both. They won't think to do this but few will turn your request for these links down.

Here are two of my short biographies. I have included the second one to show how it changes when I have submitted extracts from my book. It lets readers know in no uncertain terms how they can get their hands on it so they can enjoy more of the content they've just read. The number of words allowed for your short biography will vary. My advice is to be cheeky and submit a decent sized one. The first one below is 42 words, the second 90 words. If you have submitted a really good article your short biography should be spared any editing.

About Dee Blick

Dee is a multi-award winning Fellow of The Chartered Institute of Marketing with 31 years' marketing experience. She specialises in working with small businesses and is an author of three Amazon #1 bestselling books. Contact Dee via www.themarketinggym.org or on Twitter @deeblick.

About Dee Blick

This article is based on the Expert masterclass in Dee's latest multi-award winning book *The 15 Essential Marketing Masterclasses For Your Small Business* which is available on Amazon for £10 with 87 five-star reviews. It has been rated excellent by *The Sun, Elite Business Magazine,* and *Sales Initiative Magazine* and won *Talk Business Magazine's* Best Business Book 2013. Dee's next book: *The Ultimate Guide to Writing and Marketing a Bestselling Book on a Shoestring Budget* will be available from October 21st. Follow Dee on Twitter @deeblick.

Generate even more book sales with your PR coverage.

Every time you benefit from PR coverage it's a golden opportunity to reuse and repurpose it and so generate even more positive goodwill and more book sales.

Here's how you can achieve this:

- Use the back of any sales letters to include snippets of your press coverage. Or if that space has already been taken use the space that's usually reserved for the PS.

- Include the details of your media coverage on your website. Can you create a new page comprising a selection of articles or news for visitors to read with a downloadable sheet? How about including a list of your media coverage accompanied by the logos of the publications (make sure you get their permission). Do you need to beef up your 'About Us' page so it includes your media coverage?

- Add some of the details of your media coverage at the foot of your email signature and keep on updating it. For example: *"Have you read the latest review of my book in the XYZ blog?"* Add a link too.

- When you're networking ensure the people at the events you attend are aware of the media exposure your book is generating. This will make it easier for them to recommend your book.

- Tell your followers on social networking sites about your coverage by sharing brief details and providing the links.

- When you're speaking at an event let your audience know about your PR exposure in the first few minutes of your talk. This will enhance their perception of you as a successful author and it will encourage them to buy your book.

- Use your media coverage to get more coverage. You may start out with a little coverage in a local publication but as your confidence and experience of working with editors and journalists grows, you can become more ambitious. Use the coverage you've got to show a journalist that you are not inexperienced in these matters.

Have you arrived at the conclusion that getting PR in printed and online publications will help you sell thousands of books? Can you see how it will build your profile? And, most importantly, have you realised that it's nowhere near as challenging as you had previously thought? I hope so!

Chapter summary.

- It doesn't matter what your book is about. PR coverage in printed and online publications will help you sell more books.

- It's not impossible to get coverage in the tabloid and broadsheet newspapers but it can be tough and you may only end up with a brief mention.

- It's much easier to get significant exposure of your book in trade titles, special interest publications and consumer magazines than it is the daily newspapers.

- The approach you take for getting coverage in online publications is the same with printed ones.

- PR enhances your reputation and standing as an author.

- Don't make the common mistakes committed by some authors including sending releases with spelling mistakes.

- Never address an email to a journalist with: 'Dear journalist'!

- What does your target audience read? Create a media list.

- When researching a publication look at how you can add value to it and why they should publish your content.

- Look closely at the structure, tone and content of each publication. This will help when pitching your ideas.

- Practice your telephone pitch to a journalist. Be concise, confident and relevant.

- Read and re-read your email pitch before sending it. Is it clear, attractive, and error-free?

- Don't let a journalist down by being unavailable, late with your copy, or sending material that is over or under the agreed word count.

- Thank the journalist for the coverage. Is an email enough or could you make a special gesture?

- Press releases are still popular and accepted formats for sharing news. Make sure yours are interesting, reader relevant, concise, with a great introductory paragraph and a charming accompanying email.

- Re-purpose the PR you get by including it on your website. Talk about it when speaking, networking, signing books and so on.

CHAPTER 16

How Public Speaking Sells Books - and Yes You Can Do it!

My ability to speak in front of many different audiences helped me secure a publishing deal with Wiley. The chief commissioning editor, emphasised how important public speaking was for an author in building sales of their books and enhancing their reputation. Because I had been on the speaking circuit for a few years this made sense to me. When you secure a good public speaking engagement you not only benefit from book sales on the day of your talk and afterwards, but the organiser's publicity machine is whirring into action long before you step onto the stage. And this means book sales in the run up to the event too. For example a few months ago I was a keynote speaker at the iconic Business Show, the largest show of its kind in Europe. My books were promoted through a number of marketing channels used to promote the event. For example:

1. **Pre-show publicity.** The glossy magazine sent to everyone who registered for a ticket included generous coverage of each keynote speaker. Potential attendees could see I was an author and within a few clicks could buy my books before hearing me speak. You can read the speaker biography and the details of the talk I supplied to The Business Show further on in the chapter.

2. **The Business Show website.** My photo and details of my talks were promoted on their website which attracts thousands of visitors in the weeks and months before the event. Again, within a few clicks a visitor could be on Amazon browsing my books.

3. **Social media.** Jan, who heads up the social media campaign for The Business Show, is an accomplished and enthusiastic tweeter.

She retweeted many of my marketing tips to The Business Show's 17,000+ followers in the run up to the event.

4. **Opportunities for blogging.** Speakers could write business blogs for The Business Show website and naturally I took advantage of this opportunity! The payback for sharing this expertise was not only the fantastic exposure but the fact that my mini biography was published with each blog - I made sure it included the titles of my books.

5. **At The Business Show itself.** The show's magazine was given to every attendee and of course being a keynote speaker meant I had a packed and rapt audience because the details of my talk had been posted outside the hall I was speaking in.

6. **Social media.** After the event, on Twitter, Jan created a compilation of the best tweets from visitors and this included positive feedback on my talk.

Of course not every event you speak at will be of the size and magnitude of The Business Show. Indeed in your early days of speaking you may find yourself in front of a handful of people at a small event (which is a good place to start). But the principle remains the same. The actual speaking slot gives you a powerful platform to promote your book and there will be opportunities before and after the event to promote yourself and your book. That's why it pays to seek out speaking opportunities.

Why it's time to feel the fear and do it anyway!

Public speaking can strike fear in the heart of the most confident and accomplished person. In fact you may be reading this chapter with a sinking feeling, having arrived at the conclusion that whilst it's okay for me to stand up and speak because I'm an experienced professional, you're not and so you're not going to entertain the idea.

Let me reassure you.

I did not start out as an enthusiastic, professional speaker who was paid for my public speaking engagements. In fact it was the opposite. The thought of standing up and speaking in front of an audience was enough to make my heart pound and my stomach churn. But I realised long before I became an author that if I wanted my voice to be heard and my reputation as a marketer to spread far and wide, I had to overcome my deep-seated fear of public speaking.

That's why in this chapter I am sharing my personal public speaking tips, hints and strategies. I'm confident that if they can work for me then, with some self-belief, willingness and practice, they can work for you too. I'm not for a moment suggesting you immediately set your sights on securing a speaking slot at a huge event as a keynote speaker if you're inexperienced and only just getting your head around the concept of public speaking (although if you decide to aim high immediately then good for you!)

I took my first tentative steps by volunteering to speak at local networking events attended by small businesses. In those early days, delivering a 10-minute talk with five minutes added on for questions was more than enough. It gave me the confidence that I could speak in front of an audience without turning into a nervous wreck. I then graduated to speaking at local events and exhibitions as a seminar speaker talking for 30 minutes but, to make the transition from my 10-minute talks, I had to have a friend or family member on the front row supporting me. As my confidence grew I offered to speak at local exhibitions and at the networking events organised by the Federation of Small Businesses.

Where am I now?

Well, after honing my craft over a few years I have become a professional speaker, paid for many of my talks and booked on a regular basis to speak at company events and conferences organised by some well-known brands, often as their only speaker or as one of a small number of keynote speakers. And I actually enjoy public speaking these days - something I never thought I would say!

So, if the thought of public speaking terrifies you or makes you feel unsettled but you know deep down that it will help you sell books and build your reputation, I would urge you to set aside any doubts and fears and study the tips in this chapter before dismissing it out of hand. If you decide to give it a go, find small local events that would welcome you as a speaker so the hill doesn't seem too steep to climb. And remember that where you are now is not where you'll be in several months or even a few years time.

Accept too that whilst in your early months you may be happy speaking to a small group of people for 10 minutes, a year down the line you could be the keynote speaker at a much bigger event. Set some goals and remind yourself why you're embarking on this journey. You want your book to stay at the top of the bestsellers and your inspiring message deserves an audience.

At the end of this chapter I have shared several templates including a selection of speaker biographies and descriptions of my talks. I've included these to give you a useful starting point when creating your communications. They have helped me secure some amazing public speaking engagements including some very well paid ones.

Pitching for speaking engagements.

If you're not already an established public speaker then in your early months you're unlikely to be deluged with speaking opportunities. It's very much down to you to sell yourself to the organiser of an event whether you're interested in speaking at your local Rotary Club's monthly meeting or at a local exhibition attended by potential readers. But as interest in you grows, you should find yourself being approached by event organisers keen to book you. However when you're the new kid on the block it's down to you to be proactive and to identify the events you would like to speak at. You then have to contact the organisers and pitch to them.

How to find local public speaking events.

I took a much keener interest in the local newspapers and community magazines for details of events targeting small businesses and I used Twitter and Facebook to identify the organisers of these events. I asked business colleagues who were active on the business networking scene if I could talk at their meetings. Then, when I felt sufficiently confident to tackle bigger events, I searched online for suitable exhibitions and events to target. I looked at the publications and the websites popular with my target audiences to find details of any events being held.

For example, I was invited to speak at three of the events organised by the British Promotional Merchandise Association after discovering their regional events programme on their website and subsequently pitching my services as a speaker to their chairman. Because these speaking engagements were unpaid I couldn't give up time to speak at all of them but I was more than happy to attend the ones within a reasonable travelling distance of my home in West Sussex. I asked for and was granted some decent book promotion in much the same way as outlined in The Business Show case study, albeit on a smaller scale.

During your research you will find events that are ideal for you to speak at but the speaker line-up has already been confirmed. Don't despair - there's still something you can do. Offer yourself as a replacement speaker. If a speaker drops out you can save the day at short notice. If you're keen to do this you'll have to keep the date free in your diary and have a prepared talk. I offered myself as a back-up speaker to The British Franchise Association and because one of the speakers dropped out in the week before the event my services were accepted. I was subsequently invited as a paid speaker at another one of their events and a copy of my latest book was given to every attendee.

So, start by identifying the small events you feel comfortable speaking at.

The best way to approach an event organiser.

When I'm interested in speaking at an event, I'll find out more about it on Twitter as well as on the event website. Many exhibitions and events now use Twitter to find exhibitors and to promote their event programme to visitors. The informal nature of Twitter makes it an ideal starting point to build that all-important initial awareness and interest with the organiser or the person who's tweeting. I'll send a couple of friendly tweets expressing my interest in speaking and when I receive some interest back I will follow this up with an introductory email that includes an outline of a suggested talk I think their visitors will enjoy plus one of my speaker biographies. I also send a head and shoulders shot taken by a professional photographer. A warm, friendly, smiling photograph beats the clichéd corporate grimace any day. When my talk has been confirmed this image will be used in the promotional communications.

So, approach the organisers with your suggested talk outline and a speaker biography that shows you clearly know your stuff. Use the templates I've provided at the end of this chapter to create yours.

Don't forget your website too. If you're serious about using public speaking to sell books, it will help if you have a speaker page on your website with a video of you in action. If you're unsure what to include on this page, visit the speaker page on my website www.themarketinggym.org

Let's now look at how you can become a confident and accomplished public speaker.

No ifs or buts - you have to believe in yourself.

It's natural to have unsettling feelings about public speaking. But they're not going to help you if you allow them to go unchallenged. So greet your negative chatterbox with some positive and uplifting statements. For example, here's what I say to mine:

"I am an accomplished and confident public speaker."

"I am a talented, genuine author with an inspiring story to share."

"I'm so looking forward to meeting and greeting my audience."

"The book signing after my talk will be fantastic. I can't wait for it."

"It's going to be fantastic because I'm so well-prepared."

"I'm so lucky to be given this opportunity. Other authors would bite my hand off for it."

Make a note of your empowering slogans, practice them regularly and call on them when you drift into a negative mindset. I was told by a coach to imagine my negative thoughts grouped together on a television screen in black and white and that I should diminish them to the size of a tiny dot with an imaginary remote control. I find this technique works really well in the minutes before I'm due to speak.

Your voice is a powerful tool.

Think for a moment about the speakers you enjoy listening to. It's important that they use expressive and welcoming body language and maintain your interest with their engaging content, but if their voice is flat or they talk too fast you'll switch off. In our everyday life, we don't give our voice a moment's thought unless we're angry or upset do we? We can't do this when public speaking. Whether you're on a huge stage in an auditorium or speaking to a group of people at a coffee morning, you have to use your voice to engage your audience and keep them hooked right up to your concluding sentence.

Here are some tips that will help you use your voice as a powerful instrument when public speaking.

- Project your voice when you're in a quiet space for example in the shower, when weeding the garden, or driving. In fact anywhere you can practice speaking in different tones without being disturbed or your sanity called into question. Speak loudly then quietly. Speak with real passion and enthusiasm. Speak with a hint of drama and pathos then anger followed by joy. What do you sound like? Can you see, feel and hear how much your voice changes when you change your mood and tone?

- Select a few passages from a book you enjoy and read each one out loud. Pause between the sentences and emphasise keywords with different tones; humorous, dramatic and sympathetic regardless of the content. Repeat this several times, paying close attention to how your voice changes and the range you're capable of. This is good fun and it should make you realise how you can use your voice as a powerful instrument.

- Select a few passages from your book or another if you prefer and do the opposite of the previous exercise. Umm and err between each sentence to the point of irritating yourself. Lower the volume so you're barely audible. Rush through a passage so you can barely catch your breath. Slow down to the point where you're almost dozing off. You now know what your voice sounds like when you're not giving it your best shot. You also know what to move away from (and pronto!) when these bad vocal habits creep into your presentation.

- Watch and listen to other speakers so you can learn from their voices and how they use them as part of their stagecraft. Close your eyes so you can focus on their voice with no other distractions. Use these experiences to spend more time on vocal practice.

- Tune into your favourite radio station but instead of focusing on what's being discussed, focus on the presenter's voice instead. How are they emphasising different words? How are they varying their pitch to keep you engaged?

- At some events you'll need a microphone, so get used to holding one and moving about with it. You won't have a clip-on microphone at every event. Use a hairbrush or something similar to practice with at home.

When you take to the stage your voice has to wow your audience so if you know you've a habit of speaking too fast (like me) you're going to have to learn to slow down. If you're naturally quiet, you're going to have to turn up the volume. Your audience will respond to a warm, clear and welcoming voice; one that's never more than a heartbeat away from enthusiasm. If you've used these simple tips to find the pitfalls in your voice and to accentuate all that's good about it, you've already taken a significant step towards becoming a great speaker.

Ensure your body language is confident, warm and expressive.

It's not hard to spot a presenter who's ill at ease, their body language tells the story. Nervous and irritating body language includes pacing across the stage whilst speaking, standing rooted to the spot like a soldier on guard duty, pushing sleeves up and down, frowning intently, and erratic arm movements. Poor body language does nothing to support a speaker. In fact it has the opposite effect. A speaker who can't stand still will undoubtedly be speaking too quickly and this could mean they lose track because their own body language is unsettling them. Don't deliver half measures by talking in a wonderful, warm and welcoming voice while pacing to and fro or fiddling with your hair. Unattractive body language will undo all the good work that your voice is doing. Look upon your body language as the support act for your voice, your content and your delivery. It has to be natural and expressive.

Here are some simple exercises that will make you look good in front of any audience:

Give yourself a few minutes to deliver a presentation on one of the following topics while standing in front of a full length mirror.

- My readers will enjoy my book because...

- To me being a successful author means...

- I'm going to promote my book by...

Focus on your body language when delivering each presentation and, if you feel up to it, invite a friend to watch when you repeat this exercise so that you can nip any irritating habits in the bud. Do your movements and mannerisms support your voice or not? Is this the first time you've thought about your body language as the all-important support act to your voice?

Now repeat this exercise using the following tips - but remain silent. Imagine you're standing in front of an audience and you've just taken to the stage. Look to the middle of your audience, to the left, then back to the middle and then to the right. Make sure your smile reaches your eyes. You should do this when you're presenting for real. It will help you connect with your audience regardless of where each person is sitting or standing.

Now focus on your arms. When presenting, your arms should hang loosely by your side. But you'll need to use your arms and your hands to emphasise your key points and bring some energy to your presentation. Imagine you're drawing a large circle for your audience, then an oblong, and end with a rectangle. Be fluid in your movements. Now imagine you're describing a beautiful landscape perhaps from a recent holiday or weekend break. Don't use your voice to describe the scene, use your arms, hands, head and feet instead. Avoid sudden and exaggerated arm movements.

Now, bring your attention to your legs by feeling the ground beneath your feet. Walk around in a small space, taking a few steps to your left, then to your right, then moving forwards and backwards a little, and transferring your weight from one foot to the other.

You don't want to be rooted to the spot when presenting but equally you don't want to be like a presenter I observed recently. He covered the length of a large stage walking dramatically from left to right and then back again to the middle. He walked so much that I completely lost track of what he was saying and all I could hear was the loud click from his shoes. He gave the impression of being arrogant which I'm sure was the last thing he wanted to convey.

You'll feel more comfortable if you can get into the habit of practising your body language on a regular basis. When watching other speakers pay close attention to their body language too. I have learned so much from observing.

It won't take long before you're aware of what it takes to have a powerful stage presence. When you take to the stage for real, you won't feel unnatural or unnerved using these tools and techniques. Any awkward feelings you have now are natural. Push outside of your comfort zone and within a few weeks your progress will be evident.

Why you must look the part.

Whether we like it or not it's a fact of life that people judge us initially on what we look like and this is intensified when we're the sole focus of attention on a stage. I'm not advocating for a moment that you dress in designer clothes or don a suit but that you wear clothing that complements your complexion and physique and of course makes you feel confident and expressive. You'll normally find me on stage wearing a nice top, skinny jeans, high heels and some sparkling jewellery. You have to feel confident and comfortable in the clothes that you wear on stage and at book signings. If you don't look the part and are feeling uncomfortable you won't feel the part and this will come across to your audience.

If you're unsure about the image you want to project but are serious about public speaking to promote your book and build your expert status why not do what I did and invest in the services of an image consultant? It worked wonders for my confidence. It also made me realise the colours I should steer away from because they aged me and made me feel drab and the ones I should wear because they suited my complexion and gave me a real confidence boost.

How to deliver a talk your audience will love.

If you're invited to speak at an event resist the temptation to promote your book endlessly. The fact that you have been given a platform to speak should promote your book and generate book sales. Often at talks when I'm sharing marketing tips, I will read a short passage from my latest book if it illustrates a point I am making. This of course draws attention to my book so it's worth considering trying this yourself.

When you've been given the green light to speak at an event make it your mission to find out as much as you can about the event and your audience to enable you to deliver a show-stopping presentation.

This is what I find out from the organisers before I plan my talk:

- What is planned by way of pre-event publicity? I always request that my book's title is included in all their communications together with my speaker biography. If a book signing has been agreed I will ensure these details are included too and will request a table close to where I am speaking for selling and signing books.

- What talks have been popular at previous events and why? This helps me get on the right track with my talk.

- How long do I have to speak and will I be expected to answer questions from the audience at the end?

- Will I be speaking on my own or with other speakers? If the latter, what's the running order? This helps me visualise the event and I like to do my homework on the other speakers too.

- How many people are expected to attend and what's the profile of the attendees? It is important that I tailor my talk to meet their expectations.

- Will the audience be seated at tables or in rows? It helps to know this if I am planning on making my talk interactive.

- Where will I be delivering my talk? On a stage or standing in front of my audience with just a few feet separating us? This is comforting to know.

- Will I be provided with a microphone and if so, will it be a handheld one, a headset or a clip on? If the audience numbers are more than 60 and it's a large room I'll insist on having a microphone so I don't have to shout to be heard.

- Can I have a small table for notes and props? I don't stand behind a lectern but as this appears to be the sole presentation prop at most events nowadays I always request a small table on the stage for samples of client work and interesting props.

- If the event is a small informal one, will a flipchart stand be available? Occasionally I will bring a prepared flipchart but I never assume a stand will be available as a matter of course.

I don't use PowerPoint or any other audio visual aids when speaking but I know that some speakers use PowerPoint very well. If you're going to use it make sure you're aware of the organiser's requirements and have a backup plan lest the technology lets you down on the day. One of my marketing heroes is Professor Malcolm MacDonald. I recently had the pleasure of seeing him. He had to abandon his PowerPoint presentation at the very first slide when the technology went horribly wrong. Thankfully, he had a printed copy of his slides and was able to present what, in my eyes, was an even better talk.

With the answers to these questions, you can move with confidence to the next stage, developing your theme and writing your presentation.

Crafting a fantastic talk.

When I spoke recently at a small business marketing conference organised by The Chartered Institute of Marketing the stage was huge and, in contrast to the other presenters, I did not have any PowerPoint slides. Several members of the audience commented afterwards how relaxed I was and how they found it hard to believe I could stand up and speak without notes for 40 minutes.

My secret is simple.

Rigorous practising aside, I only talk on subjects I am passionate about and that I know inside out. I can then ad-lib with confidence knowing I'm not straying dangerously towards the limits of my expertise, which puts me in danger of waffling or going blank. I also keep my talks very simple. I don't cover more than half a dozen key points in any presentation and these points are always in a logical order so they unravel like the plot of a story that makes sense to me and my audience.

However a few months ago and against my better judgement I moved away from my tried and tested approach of keeping it simple and decided to add more content to a talk I was delivering at a regional exhibition. Although I managed to pull it off, I was uncomfortable throughout because I had too much to remember and I felt as though I was rushing my presentation to squeeze everything in. Not a pleasant experience! So, my advice is to keep your talks simple too and to trust your knowledge and experience. Half a dozen key points will be more than enough to inspire your audience. Have a few extra nuggets in reserve should you unexpectedly find yourself with more time because a speaker has dropped out or you've reached the end of your talk and have time on your hands.

Here are some tips to help you plan a memorable talk.

- **Be relevant.** Your presentation has to meet the needs of your audience and it has to be pitched at a level they will understand and appreciate. And of course it has to be entertaining. These things should be at the front of your mind when crafting your presentation.

- **Be clear about the purpose of your talk and how your audience will benefit from listening to you.** For example at The Business Show I found out beforehand that my audience was likely to comprise small business owners and start-up businesses. If I focused my talk on sharing case studies from big budget marketing campaigns I would not be popular because my audience would struggle to identify with my content. The purpose of my 30 minute talk therefore was to share practical marketing on a shoestring tips for small businesses. For the last five minutes I performed a light-hearted exercise with a member of the audience so I could end on a memorable note. Throughout my talk I used case studies to show how a small business can succeed when they put my marketing tips into action.

- **Can you reinforce any tips you're sharing with a case study or some interesting facts?** I often find that the parts of my talk that are most commented on afterwards are the ones I have illustrated with a client case study or a thought-provoking fact.

- **If it's not appropriate to share tips,** can you tell a story that will underpin your central message and add authenticity to your content? If you have been invited to talk about your book your audience will warm to you if you can share your writing journey warts and all! Stories are memorable and they can be captivating so don't shrink from telling yours - but keep it fast-paced and concise.

- **Can you enhance your talk with a little audience interaction?** Asking a question that requires a show of hands is a simple way of involving your audience.

- **Avoid jargon at all costs.** Engaging presenters do not set out to bamboozle their audience in the mistaken belief they are demonstrating how clever they are with their elaborate explanations.

- **Can you read excerpts from your book?** Your audience will really appreciate this touch. I do this at many of my talks. It's a subtle but effective way of promoting your book and adding extra sparkle to your talk.

Structuring your talk.

I follow a simple three-part structure for my presentations regardless of how long I'm talking for and who I'm talking to. The first part of my talk is my introduction. This is where I thank the organisers for inviting me and share a few of my credentials as an author and marketer. I talk a little about my book, the PR it has attracted and awards it has won. I let people know I will be signing copies in the break afterwards. If I don't want to be interrupted with questions during my talk I will explain that time is available at the end for questions and/or I am happy to answer questions in the break. I go on to outline what my talk is about and how the audience will benefit from it.

The lion's share of my talk falls within the second part, the subject matter I am going to cover. It's usually marketing tips in one form or another. I will include some client campaigns which go down really well or, if I'm talking about my journey as an author, I will read out some of the notes from my ideas book and chart the highs and lows of my book writing journey.

The third part of my talk is my close. I will conclude by thanking my audience, inviting them to chat with me in the break and to connect with me on Twitter. I will also mention my book again and where I will be signing copies of it.

How to achieve Zen-like calm? Practice!

Once I have drafted my presentation and reduced it to bullet points I spend a few hours, usually broken into 30-minute sessions over several days, practising it in my head and out loud. I can't emphasise enough the importance of doing this. The reason why I am so relaxed when presenting without notes is because of those all-important practice sessions.

However I did not start out speaking without notes.

In my early years of speaking I used various memory aids including cue cards and flipcharts before graduating to just one cue card and then to presenting without notes. I have seen other presenters using their Tablet or mobile which looks pretty cool but I'd encourage you to work with whatever makes you feel confident and comfortable. Don't shrink from using memory aids but use them as a support rather than a crutch. They are there to jog your memory when you're presenting.

Memorise your introduction and the introductory line to each new point, story or case study. When you see a speaker on a stage sounding and looking confident despite a lack of notes, it's usually because they have spent time rehearsing and they feel confident as a result. Don't stint on practising! Because I do a fair amount of driving I'm quite happy talking through a presentation in a traffic jam, making good use of what could be wasted time.

Go live!

Unless you're one of those lucky people who rarely suffer nerves in high pressure situations, take it from me that it's natural to feel nervous before your presentation. I've spoken at dozens of events and still have that peculiar out-of-body feeling when I hear my name being called and I'm making my way to the stage. Thankfully the nerves soon disappear as the adrenaline kicks in.

Here are my tips to help you deliver a great talk and feel confident and in control throughout.

- Arrive early at the venue, freshen up in the washroom and familiarise yourself with the surroundings. If you can, check out the room you're speaking in beforehand.

- Let the organisers know you have arrived. Ensure your requests are in hand and reiterate how you would like to be introduced.

Remind them of the title of your book and that you will be signing copies afterwards. Don't assume they will remember these details.

- If your mouth feels dry take a few sips of water before you start and have a mint. At this stage it's natural to be acutely aware of every sensation in your body and for every uncomfortable feeling to be intensified. When you take to the stage, your dry mouth will ease but make sure there's a glass of water close by.

- In the minutes before you start bring your breathing under control by focusing on the cool sensation as you breathe in through your nose and the warm sensation as you breathe out. If any negative thoughts creep in, greet them with your positive affirmations. Don't worry if your heart is beating fast. It's not going to kill you and it will soon calm down when you start speaking.

- Smile when you're called to the stage or the space where you are presenting and maintain it. It will trigger your body to release a flood of positive, feel-good endorphins. Walk purposefully to your place and feel the ground beneath your feet for a few seconds. Pause, look to the middle of your audience, to the left, back to the middle and then to the right. Then open your mouth and speak.

- If you still feel nervous after delivering your opening lines, don't fret. It can take a few minutes to feel at ease. You have practised your opening lines so your audience will be none the wiser.

- Keep smiling throughout your talk, self checking as you move along. If you're aware of speaking too fast simply pause and slow down. Is your voice a little flat? Inject some volume, rhythm and enthusiasm. Rooted to the spot? Move around a little. This is your stage and you, not the audience, are in control. You know that you are perfectly capable of adjusting your voice and your body language in seconds.

- What happens if your mind goes blank? Well firstly be reassured that this happens to most speakers. I have yet to deliver a talk when my mind has not gone blank momentarily before I remember my next point. But this did unsettle me in my early days of speaking. If you lose your way completely just say something like "bear with me, I just need to check where I am" to your audience with your warmest smile. No one will mind. You can also buy time by asking the audience a question and inviting responses so that you can look more closely at your memory aids to get your bearings.

  You're allowed to be human. Many of the audience members will be looking at you thinking "I could never do what she's doing. You wouldn't get me up there speaking," so accept these little quirks. They show you're human. Sometimes you will deliver a talk and feel on top of the world. At other times you will deliver the same talk and stumble in places and feel flat afterwards. This is only to be expected. All speakers have their good days and average days.

- Don't allow yourself to become distracted by any disconcerting behaviour such as a member of the audience yawning or even walking out half way through your talk. Every speaker experiences this. I've learned not to take it personally and neither should you. Focus on the people who are smiling at you and nodding their heads in agreement. You can't please everyone.

Useful speaker communication templates.

Your speaker biography.

Whether you've been approached by an event organiser or have found an event you're keen to speak at, you need a speaker biography that'll be informative for both the organiser and the audience. The benefit of having a prepared speaker biography is that you can send it at a moment's notice and, if you've spent a little time whipping it into shape, the likelihood is it will be spared editing. I have one main speaker biography that I adjust for each event. For example, in the past year I have spoken at two events attended by franchisors so I've tweaked my speaker biography to include a paragraph covering my experience working with franchisors and franchisees. Make it easy for the organisers to promote your biography.

You'll see that I don't shrink from promoting my books and outlining my expertise as a marketer in my biography. Don't be a shrinking violet! Promote your book and update it with any good news such as winning an award or a critic raving about it.

My main speaker biography (260 words).

Dee is a Number One bestselling small business marketing author, regarded as one of the most respected and influential marketers in the UK. She's the author of three books including: *The 15 Essential Marketing Masterclasses For Your Small Business* (Sept 2013). Rated 'an excellent read' by *The Sun Newspaper, CityAM, Elite Business Magazine,* winner of the Bookbag nonfiction book award and one of *Talk Business Magazine's* 'Best books of 2013. It's endorsed by The Chartered Institute of Marketing. Her previous book, *The Ultimate Small Business Marketing Book* has sold 20,000 copies to date and remains an Amazon No. 1 bestseller. It has now been translated into Mandarin after Dee was offered a publishing deal by CITIC publishing in Beijing. It is also required syllabus reading for business and marketing students at The University of Texas.

Dee is the marketing blogger for Barclays Connector website, the marketing contributor to the Microsoft book *Key Metrics for Business Success* and video blogger for The Institute of Directors. She blogs for The Forum of Private Businesses and whichfranchise.com.

Dee is a Fellow of CIM with 30 years' marketing experience, mostly gained working with small businesses. A sales-driven marketer, Dee's generated £12million+ sales. She's renowned for her down to earth approach to marketing and for helping small businesses get incredible results on small budgets. Dee's tips are practical, you don't need marketing qualifications to implement them and they cost little—the biggest investment being your time. Dee dispenses marketing tips that work and that generate sales on a shoestring in the real world.

Why you also need a smaller speaker biography.

Sometimes an organiser will specify the word count for your biography and you can't get away with so many words. In my experience, 100 words is the most frequently allocated word count. The biography below is one of several I use because again I will tailor it to reflect the event I am being invited to speak at and the profile of the audience.

My smaller speaker biography (100 words).

Dee Blick is a Fellow of The Chartered Institute of Marketing with 30 years' marketing experience. Dee is the author of the award winning book: *The 15 Essential Marketing Masterclasses For Your Small Business.* Rated 'an excellent read' by *The Sun Newspaper, CityAM, Elite Business Magazine* and winner of the Bookbag nonfiction book award, it has been endorsed by CIM with the CIM logo on the cover. Check out the reviews on Amazon to find out what readers of her book have to say about it! Dee's previous book, *The Ultimate Small Business Marketing Book* is an Amazon No 1 bestseller.

How to 'sell' your proposed talk so the organisers can sell you.

You have to make the subject matter of your talk as interesting and appealing as possible. If you're pitching to an event organiser the way you present a potential talk is important because they're usually inundated by people wanting to speak. Your pitch has to stand out.

If an organiser has offered you a speaking slot, you want make it easy for them to market your talk effectively so it's packed out. Here's a description of one of my talks that I created after I had been given the green light by an organiser (although it could just as well have been a pitch to the organiser). My keynote talk was standing room only and I suspect this description helped fill those seats. The organisers did not make any changes to it. Can you see how I have used 'you' and 'your' throughout and how I manage to share some of my credentials in the second paragraph, again referring to my status as a bestselling author? At the end I promote my book and include the special price. I have used a number of descriptive words and phrases to intensify the impact of the key points and have emboldened these for your benefit.

The 7 essential steps to making money from marketing.

You love your business so don't shortchange it with tick box marketing. You have to profit from your passion!

In this 30-minute marketing masterclass multi award winning Chartered Marketer and international bestselling business author Dee Blick will share many practical, expert, and commonsense marketing tips - with real client case studies that bring the **tips to life.**

She'll cover:

- Why you need to identify your **marketing comfort zone** and break out of it.

- The value in auditing your marketing - **out with the old, in with the new** and improved.

- Why you must have a **robust** and **compelling** positioning statement.

- Why you don't have to be unique to be successful.

- Why and how you can find your **starving crowds.**

- Why the continuum of behaviour is your most **powerful marketing ally** and how you can use it to build shoestring campaigns.

- Why traditional marketing is still generating sales by the **barrel load!**

Bring a pad and pen and stay on afterwards to chat to Dee about your marketing and buy a signed copy of her **latest bestseller** *The 15 Essential Marketing Masterclasses For Your Small Business* for just £10.

How to provide a combination description about your talk and about you.

Sometimes you'll be asked to provide a combination description that includes your smaller speaker biography and the details of your talk. I am always surprised when a speaker does not take advantage of the maximum word count they have been given. The words you provide will be lifted in their entirety for use in all the event publicity. Take advantage of that precious word allowance but don't use most of it for your mini biography unless told otherwise by the organisers. Some people will attend your talk because they want to see you in action, some because they are interested in your subject matter and some because they like the sound of you and your talk.

This is what I submitted for *The Business Show Magazine* to their exact word count of 300 words. Look at the descriptive words I have used to make my proposed talk sound enticing. For example *'a powerful blend of small business case studies and practical marketing tips'* has more impact than *'small business case studies and marketing tips.'*

About Dee Blick.

Dee is a multi award winning Fellow of The Chartered Institute of Marketing with 31 years' marketing experience, mostly gained while working with small and medium sized businesses. She's also the international bestselling author of *The Ultimate Small Business Marketing Book* (published in China) and the award winning sequel *The 15 Essential Marketing Masterclasses For Your Small Business* - voted *Talk Business* magazine's Best Business Book 2013 and rated excellent by *The Sun, Elite Business Magazine* and *B2B Magazine*. Dee has worked with hundreds of small businesses on a one-to-one basis and is internationally renowned for sharing powerful, practical and easy-to-implement marketing on a shoestring tips, reinforced by genuine small business case studies. Dee is not a theoretical marketer. Every day she works with small businesses on a retained basis and has generated £12 million sales in the past 31 years. What she has to say is well worth listening to because it delivers results.

Powerful Marketing Shoestring Style.

For any small business marketing is not an option: it's vital if sales are to soar! And today savvy customers want it all: exceptional value products and services backed up by an attentive customer service - with tantalising marketing messages delivered through relevant and engaging channels to pique their curiosity and motivate them to buy. Using a powerful blend of small business case studies and practical marketing tips, Dee will share how you can grow your small business on a shoestring budget, how you can avoid the mistakes many small businesses make and why 'The Power of 3' should underpin your shoestring marketing campaigns. She'll show you how you can create a powerful, theory-free marketing plan, why you don't need a USP to be successful, and why being brilliant at the basics drives sales.

Review your writing and add the Wow factor.

Don't be content with your first draft. Review it and make sure every line has the Wow factor. Have you made your sentences sing by adding descriptive words and phrases? You want this talk to be standing room only! The words and descriptions you use can ensure this happens.

Finally, here is a talk outline I created for a talk I was delivering at a Chartered Institute of Marketing conference for small businesses. It's just 170 words.

The 7 marketing secrets of successful small businesses.

In tough times you have to be really smart with your marketing. Customers know they are in demand. Should you dive straight into tactics: advertising, networking and PR, spend all day on Twitter or stand back and actually plan your marketing so you know who you want to reach, why and where? In this lively and engaging talk, Dee will share many top tips that work in the real world. Tips you can use to generate sales on a small budget. Dee will give real-life examples of how small businesses have used her tips and strategies and will explain why traditional marketing is still generating sales by the bucket load. Bring your pad and pen and chat to Dee after her talk. You can also buy a signed copy of her latest multi award winning best seller *The 15 Essential Marketing Masterclasses For Your Small Business* at the amazing price of £5 thanks to a generous subsidy from Cim Eastern (rrp £15).

Without a doubt public speaking deserves a place in your book promotion marketing plan. So, take the plunge and give it a go and let me know how you get on too.

Chapter summary.

- For any author a public speaking engagement is usually just one part of an altogether bigger promotional machine.

- It's natural to feel nervous about public speaking but it's worth pushing ahead because it will boost your author profile, build your expert status and help you sell more books.

- Feel the fear and do it anyway! Start small, working your way up to the bigger talks when you feel sufficiently confident.

- When you're starting out it's down to you to pitch your speaking services to event organisers.

- Consider offering yourself as a replacement speaker but be prepared to talk at a moment's notice.

- Research events you'd like to speak at on social media and build a relationship with the event organiser.

- Create a set of positive empowering slogans to call upon.

- Your voice is a powerful instrument and it only takes a little practice for you to realise this.

- Your body language is the all important support act for your voice.

- Study other speakers. What can you learn from them to further improve your stagecraft?

- Could an image consultant give you an extra confidence boost?

- Before creating your talk find out as much as you can about your audience.

- Suggest a book signing to the organisers.

- Think about the structure of your talk. Plan it out and use case studies or facts and figures to give it a boost.

- Consider using your book as a prop during your talk by reading excerpts from it.

- Practice your talk in a quiet environment. Use cue cards, your mobile, iPad and so on. Have a back-up plan if you're using PowerPoint.

- Ensure the organisers are reminded of your requests when you arrive at the venue.

- Use your breathing exercises and positive sayings before you take to the stage.

- Self check throughout your talk and don't be afraid to adjust your body language and voice.

- If you forget something buy time by asking a question or pause to gather your thoughts.

- Make sure you promote your availability for public speaking and book signings on your website.

CHAPTER 17

How to Promote Your Book on the Radio

I was recently invited by BBC Radio Sussex and Surrey for a 25-minute live on-air interview to share my journey as an author and my publishing deal in China. I arrived early, excited and a little nervous. Personally I find live radio more daunting than pre-recorded television simply because you can't afford to put a foot wrong and you have to be clear and concise from start to finish. For this interview I didn't know the questions I was going to be asked and so couldn't prepare any answers. Before the interview began I managed to spend a few minutes with the presenter and used this time to give her a thumbnail sketch of my story. I also gave her a copy of my book in the hope this would encourage her to give it some extra air time which it did. Before she started interviewing me she described the cover in detail, even reading out the cover testimonials. It was an enjoyable experience and despite being asked a volley of interesting and challenging questions I managed to answer them without faltering. I was asked to stay on for an impromptu phone-in which was nerve wracking because the first caller had a real bee in his bonnet. On the way home I replayed the conversation with the presenter and realised there was no way I could have handled an interview like that or a phone-in when I first thought about approaching radio stations to market my book.

I started out by seeking opportunities to speak on community radio stations because I knew from listening to several that they were always on the lookout for interesting people to interview and many of the interviews were pre-recorded. All in all a good starting point for any author with no experience of being interviewed on the radio.

So don't let it worry you if the thought of being interviewed on live radio makes you a little nervous. Do what I did and cut your teeth on the smaller stations so that when you're presented with a golden opportunity to talk about your book on a much bigger station you can accept it with both hands. But if you're offered a live radio interview on a big station my advice is to grab it and in the time before your interview, study these tips. You'll also benefit from the tips on how to project your voice in the previous chapter.

Here's how you can promote your book on the radio. The process is similar to the one I follow when approaching a journalist or an editor.

- Identify the community radio stations you think may be interested in hearing about your story. Search the internet and use social media to locate these stations and create a shortlist. You'll find useful information on their websites, including the stories they're looking for and how they are structured.

- Tune in and listen. Do they have programmes that promote interesting people, local or not? How are these interviews structured and how long do they last for? Get under the skin of each radio channel, the team and the presenters so you can fine tune your imminent pitch.

- Answer the following questions before pitching: how can I add value for this station? Why would listeners be interested in hearing about my book and my journey as an author? Do they have any particular programmes that would be suitable for me to take part in?

- Rehearse your interesting pitch before pitching it! Local radio stations tend to be on the lookout for genuinely interesting stories and news to spice up their content and the more people-oriented these stories are the better. This gives you a definite advantage as an author. So when you've mapped out the reasons why they should interview you, it's simply a matter of picking up the phone or sending an email to pitch your idea. If you want to share some news about your book you may need to speak to the newsroom. If you have an idea for a programme you may need to speak to the researcher. That's why it's important to find out how each station is structured before making your initial contact. At the end of this chapter I have included the email I sent to BBC Radio Sussex and Surrey after they had interviewed me by telephone on International Women's Day. In this email you can see how I suggest they interview me on their popular early morning programme. I simply took advantage of the opportunity when I was interviewed by them on the telephone to pitch for a much bigger share of air time. How did I manage to squeeze this in? It was very much a case of thinking on my feet! When the researcher thanked me for my input at the end of the call I asked if I could send an email about my experiences as an author, explaining why I thought their listeners would be interested in my book launch in China. I also spoke briefly about my love of writing from an early age. It did the trick. Use the structure of this email to compose your pitch whether you're talking it through on the telephone or sending an email.

If you receive a warm reception and it's all stations go (pardon the pun) find out if your interview will be live or recorded. Maintain your composure if you're told you'll be on a live show. It's then time to do some preparation so that you can deliver a sterling performance on the day.

Here's how you can do this:

- Don't prepare a script. This will not inspire the presenter or engage the station's listeners. Instead, compile a sheet of bullet points in a font and point size you can read when glancing down. It's easy to get carried away during a radio interview only to realise afterwards that you were rambling and didn't touch on your key points. The station's listeners can't see the crib sheet and the presenter won't mind.

- If you don't know the questions you're going to be asked prepare for some of the obvious ones such as: "What made you write your book?" "Where did you get your inspiration from?" "Tell our listeners about your book." "Have you always wanted to write a book?" "What reaction has it had so far?" "Who buys your book?" And "Did you enjoy writing at school?" Rehearse your answers in the days leading up to your interview, talking them through as though you were in the studio. When you're on air, these words will seem familiar which is reassuring.

- Confirm the date and time of your interview with the presenter or your contact a few days before the interview.

- Tweet about it and ask the station to retweet your tweets. This simple act alone will generate book sales.

- Arrive early so that you can find a place to park if a space has not already been allocated. Aim to get there an hour earlier than required and find somewhere quiet to run through your notes. Use the positive self talk tips in the previous chapter to keep nerves at bay before adrenaline kicks in.

- Book in with the radio station reception half an hour beforehand unless you've been given different instructions. You may be lucky and get to speak to your presenter or it will simply be a matter of waiting in reception and keeping the butterflies at bay.

- Time permitting run through your expectations of the interview with the presenter before you go on air. Give them a copy of your book after engaging in the usual pleasantries. The presenter is more likely to talk about it if they have a copy in their hands and, it's likely they will allocate more discussion time to it too. Make sure that the presenter knows your full name and why you wrote your book.

- When you're on air concentrate on speaking clearly and with passion. It's easy to umm and err but pause instead. Don't rush through what you want to say. Emphasise keywords but above all be enthusiastic. You will sound confident and people will enjoy listening to you.

- If you're asked a question and your mind goes blank, simply respond with: "I'm not sure I can do that question justice... but what I would say is..." and move to a related subject that you feel confident talking about. This happens to me now and again and it's really not a big deal unless I make it one. If you can mentally prepare for the odd glitch beforehand you're more likely to handle the odd sticky patch calmly and with confidence.

- Maintain eye contact with the presenter throughout the interview. They have to communicate with you when you're talking by using non-verbal signals. You need to pick up on when it's time to have a break for the music, news, travel and weather alerts, or when you're talking too much. You don't want to be cut off midway through a sentence because you drifted into your own world and didn't spot the presenter frantically trying to get your attention. It's up to you to make their job easy.

- In the break check that your presenter is happy with what you've said so far. Don't be afraid of suggesting they ask a question you'd really like to answer or that they give you a little more time to expand on a previous point. Is it okay if you give the station's listeners your social media addresses and your website or blog details so they can contact you? By this stage, you'll have built a rapport with the presenter and should find them more receptive to these requests.

- When the interview has ended be charming and thank the presenter. Tell them how relaxed they made you feel and why their questions were the ones you had been hoping for. Small touches make a big difference in these intimate situations.

- There may be an opportunity for you to return for another interview so if you feel this is the case, suggest it. At this stage, a tentative yes is all that's needed. You can begin your charm offensive for round two further down the line.

- Let the appropriate team members at the station know that you're more than happy to be a trusted voice they can call on at any time when they have a topic that falls into your area of expertise. You'll be added to their database of trusted experts. For example, I've been contacted by BBC Radio 5 Live on the strength of being an expert contributor on BBC Radio Sussex and Surrey.

The winning email that got me the interview.

This is the email I sent to the researcher after briefly suggesting they interview me. I was asked to send an email outlining my story and why I would make for a good interview. This email is a not inconsiderable 501 words. You may think it's too long but it worked. Within a few hours I received the confirmation details of my interview. I knew when drafting this email that it was important I share my story in some detail so that the researcher could confidently arrive at the decision to devote an entire show to me. I'm not suggesting you send something as long as this when you're pitching to a radio station from a cold start. However, if they have shown an interest in your story and your journey don't be afraid to write something of substance to clinch that interview!

Dear XXX
It was lovely taking part in your show this morning. Thank you so much for thinking of me.

I would love to do a show with you sharing my story from very humble beginnings. If I can inspire others that success is out there and you don't have to be born with a silver spoon to realise your dreams that would be great.

I had a working class upbringing and loved to write from a very young age and so sought comfort in this, especially as I was bullied at school (ginger hair!!) I was the only girl in my school to get a distinction in creative writing. I was the nerd writing stories and mini books when the other kids were out playing.

I went to university (first person in my family) and tumbled into marketing only to discover I had a real skill for creative writing that brought home the sales big time. I reached a very senior position but gave up the career to be a mum.

I started my own marketing business but developed chronic RSI in my arms and shoulders which threatened my writing career. I could no longer type, struggled to handwrite. After being upset about this for several months, thinking it was the end of my career, I trained myself in Dragon Speech Recognition Software and my writing took off. I'd always wanted to write a book but lacked the courage then Dad died and I decided to go for it. I am the woman who has written three books without actually writing a word!

I self published book one and received several blows including being told my book was no good, I'd never sell books and folk saying they would help me to promote it fading away. My second book hit the top 150 of Amazon books and has been picked up by China and the contract is all sorted, advance paid. It's the UK's number one bestselling small business marketing book. Readers comment on how they like my conversational style which is handy as I dictate.

I landed an international publishing deal with the world's biggest publisher of business books, Wiley & Sons, for my current book, number three. They actually approached me. I am now writing my fourth book about how to write a bestselling book and market it on a shoestring budget.

Lots more *(name)* but I don't want you dozing off. My story has been one of having to overcome obstacles and having to believe in myself when I was the only one out there touting my books. It's been a magical journey. I'm never driven by money, ever. I am an obsessive writer, driven by reader delight! Yet writing is my hobby, what I do in my spare time as I have a successful full-time marketing business.

I look forward to hearing from you about when you want me to take part in your show. Have a lovely weekend and thank you again.

Kind regards,

Dee

Keep on listening to those radio stations so that you can identify opportunities to speak. Once you have appeared on the radio and made a great impression with everyone there's every chance you'll be invited back and any further ideas you have will be given a fair hearing.

Chapter summary.

- If you haven't spoken on the radio before, start by pitching to the small, friendly community stations.

- Do your homework on the stations you would like to appear on. Find out who the presenters are, what they cover and their approach to interviews.

- Before pitching, answer the question: 'Why should this station interview me?'

- Find out who you should pitch your idea to and the best way to contact them.

- Your email or telephone pitch should tell an interesting story about you as an author and not just focus on your book. Your journey may be of more interest to a presenter than your book.

- Create a sheet of bullet points and practice your answers to the questions suggested in this chapter if you don't know what you'll be asked.

- Arrive early so you can park, say hello, calm your nerves and hopefully introduce yourself to the presenter.

- Before the interview starts, give a copy of your book to the presenter.

- When talking be aware of your tone of voice, your pace and volume. Make an effort not to umm and err.

- Maintain eye contact with the presenter to pick up on any non-verbal signals.

- Catch up with the presenter in any breaks. Are they happy with your answers? Suggest other questions.

- When your interview has concluded be fulsome in your thanks and don't forget to offer yourself as a trusted voice for future shows.

CHAPTER 18

The Exhibition Skills Masterclass

Ten years ago I developed an exhibition skills workshop to help 15 start-up businesses exhibit on a shoestring at a large exhibition in Sussex. Despite the lavish displays elsewhere the busiest stands at the event were without a doubt the ones manned by these 15 businesses. I've since delivered this workshop to businesses of all sizes. Whilst many had exhibited before, they could see how it was possible to become even more effective at exhibiting and on a shoestring budget.

But, it was only when I became an author that I realised how valuable exhibitions were. In the past six years I've benefited from promoting my books as an exhibitor, mostly at local exhibitions. I've sold hundreds of books, promoted my services as a professional speaker and built awareness of me as an author and a businesswoman. I've met many readers and built relationships with local journalists and editors. My book sales on Amazon have increased in the week before an exhibition, on the day itself and in the week afterwards. Whilst I've exhibited at 12 exhibitions in the past six years, I haven't paid a penny. Instead I've approached the organisers and offered my services as a speaker in exchange for a free stand. I've also thrown in other extras including copies of my book for the prize draws and sharing my exhibition skills tips with the exhibitors. I would encourage you to negotiate too before reaching for your chequebook. What can you offer that would appeal to the organiser of an event you would like to exhibit at?

And so in this chapter I share my step-by-step approach to exhibiting on a shoestring budget so that you can promote your book without it making a dent in your pocket. We'll look at how you can use an exhibition as a platform to generate awareness of you and your book and how you can benefit from book sales on your stand and online.

But first, why do some authors walk away at the end of an exhibition having achieved only a handful of book sales if that?

Here are some of the reasons:

- The exhibition was unsuitable because the visitors did not meet their profile of ideal reader.

- They did not view it as a marketing exercise requiring planning from start to finish. They simply pitched up on the day with a few boxes of books, a bowl for business cards and some sweets for the 'grab and go' brigade.

- Their stand was drab and flat. It did not draw visitors to it. In fact it acted as a deterrent despite the great book hidden behind the dreary facade.

- They did not make it clear in the communications promoting the event that they would be selling books. Visitors were not primed to buy.

- Their body language was far from friendly and they were too busy eating, drinking or checking their mobile to pay attention to their visitors.

- They had not mastered the skill of describing their book in a few minutes. They either spent too much or too little time talking about it.

- They were only interested in talking about themselves and their book.

- They packed up early and missed out on the one key person of influence who could have made all the difference.

- They did not consider the additional benefits that were on offer to exhibitors such as opportunities to speak at the event, to sponsor it and to have a book giveaway in exchange for some promotion.

Don't make these mistakes! You've invested your precious time and (hopefully not too much) money exhibiting. Make it your mission to sell books and build your reputation as an author.

How to find the right exhibition for you and your book.

I found the events I was interested in exhibiting at through a process of searching online, reading the business pages in local newspapers and magazines and watching what was happening on Twitter in my local area. By the time you're considering exhibiting as a marketing activity you know who your ideal reader is. It's then a straightforward process of tracking down the exhibitions that will appeal to them. Whilst there may well be no shortage of exhibitions, you must consider the merits of each one in detail so you don't fall into a time wasting trap. Understanding the profile of the people that the organisers are targeting has to be your first priority. They have to match your profile of ideal reader. That said, I've shied away from exhibiting at some of the big national events even though they were targeting my ideal readers because the cost of exhibiting was too high. If I like the look of one of these I will offer my services as a keynote speaker instead.

So don't sign up to an event simply because it's targeting your ideal readers. There are more questions you need to ask the organisers including:

- **How is the exhibition structured?** For example, is there a seminar programme and a networking area to encourage visitors and exhibitors to network? Will there be wireless facilities, nice refreshments and - the icing on the cake - great keynote speakers to pull in the crowds? Is the venue attractive and spacious? How easy is it to reach? Consider these points when evaluating an exhibition. If it doesn't appeal to you it's unlikely to appeal to visitors.

- **Are you charging visitors an entry fee?** I attended a local exhibition recently and was shocked when told by the organiser it would cost £3 to browse the stalls inside the small hall. This explained the lack of visitors. If there is an entry fee, you have to be confident that the event will still be popular with visitors and that it won't act as a deterrent.

- **How much will it cost me to exhibit?** Don't just look at the cost of the floor space. This may be the first in a line of expenses. You may have to take the following into consideration:

  - Insurance. At one event I was told I needed public liability insurance and had to increase my cover from £1 million to £5 million.

  - Buying a sturdy fold-up table for displaying your books. You may only get the floor space and nothing more.

  - Overnight hotel stays, meals, travel expenses and parking.

  - Investing in pop-up banners and other marketing collateral.

After listing your expenses the final figure may surprise you. Divide it by the number of books you'll have to sell to break even. If this is your first exhibition and you're using it to make a splash about your book then making a profit may not be a key priority. But you should aim to cover your costs.

- **How are you marketing the exhibition to potential visitors?** A good organiser will use several marketing channels to promote their exhibition including social media, advertising, business networking, direct mail, PR, email marketing and their website.

- **How are you promoting the exhibitors?** A proactive organiser will promote their exhibitors before the event. You will sell books as a result of this to people who are unable to attend but are nevertheless keen to buy your book. And of course some people will attend the event just to meet you!

- **Is it an annual event?** If it is discover how popular it has been in previous years. The organisers will have visitor numbers for previous events and a list of past exhibitors. If the year-on-year visitor numbers are declining you'll need some convincing that this year's event will buck the trend.

- **How open to negotiation are you?** You're at your most powerful when interested in taking a stand but it's in your interest to make the exhibitors keen to have you. So when negotiating, talk about the benefits of having you as a keynote speaker, or if that's not possible, suggest a seminar with a book signing afterwards. Offer some free books in exchange for this gesture being mentioned in the communications promoting the event.

- **Can I see the floor plan?** It's a good idea to be close to the networking or refreshment areas because these areas attract high footfall at all times. And if you can have a space on a corner because it will give more room for visitors to browse your book.

Exhibition booked, it's time to get organised!

The exhibition checklist is king.

Planning an exhibition is not that dissimilar to planning a wedding. The time you spend before the event ensuring that no stone is left unturned will ensure a flawless performance on the day. Here's a checklist I use before every exhibition. Use it and you won't forget anything!

Exhibition Checklist

	Y/N	Additional info
Stand booked?		
Entry time confirmed?		

Stuff to Take

Black box	Clipboards	Bookmarks
Desktop Diary	Fabric in book colours for dressing stand	Bowl for business card draw
Pens/Stapler/Clear folders	Fabric in book colours for dressing small boxes	Promotional gifts (mugs and pens)
Helium balloons	Pop up banner	Two shoe boxes for displaying books
Two circular biscuit tins for displaying books	Recipe bookstand for displaying two books	Four sample books for visitors to peruse
Leaflet dispensers to display my Amazon review flyers	£150 of loose change and notes	Useful contact names and numbers
Business cards	Prospect sheets	Mints

Create an outstanding stand and boost your book sales.

Small is beautiful so if you have a small space and a small table (pretty standard nowadays for local exhibitions) you can still create a buzz around your stand and your book. Don't be content with arranging books in piles and fanning out your promotional material. This will not entice visitors to stop, chat and buy!

Instead:

- Buy four pieces of decent quality fabric (ideally plain cotton with a satin finish) that match the colours on your book cover. They should be neatly trimmed and large enough to cover your boxes with some surplus. If the organisers are not providing a cloth that covers your table and reaches the floor, buy a piece of cloth that does and use the space underneath for storing boxes of books out of sight.

- Place two shoe boxes and two circular tins underneath your fabric to give height and variety to your table and to draw attention to your books so they can be seen from afar. You can then practice arranging small piles of books on them.

- Have a couple of acrylic literature dispensers for the sales literature you'll be creating to promote your book.

- Consider adding some low cost extras such as bookmarks, props that tell the story of your book, a striking poster depicting its position on Amazon and a flower arrangement in your book cover's colours.

- Make your stand even more attention grabbing with three helium balloons promoting the title of your book and, if it's true, the phrase '#1 bestselling author' in a bold contrasting ink. If you're celebrating the launch of your book why not have a large balloon with the words 'My book is being launched today!' or something similar?

- Have room for a pop-up banner that has an image of your book and you plus a few benefits. If your book is already a bestseller this should also be on your banner. Make sure it's in full view of visitors (i.e. not located behind your table so it's only partly visible)

Your exhibition stand has to showcase your book so that visitors stop and admire it long enough for you to strike up a conversation.

Some low cost sales literature to consider.

If you've followed my tips on making your stand eye-catching then your book should sell itself. Investing in masses of promotional literature is not necessary. However there are a few items that you can create. I fill my leaflet dispensers with two different flyers, each one printed on A4 paper weighing 180gsm so it feels nice. One comprises extracts taken from eight of the best five-star reviews of my book on Amazon with a clear call to action: 'Buy my book at the special price of £XX today.' I include my contact details, the title of the book and its availability on Kindle. The second flyer includes extracts from the best professional critics' reviews of my book. I also include details of the awards my book has won and add my contact details.

Both work well in starting up conversations and I make sure that a visitor walking away from my stand empty-handed has both copies in the hope they will be tempted to order my book at a later date.

You can create these flyers on a modest budget but it's worth paying a designer to add the finishing touches. If you want to use them for other events and book signings don't date them by including special offers that are restricted to a particular event. Write the details of any special offers on plain postcards, folded in half so they can be placed by each pile of books. At my last event when I was promoting my three books I had several postcards with the following in my husband's neat handwriting:

Special Horsham Microbiz offer £XX—cheaper than Amazon!

Buy any 2 of Dee's books today for £XX—save £X!

Buy all 3 of Dee's books today for £XX—save £X!

Get your signed copy of Dee's latest multi award winning book today!

Other promotional literature to consider.

You may want to consider giving bookmarks away, having business cards that advertise your books, or maybe colourful flyers with one side replicating the front cover of your book and the other summarising the content with a great quote from a critic. Keep it simple. An attractive stand with artfully arranged piles of books, a few flyers in dispensers plus handwritten postcards advertising special offers should be more than enough to help you sell lots of books and boost your online sales too.

Inviting people to your stand before you exhibit.

Why not promote the event you're exhibiting at to your database and on social media? A couple of emails, one sent a month before the exhibition and one in the week before, will bring more people to your stand keen to buy your book and, if you're delivering a talk, to hear you speak. Post several messages on social media promoting the event, explaining why your followers should visit you.

If you don't have a database, make a list of:

- People who've expressed an interest in your book.

- The people you've met at networking groups who were interested in you and your book.

- The people you know who could recommend your book to their followers, members or clients.

- Your lapsed clients, existing clients, warm prospects and hot prospects; potential candidates for your book.

Don't just rely on email. Pick up the phone and let these people know why they should come.

How to run your stand on the day.

- **If you're allowed to, set up your stand the night before.** Keep your books out of sight to arrange in the morning. Arrive at early doors so you can add the finishing touches. You're then ready to greet people in the first few minutes of the exhibition opening.

- **Talk to the exhibitors around you during the day.** Being friendly can lead to more book sales especially at a local event where you're a familiar face.

- **Don't be alone for the whole day.** You'll need a partner to ensure the stand is manned all day long. There will be busy periods, for example when a seminar finishes. You don't want a packed stand with only you to juggle talking, handling the money, and signing books. Some visitors will want to talk to you about your book and your journey as an author which is why an extra pair of hands is important.

- **Smile at people as they go by.** Commonsense I know but a warm smile goes a long way in building rapport.

- **Don't eat or drink on your stand and resist the temptation to check your mobile every 10 minutes.** Don't lose book sales by being distracted.

- **Have a 'freshen up' kit.** Standing in a warm environment can make you feel stale. Be aware of coffee breath too!

- **Tidy your stand as the day goes on.** Keep topping up with books and ensure your sample books are in full view. I put stickers on my sample books with: *'Amazon No 1 Bestseller. Please pick me up and read me!'*

- **Take short breaks whilst the seminars are running.** People tend to come pouring out after a seminar has finished and most of your book sales will be in these busy patches. If you leave the stand take a few books, your flyers and bookmarks. I've brought many people back to my stand by doing this.

Rapport sells books.

People will warm to you and be more likely to buy your book if you focus on making them feel good about themselves.

So pay a genuinely nice compliment to each visitor and maintain your interest when they're talking to you. You'll have to work at this because it can be challenging to keep on chatting to one person when you can see other people gathering at your stand and you don't want to miss a book sale. Remember to nod, to acknowledge what's being said and to be enthusiastic. It pays to be aware of your body language too. It's easy to become too relaxed and to slip into body language that conveys you're bored or tired even though you're feeling warm and friendly.

Have some useful 'conversation starters' and fillers in mind.

Knowing how to start a conversation avoids those sometimes awkward moments when a person has approached your stand, you've given them your best smile and then silence descends and hangs in the air. Often a visitor will be interested in your book but a little tongue-tied. It's your job to take the lead with some conversation starters.

Here's how I do this:

- "What has brought you here today?"

- "Where have you travelled from?"

- "Are you coming to my seminars?"

- "Do you have your own business?"

- "Have you come across any of my books before?"

- "Are you enjoying the exhibition so far?"

Make it easy for visitors to understand what your book is about.

You haven't got all day long to sing your book's praises. At best you have a few minutes to wow a visitor so use the following guide to talk about your book without overwhelming them.

- Tell them the title.

- Let them know in a few sentences why you wrote it and what it's about.

- Explain who your book is aimed at, how your readers benefit from reading it and why it's different from other books covering the same subject.

- Tell them how it has been received. If it has achieved bestselling status, won any awards, had rave reviews from readers, bloggers, and journalists be sure to mention this. Don't hesitate to share good news.

- Round off by letting them know about any special offers or discounts you're offering today.

Have a copy of your book in your hands whilst you're talking so you can flick through it and draw the visitor's attention to any sections you think may appeal to them. Then, **put your book in their hands** so they can look at it from close quarters and feel the pages. This simple act usually clinches the sale!

Use a welcoming and positive tone of voice.

Your voice is a powerful tool and it can maintain the interest of any visitor.

- **Speak in a warm, enthusiastic voice** at all times - when you're leading the conversation and when you're responding to a visitor.

- **Enthusiasm is vital!** If you can't be enthusiastic about your book you won't inspire a visitor to buy it. As Henry Ford said of enthusiasm "With it there is accomplishment, without it only abilities." You can convey enthusiasm by emphasising key words in an enthusiastic manner. "I think you will *really enjoy* my book."

- **Most of us 'umm and err'** so be aware of this natural but irritating tendency and make a conscious effort to... pause... instead.

Demonstrate you're a good listener.

Common courtesy aside it pays to listen to every person who visits your stand because you'll be able to tell if they would really benefit from buying your book. You can then promote it with confidence.

It's easy to show you're listening. Pause after the person has finished speaking and use verbal and non-verbal signals. Nod your head, smile slightly; say 'yes' or 'no' in a lower tone of voice as the conversation is progressing.

When combined with your meticulous exhibition planning, these simple but powerful tips will win you many new readers. Be prepared to go the extra mile and radiate enthusiasm and warmth from early doors to close.

Chapter summary.

- Exhibitions can help you sell books, meet readers and boost your profile.

- Avoid the mistakes made by other authors, including a lack of planning, a boring stand, and poor rapport-building skills.

- You can find local exhibitions easily. Search online, read the local papers and research on Twitter.

- Keep costs down. Look for local exhibitions and offer to speak at larger regional and national exhibitions.

- Do your homework on each exhibition before signing up to it.

- Negotiate! Offer to sponsor the event, speak at it and give some books in exchange for a free stand.

- Use an exhibition checklist so you don't forget anything.

- Make your stand a magnet for visitors with props including shoeboxes, biscuit tins, a lovely cloth, pop-up banners and balloons.

- Create a couple of flyers promoting your book and consider bookmarks and special offers on plain postcards.

- Practice explaining what your book is about and why you wrote it.

- Be warm, friendly and welcoming to all visitors. Build rapport by asking questions, listening and smiling.

- Don't be afraid to sell your book! Put it in the hands of a visitor when talking to them.

- Be a good conversationalist and an equally good listener.

CHAPTER 19

How to Promote Your Book With Networking

As a businesswoman and an author I've always been a fan of networking not least because it seems to provide the best of both worlds; the opportunity to promote your book to a group of people, all wrapped up in a semi-social setting. You don't have to delve into the murky depths of hard selling either. Networking is an enjoyable way to spend your time with the cost of attending networking events modest in comparison to other marketing tactics.

By attending an eclectic mix of networking events I've managed to sell hundreds of books and met some really interesting people that I have gone on to work with, with a fair few recommending me for public speaking engagements. As I mentioned in Chapter 16, I owe my public speaking career to networking.

If you're writing fiction I can understand why you may be tempted to dismiss networking out of hand because it's fair to say that most of the networking groups nowadays are primarily aimed at business people (which of course makes networking ideal if you're writing a non-fiction book). But even if your book is a work of fiction you may be pleasantly surprised to find some networking groups and events in your local area that attract your ideal target audience. You won't know until you start digging.

Where I live in Sussex, networking groups and events are abundant and include for example:

- A thriving Mumpreneur networking group aimed at working mums, with weekly meetings that take place throughout the county and beyond. www.agoodgossip.co.uk

- A 'First Friday' group - an informal gathering of business owners who meet on the first Friday of each month. www.firstfridaynetwork.co.uk

- A women's social network - strictly no business and aimed at women of all ages who enjoy socialising in the company of other women.

- Writers' groups. www.horshamwriters.co.uk

- Women in Business groups. www.wib-sussex.co.uk

- Events organised by the local Chamber of Commerce.

- Business Improvement Groups.

- 4Networking. More on this group later!

- BNI. www.bni.co.uk

And I am only scratching the surface here. No matter who your book is aimed at I would wager there's a networking organisation or a group that's not a million miles away from you that will attract your profile of target readers. And you have to be there! At the most, attending an event should only cost you the price of a breakfast, lunch or evening meal and you should sell books and find enthusiastic advocates of your book.

Some networking groups require an upfront commitment from you and a membership fee to cover membership which can be for as little as a few months or an entire year. You can usually attend at least one meeting before signing up as a member. I would encourage you to do this. Other networking groups run on an informal basis. You simply turn up if you feel like it and you pay on the day.

The likelihood is that you will not want to network hundreds of miles away from where you live. So, use the internet to draw up a shortlist of all the networking organisations and the networking events in your area and whittle it down to the ones you're reasonably confident will be attended by people who match the profile of your target readers. Ask your local Chamber of Commerce for a list of events they organise and keep your eyes peeled on the business pages in local publications. Twitter is incredibly useful for finding out more about networking events and organisations in your local area too.

Don't worry about being tongue-tied when you attend an event. If you're new to networking it may take a little time before you feel completely at ease. Prepare beforehand to keep the nerves at bay. For example if you use the tips in the previous chapter you should find it easy to paint an enticing picture about your book. Similarly the tips in chapter 16 on how to use your voice and body language will help you deliver an engaging and memorable brief presentation. (At most events you're usually given 40-60 seconds).

When I was planning this chapter, I was keen to tap into the expertise of two of the most influential and respected networking experts in the UK and it just so happens that I know them so it was an easy ask! Brad Burton is a very successful international author and the founder of 4Networking. Stefan Thomas is a director of 4Networking and author of the bestselling book *Business Networking for Dummies*. I hope you find their practical tips on how to promote your book through networking helpful. It's reassuring to see that they both emphasise the importance of being helpful, genuine and friendly. You don't need any complicated tricks up your sleeve to make people warm to you and want to buy your book. But there are some simple things that you can do to successfully promote yourself and your book.

Why it pays to blend your networking.

If you decide to join a networking organisation such as 4Networking this should not stop you from attending other networking activities and events. Your local Chamber of Commerce and Federation of Small Business may organise evening and lunchtime networking events where you pay a one-off fee to cover refreshments. So find out where your readers network, pick up the phone, introduce yourself to the organiser and go along armed with your books, a warm smile and enough loose change!

I confess to being a networking butterfly. Whilst I am a member of our local Women in Business Group, I also attend many local networking events on an informal basis with the aim of promoting my books and my author profile locally.

Top networking tips from Stefan Thomas.

I first met Stefan at The Business Show where he was speaking about networking. It was just before the launch of his new book, *Business Networking for Dummies*, which has since become an Amazon bestseller and a WH Smith's bestseller too. Here's my interview with him.

Q. For authors unfamiliar with the concept of business networking, can you explain it in a nutshell?

A. In its simplest form business networking is simply any activity where you're interacting with others in a business environment and taking the opportunity to form new relationships or strengthen existing ones.

Business people may find networking opportunities in many places and at many events - in the course of a day's work, at conferences and industry events and, more recently, through social media.

But narrowing the definition of 'business networking' further still, nowadays it's referred to when describing organised networking events that take place primarily for the purpose of networking with others.

In recent years, organisations such as 4Networking and other groups have organised regular events with the sole aim of enabling business owners irrespective of size, sector or gender to meet, engage with each other and do business in a semi-social setting.

Q.What are the benefits of networking in general?

A. Most people will turn up to their first business networking event looking for more business. One of the biggest benefits of business networking is that when approached with the right mindset a business owner can get more business from their network for a small outlay, but there are other benefits too. Business networking is a simple and enjoyable activity that keeps a person's network stable provided they make the effort to actively network. Many also benefit from a growth in confidence and personal skills. Most business networking events involve some sort of pitch (at 4Networking it is called the "40 second round") so over a period of time a person can improve and refine their pitch - which benefits them in their everyday life too. It's no longer daunting when pitching to a prospect or presenting a meeting. Surrounding yourself with other businesspeople with a range of skills and experiences is incredibly useful for any business owner but especially for someone new to business.

What's more any business owner will have to select suppliers at some stage for their business and a networking environment facilitates this. Instead of choosing unknown people from a directory you can choose suppliers from your networking contacts, the people you have come to know, like and trust. You have the opportunity to get to know people and witness firsthand the level of respect they command from others before you engage them which has to be better than selecting someone from an advert.

There are many other benefits too, perhaps an overlooked one being the sense of camaraderie. Working on your own can be isolating so attending a buzzing networking meeting is a real highlight. As an author I know how lonely it can be to write a book and how those four walls can drive you crazy!

Q. Why would an author benefit from business networking?

A. Using business networking events to promote their book is a no-brainer for any author. You have the opportunity to meet people on a regular basis; people who will buy your book and introduce it to their own contacts. You get to talk about your book for 40 seconds every week to a captive audience. At 4N we also have a speaker slot where a member delivers a short presentation of 10 or 15 minutes. An author can take advantage of this to promote their book which will boost their book sales.

I've been invited to speak about my book and share networking tips at other events on many occasions simply because my networking contacts have recommended me to their contacts. At some of these speaking engagements the organiser has placed a bulk order of my book which helps in boosting my Amazon rank.

Just a quick tip, when anyone at a networking event mentions they've read my book, I will ask them to post an Amazon review. I gently remind them with a follow up email, thanking them for buying my book and asking for the review again. I've had amazing reviews from people who would've not got round to it had I not asked them personally and followed up.

Here's something else though. If you're currently at the early stages of writing your book it's never too early to start networking and telling people about it. Then as soon as your book becomes available you have an audience keen to buy it. I managed to get a high number of pre-orders on Amazon by talking about my book from the moment I had been offered a publishing deal from Wiley.

Q. What are the networking mistakes you see people make when networking; mistakes that an author should avoid?

A. The biggest mistake is approaching networking thinking only of what you want to get out of it. Of course you want book sales but you can't just stand there week in and week out saying 'buy my book'!

Every person at a networking event has their own agenda so if all you do is think about yours, you're unlikely to be successful. Think instead of how you can help other people achieve what they're looking for.

That said if your ultimate intention is to sell books you should not be afraid to ask for the sale! The social aspect of networking can mean you never actually get round to selling, but when the moment is right, if you know your book is perfect for a person, you must say so. It really is a fine balance - treading the line between being too salesy and not salesy at all.

Q. What are the traits and behaviours of successful business networkers?

A. The most successful networkers realise that networking entails effort and that it's not enough to turn up and stand in the corner. Successful networkers find out what other people want from the relationship; they keep in regular touch and are open to the possibilities of working with others. They don't prejudge the other people in the room. They push out of their comfort zone and walk up to people to join in with the conversation rather than waiting to be approached. They can sell; they can listen and they like to help others.

Q. How should an author approach business networking so they can build a strong reader base?

A. Get stuck in; provide value. What is your book about? If it's about finance, be free with the advice you give to people about finance. If it's about presentation skills, help other people in the room with their presentation skills. If it's about marketing, share marketing tips. Embody the spirit of your book.

Once people have seen that you're a product of your book the likelihood is they will buy it whether their intention is to learn more, or they just want to say thank you.

An author should go to a networking event well prepared with a small stock of their books, a few sample copies for people to look at and a nice pen for signing. If you have literature, even better. Not every person will buy your book on the day but they might buy it later. A nice leaflet or a bookmark acts as a handy reminder.

Because I have been promoting my book from its early stages I have built up a head of steam so that at most of the 4Networking events I attend there's always someone in the room who has a copy of it and some bring their copy for signing. This encourages others to talk to me and buy a copy.

Make sure that you join up your real life networking with social media too. The people that have not bought your book will be gently reminded through your social media activity and the ones that have will be most likely posting lovely messages that you can share. It's only a matter of time before the people sitting on the fence buy it!

So, share your expertise to help others, focus on giving value and take the opportunity to introduce your book to as many people as possible. And keep in touch on social media.

Q. At most networking groups members are given the opportunity to stand up and promote their business. Can you share a few tips so an author can make their presentation memorable?

A. Be authentic. Speak with passion about your book. How will your audience benefit from reading it? Be specific. And share your positive

Amazon reviews too. Reading out a great review works wonders. For example I read out a review in which one of my readers said he'd got more value from my book at just £12.99 than working with a business coach for two years at a cost of several hundred pounds.

And always include a call to action. People often forget to do this. For example *"if you want to find out how Steve White rated my book, or you would like to ask me how you can benefit from a copy too please ask for a one-to-one meeting"*. Make sure your book is in your hands when you're talking about it.

Q. Can you tell me about 4Networking and how an author can get in touch with you?

A. I'm really chuffed to be a Director of 4Networking, having joined as a member back in 2007. We now run over 5000 breakfast, lunch and evening networking meetings across the UK.

All of the meetings include many different business people and at each and every meeting you get the chance to promote your business or your book (or both!).

Each meeting includes time for open networking, a 40 second introduction round, a 15 minute presentation by a member and, uniquely, three one-to-one business meetings with other members in the room. A huge benefit of 4Networking is that a member joins the network rather than just one group. This means that any author can promote themselves locally, regionally or even nationally, all for one membership fee. They can attend any meeting anywhere.

The simplest way for anyone to get in touch is to check out our website at 4Networking.biz. You can see where our meetings are held across the UK and you can register for free and engage with our members online. If anyone wants to contact me personally say hello on Twitter where I am @noredbraces.

Wise words from another true networking guru, Brad Burton.

I spent some time recently with Brad Burton, the charismatic founder of 4Networking. I was keen for him to share his tips on how an author can sell their book when networking and he did not disappoint.

This is the raw transcription of our interview delivered in Brad's unique way...

"Did you know my first self published business book 'Get Off Your Arse', is the highest rated and reviewed business book on Amazon?" So what?

"When I published my first book, *Get Off Your Arse,* I was excited. I was hell-bent on packing as much information as I could into my 40-second pitch and was forever thrusting my book into the hands of anyone who would listen... *"And in it you'll learn this, and that, and also this, and also that..."*

"In the early days I was like an over-enthusiastic teenager. It paid off occasionally but it was all a bit clunky.

"Now I'm on my third book I've learnt that you can't bore someone into a sale. Be relaxed. Curb your enthusiasm (which is counter-intuitive to someone like me given I've built my career on enthusiasm and energy).

"When you network you will get many opportunities to talk (not pitch) about your book.

"Would your approach work on you?

"If another author sat opposite you and said the very same things you're planning on saying, would you buy their book? If not, what would encourage you?

"The great thing about networking is that you can continually adapt your formal and informal presentations whether you're talking to the group or on a one-to-one level. Don't beat yourself up about the fact that you'll occasionally get it wrong, especially in your early days.

"If you want to sell more you have to sell less. My primary reason for writing books was to build my credibility. There's just something about meeting an author that instantly moves them up the credibility steps. Why do I say this? Because it's how I feel every time I meet an author. After building credibility my goal was unsurprisingly to sell my books. Today it all seems to work really well and I sell thousands of books.

"I use my books as a hook for credibility. When I'm speaking at a networking group I'll simply flash the cover and leave it at that. When I have one-to-one meetings with people I'll place my book casually on the table and occasionally allude to it.

"In terms of book sales, the most I've managed to sell at a networking event is 50 from a room of 300. One of my friends, Sharon Wright, has a much higher hit rate with her self published book, *Mother of Invention*. When presenting she'll say words to the effect of, "I don't have time to go into this right now, but if you want to know more, it's in the book."

"She'll repeat this several times during her presentation. Does it work? In a room of 120 I saw 113 people buy her book netting her a cool £1,130 which is not bad for 35 minutes work. She now has 113 people who have paid to market her business!

"At this event I could see how Sharon's focus was on selling books and giving sound advice. The table at the front was stacked up with her books and she made it clear she was signing books immediately after her talk. She created the conditions that make people want to buy.

"Authors benefit from networking because networking events appeal to non-salespeople. But if you're going to give it a go think about what you're going to focus on when you stand up and talk about your book. What do you and your book offer that I can't get anywhere else? You should major on this during your 'stand up round' at a networking event.

"And be authentic! Spend 100% of your time, being 100% you. Don't put on a posh author's voice, pretending to be something you're not. That's exhausting and disingenuous. Perhaps it was only me who did this when I first started networking in a bid to suppress my Coronation Street voice.

"Don't be what you *think* other people want you to be; be you. I realise now that my 'realness' is what people love about me and my books. Others are not so enamoured with my approach. So what! There's a big wide world out there. You can't sell to everyone. So don't try to.

"Be likeable. Would you buy a book from someone you don't like? No of course not. If the buyer doesn't like the seller it's going nowhere.

"I've heard some authors say that networking doesn't suit them and their book because the event attracts the 'wrong sort of people.'

"Let's say a target audience for your book is solicitors, but there aren't any solicitors in the group you're attending. Before saying 'It's not really for me... Networking doesn't work...' well neither does Google if you don't ask the right questions. And that's what networking is; Google but with people. Asking questions elicits more answers, more links, moving you closer to your destination.

"If you had the opportunity to stand in front of the group and ask, "who here personally knows a solicitor?"

"Eighty percent of hands would go up.

"It's not just the person you're talking to; it's all the people they know. This is a cornerstone of networking.

"Ultimately it comes down to you - what you say and how you say it - that will have a massive impact on whether networking works for you as an author or not. I can guarantee one thing though; there are more people at a networking group who might want your book than you'll find sitting in your home office, dressing gown on, waiting for the phone to ring. How do I know? I was that person.

'I've been to networking events before but they don't work for authors!

"So what bit of talking to people about you and your book isn't working?"

Many thanks to Stefan and Brad for their brilliant networking nuggets. I hope you've been persuaded of the value of networking in helping you to promote your book and are now keen to give it a jolly good go.

Chapter summary.

- Don't dismiss networking if you're writing a fiction book until you have researched all the networking opportunities in your local area.

- Make a list of the events and groups you are interested in attending. This should include details of informal networking events and networking organisations where you pay a membership fee.

- Use the tips provided in this book to practice your voice tone and body language so that when you are given the opportunity to talk you can make a great impression with your audience.

- Make sure that you can describe what your book is about, who it is aimed at, and why it is so appealing in as little as 40 seconds.

- If you decide that networking is for you, blend your networking activities. So if you join a networking organisation, don't let this stop you from attending other informal networking events.

- Networking is not just about selling books. It will build your confidence as a speaker and it gets you out of the house.

- Think about how you can help the people who you are networking with. What you give out, you will get back.

- Ask for Amazon reviews from the people who buy your books at every networking event you attend.

- Share your expertise. Be a walking ambassador for your book.

- Be 100% you. You don't need to put on a posh author's voice.

- Don't dismiss the people in your group. Virtually every person will be connected to at least one of your ideal readers.

CHAPTER 20

How Social Media Can Build Your Book's Success

I met Nicky Kriel several years ago at a 4Networking meeting. I had been aware of her beforehand because she had sent me a lovely tweet telling me how much she appreciated my first book. Nicky has since become one of the most influential social media marketers in the UK. Her advice is sought by global brands, small businesses and individuals alike because what she says makes sense and is devoid of jargon. She's one of those rare people who are extremely knowledgeable and up-to-date on social media whilst not making it appear in the least bit daunting. Nicky practices what she preaches which makes her a credible social media guru. Her first book, *How to Twitter for Business Success* is more or less permanently in the top 10 books in its category on Amazon. I was thrilled therefore when Nicky agreed to write this chapter. This is what she had to say to my questions.

Q. How have you used social media to promote your book *How to Twitter for Business Success*?

A. I would love to say that I started with a grand plan for marketing my book, but the truth is that I got so busy writing it that it was nearly done before I started. Luckily for me, I already had a strong presence on social media and my blog had a very good reputation with thousands of visitors flocking to it every week so I wasn't starting from scratch. Plus I had Dee as a role model.

This is what I did:

Before the book came out. I told people on my social media platforms that I was writing a book and asked my community what they would like to see in it. I shared the writing process with them; the frustrations of editing, the pain of proofreading and the excitement of the artwork for the front cover. I also wrote blog posts about my book which I shared on social media platforms. As soon as the book was available, I let my community know. As a result I had people buying the Kindle version within minutes of it being published.

Within the book. I mentioned my Twitter account and encouraged people to connect with me several times throughout. I also asked people to 'send me a tweet telling me you're enjoying this book' in the chapter 'Tons of things to tweet about'. It's amusing to see how many people send me a tweet when they reach that page. It's so lovely to connect with readers and of course when readers do connect with you on social media it's a great opportunity to share their words. The impact when someone raves about your book is much greater than when you do it. So make it easy for your readers to connect with you. In hindsight I should have also created a hashtag for the book on Twitter and encouraged people to chat to me on my Facebook author's page. Why don't you create a hashtag before your book is published?

Book launch. I probably wouldn't have had a book launch had it not been for Dee's persuasion but I'm so glad I did. I would highly recommend you have one too. In life it's always good to celebrate key moments and giving birth to a book is no different. It also gives you a great story to share on social media. I created an electronic invite which I sent to my email list, but I also posted on Facebook, LinkedIn and Twitter. This resulted in a well-attended, lively event. I also invited the local press along and made sure that I had a videographer and a photographer to capture the moment. Social media is increasingly visual so it's always worth having images that you can share. A video is perfect for your guests to relive the event and once it's uploaded to YouTube, it's easy to share on social media.

In this launch phase I contacted bloggers that I already knew through my social media activity and asked each one if they would review my book. Most of them obliged and one even created a video review because she liked the book so much. It's incredibly powerful having other people talking about your book and once your content is online it stays there for years.

Creating a social media footprint. My book title was chosen with search in mind. I knew how important it was to get the keywords that people would search for in the title and strapline. However it's not just the search engines that you need to consider if you want your book to be found. People spend an increasing amount of time on social networks. So create a social media presence for your book that enables people to find it on whichever platform they prefer to use. Many of your potential readers will be online. The place they are most likely to be hanging out on will depend on the type and genre of your book. I go into more detail about ideas for Facebook, LinkedIn and Twitter further in the chapter but you could also consider the following:

- Creating a Pinboard on Pinterest which allows you to keep everything about your book in one place. I've created a place to pin all photos from readers, photos of press coverage, radio interviews, blog posts written about my book, online coverage and video interviews on a virtual pinboard. What's great about Pinterest is that you can add links to Amazon or wherever your book is stocked so that people can click directly from Pinterest to buy your book. Take a look at what I've done on Pinterest for inspiration: http://www.pinterest.com/nickykriel/how-to-twitter-for-business-success-book/

- Creating at least one video for your book and optimising it so it can be found on YouTube. I have a video trailer for the book, a video for the book launch plus a video of the photographs readers have sent me. Make sure you include your book title in the title of the video and in the description. Add a URL to where people can buy your book into your description of your video so if someone watches it on YouTube they can click through and buy it with ease.

- Create a presentation on PowerPoint about your book and share it on Slideshare, a presentation sharing platform that's almost exclusively business-focused. The added benefit of doing this is that you can add Slideshare to your LinkedIn profile and share it on Twitter and Facebook too.

- Add a profile to Goodreads and get yourself verified as a Goodreads author with your ISBN. Goodreads is a social networking platform exclusively for people interested in books. You can connect with a wide variety of readers and authors on the platform and there are active discussion forums taking place all of the time. A word of warning however: Goodreads reviewers tend to be harsher than the reviews you find on Amazon because they're avid book-readers.

- Write blogs on your website sharing your author journey, top tips and even excerpts from your book.

Q. How have you used social media to maintain interest in your book?

A. Relentlessly promoting your book becomes ineffective after a while. You need a better long-term strategy to keep your book at the top of potential readers' minds. Good reviews are useful to share and remind people that you have a book without overtly saying 'buy my book'.

When a reader contacts me (usually on Twitter) I always respond to their tweet and will sometimes ask for a review, at other times a picture. The reviews are so important. Many of my readers tell me they've bought my book as a direct result of my Amazon reviews.

If they send me a picture, I always ensure that I focus on them and their business rather than my book. People can see my book in the photograph.

I've been delighted at the pictures I've been sent. When I originally asked for photos, I expected to see someone holding my book or a picture of it on a table, but my readers have been creative and competitive. The very first pictures I received were from a reader in Phoenix, Arizona in the USA. She sent me 12 pictures of my book posing next to a cactus and on a cowboy saddle amongst other places. To date my book has been in a hot air balloon, underwater in a pool, arriving in New York at dawn on the Queen Mary II, at a Real Madrid game and in a wicker casket. Last year I had great fun going around Madame Tussauds with a friend, so I now have a few snapshots with 'famous people'.

I share these photos from readers with links to their websites on my personal profile on Facebook, my Facebook business page, Twitter and Google+. Social media is fast-moving so I will pin my photos on Pinterest which also allows me to place the location of my pins on a map - this is great as the images are from all over the world!

I've also used the photos to create a video for YouTube to say 'thank you' to all my readers. Sometimes I'll take photographs of my book in unusual places and I will share these on Instagram as well as Twitter and Facebook. My friends and followers love seeing where *How to Twitter for Business Success* will pop up next.

Q. What are the biggest mistakes you see authors making on social media?

A. The five biggest mistakes I see authors making are:

1. Failing to build their social media platforms before their book is published. It takes time to build your platforms from scratch; to learn the etiquette of the platform; to build an audience and form

a relationship with potential advocates. If you haven't started using Social Media start NOW!

2. Delivering a constant stream of sales pitches. Many authors only tweet or post messages asking people to buy their book. People don't want to be sold to or spammed. Get the balance right by creating helpful and engaging posts. There are different thoughts on what the ratio should be but aim to have at least three or four helpful, friendly and useful posts to one promotional post about your book.

3. Creating accounts for the book or the characters if you're writing a fiction book instead of creating the account and making it clear it's you the author posting. Whilst this can work my experience is that people would rather get to know you the author and this awareness-building will help when you start working on your next book. Putting yourself out there may seem scary if you're an introvert, but think of it, would you prefer to meet a person or a book?

4. Not spending time building relationships. Many authors look upon social media as free advertising and only use it as a one-way broadcasting tool. Social media is about being sociable. You'll get much better results from building relationships than you will constantly promoting your book.

5. Ignoring their readers by setting their social media up on auto pilot. Tools such as Hootsuite enable you to broadcast the same message to multiple platforms and you can schedule posts, but don't use a platform if you don't intend to visit it regularly. Readers will talk to you using the platform they're most comfortable with using. If someone takes the time to reach out to you as an author, the least you can do is talk to them. It leaves a bad impression if you ignore your readers because your only presence on a social channel is by automated posts.

Q. What are the key benefits of sharing your expertise as an author on Twitter, Facebook and LinkedIn and how do they differ?

A. Being a credible author gives you authority on a subject. Before your book is published you should establish your online credibility as an expert in the field that your book covers. This means ideally sharing your knowledge and expertise on social media before your book comes out.

Each platform is different. Facebook has over a billion active users each month so it's highly likely your readers will already be on Facebook. As a platform it's very chatty and very visual. It's a good place to build a community and build relationships with your readers.

LinkedIn tends be more formal - think business networking. It's a great place to establish your business expertise and to find people who can help you throughout the book production process.

Twitter is quick and fast-flowing; brilliant for building awareness and making contacts with people and for speaking to journalists.

If you only have the time to focus on one channel I would advise that you take the time to add your book to your LinkedIn profile; remember to tell your friends on Facebook but invest your time on Twitter. It's second to none as a PR and marketing tool.

Tips for LinkedIn.

If your book is business-related, LinkedIn is a great place to build your credibility and your readers are likely to have a LinkedIn profile. Even if you don't plan on using LinkedIn proactively, make sure you do the following:

- Have a LinkedIn profile! If someone searches for your name on a search engine, one of the top results will be your LinkedIn profile.

- Make sure you have a recognisable picture on your profile (I use the same one across all my social media profiles. It's the same as in my book and it helps in creating a brand consistency).

- Make sure you fill in your profile thoroughly.

- Add the word 'author' into your headline.

- Add the book title and some nuggets about your book in the summary section.

- Add additional media about your book such as photos, videos or Slideshares to your profile summary.

- Fill in the publications section.

- Make sure that your profile illustrates why you are an authority on your subject.

If you want to use LinkedIn more proactively:

- Post updates about the book especially press coverage, interviews, awards and blog posts written about it.

- Connect with people who can potentially help you. You will find people on LinkedIn who can help you every step of the way of your book's journey.

- 'Inmail' connections that you haven't spoken to for a while and ask them how they are and what they are up to. They're likely to respond, asking you what you're up to, giving you a perfect opportunity to tell them how excited you are about your book.

- Join Groups on your subject and contribute to them. If you're helpful, people will view your profile and will see that you're an author.

Tips for Facebook.

No matter how excited you are about your book, remember to keep your posts on your Facebook profile balanced. If you have spent time building relationships on Facebook, you'll find your friends on Facebook are more likely to buy it than any other group.

- Share the writing process with your friends; the book cover, the launch event, newspaper coverage and great reviews, but remember they want to hear other news about you too.

- Remember to interact and comment on your friends' posts to increase your visibility in Facebook. Not everything published on Facebook will appear in your newsfeed. Facebook applies an algorithm and will choose what appears to your friends depending on your relationship (amount of engagement and interaction, not real feelings) and how much interaction a post gets. So make sure you spend time building relationships.

- At the time of the launch, why not change your profile picture to your book cover or an image of you holding your book? Your friends will then see that you have a new book.

- Set up your book launch as an event on Facebook and invite your friends to attend. This will increase its visibility.

- Create a Facebook business page where you can post to your heart's content about your wonderful book! It will also allow readers who are not your friends on Facebook to communicate directly with you. Make your readers the focus on this page. The advantage of a business page is that everything you publish is by default public and can be found on Facebook search and through search engines.

- Your Facebook cover picture is a great space to show pictures of your book launch. Every time you change your cover picture, it's posted in the newsfeed. Remember to add a URL to the place where people can buy the book in the description of the cover picture.

- Visual content gets more shares and likes so think of creative ways to include visuals. I am still getting interesting pictures, but I also screen capture some of my Amazon reviews. You might want to add a quote from your book on a beautiful background.

Tips for Twitter.

You would be forgiven for thinking that because my book is about how to Twitter, that the people who need it the most are not on Twitter, so Twitter is not the right place to promote it. But guess what? Many of my readers were recommended my book by my Twitter followers and, many of my readers are complete beginners to Twitter. I love Twitter because you can share news about your book as it happens and it's probably the easiest way for readers to connect with you.

- Add the book into your bio or at the very least include in your bio that you are an author.

- Talk to your readers - there's something quite special when a reader tells you how amazing your book is. My relationship with Dee started when I wrote a tweet telling her how wonderful her first book was. I've often had casual chats on Twitter about my book resulting in a significant amount of business later.

- Follow your readers back on Twitter. It sends a message that you're approachable.

- Create a Twitter list of your readers so that you can find them later and re-engage with them.

- Add lovely tweets about your book to Favorites. This bookmarks them for future reference and each tweet is a review that could potentially be used later to market your book.

- Retweet your readers' comments so your followers get to see the comments too. This also acknowledges their tweet and increases their visibility on Twitter.

- Post pictures of your book and readers' pictures. Pictures get more retweets and clicks than text-only tweets.

- Search for your name on Twitter. Not everyone will use your Twitter name when they're talking about your book and you don't want to miss their tweets. I use a tool called 'mention' which emails me when people mention 'Nicky Kriel' on social media. I discover many tweets I would have otherwise missed.

- I've had many invitations to be interviewed for podcasts through Twitter. Podcasts offer you a great opportunity to be introduced to a completely new audience.

Be open to the opportunities that Twitter can bring. Amazing things can happen.

Q. Is Google+ a useful channel to promote your book? If so, can you share some practical tips on how an author can get started?

A. I don't think Google+ can be ignored. It may feel overwhelming with all the different platforms to consider, but if you want your book to be found you need to consider Google+ for Search Engine Optimisation (SEO). Google+ is owned by Google after all. It has very large numbers of active users, far higher than Twitter and LinkedIn. If you claim your Google+ authorship, your picture will pop up in Google searches. Posts with pictures get a significantly higher click-through. If you have a website dedicated to your book why not consider setting up a Google+ business page for your book which will help your website to be found once it has been verified.

Two of the strengths of Google+ are Communities and Google Hangouts.

There is a community for almost every interest group (not dissimilar to LinkedIn groups) so I would encourage you to find a community of like-minded people with the aim of becoming active within that group. There are several communities for authors and they tend to be active and supportive.

Google Hangouts enables you to interact with your readers face-to-face. They are similar to Skype video but are more advanced. The brilliant aspect of Google Hangouts is that you can record them directly onto YouTube, so it's a free way to capture video interviews. I have learned so much about marketing my book through listening to other people's Google Hangouts. I would thoroughly recommend you use them too.

Even if you don't plan on being highly active on yet another platform, you can use Hootsuite which I mentioned earlier to post the same content you are posting to Facebook and LinkedIn to your Google+ company pages. Almost every post that you read will allow you to +1 it, which means that you can post it to your Google Profile. Every time you search on Google, you can see your notifications and react to them. Get into the habit of making regular searches so you're not ignoring people. I am constantly surprised by how much interaction I get from my Google+ posts, so it's worth taking seriously.

I hope that after reading this chapter you're not feeling overwhelmed by all the things I've done on social media. Please rest assured that I didn't do it all at once and I didn't start from scratch. And I had to put my L-plates on and learn about marketing my book using social media. If you can devote most of your time on social media to one or two channels, confident they are the ones where you'll find most of your readers, you're off to a very good start. But explore the other channels too before discounting them.

Many thanks to Nicky for her fantastic and practical advice. I realised when I was reading through her chapter that there's plenty more I can do on social media to promote my books so I hope you're feeling similarly inspired.

Chapter summary.

- Promoting your book on social media should ideally start before it is published.

- Share your book publishing journey on social media; the highs and the lows, to build engagement with your community.

- Video your book launch sharing it on YouTube and across all your social platforms.

- Consider creating a Pinboard on Pinterest. You can add links to Amazon to convert interest into sales.

- Any PowerPoint presentations about your book can be used on Slideshare and posted to Twitter, Facebook and LinkedIn.

- Don't use social media if all you're going to do is broadcast selling pitches of your book. Be sociable!

- Let people get to know you as an author. Don't hide behind images of your book or characters.

- Beware the dangers of over automating your messages. You could be seen to be ignoring your readers.

- If your book is business-related, LinkedIn is the place to build credibility and connect with readers. Make sure your LinkedIn profile conveys that you are an author.

- Use Twitter to build relationships with your readers and think about quirky ways in which you can promote your book.

- If you're already on Facebook don't overload your friends with posts about your book.

- Google+ is worth exploring not least because when your name is searched on Google, your posts on Google+ will feature high up in the search results.

- Don't be overwhelmed by social media. You don't have to do everything at once. Commit your time to one or two channels and explore the others.

CHAPTER 21

How Intelligent Blogging Boosts Book Sales

I 'met' Bryony Thomas on Twitter a few years ago. It was clear to me from the outset that she was a gifted marketer. Her first book, *Watertight Marketing*, has certainly given mine a run for their money. It's more or less permanently in the top 20 bestselling small business marketing books on Amazon.

I discovered as I got to know Bryony that she had a real talent for blogging; not only that but she had managed to secure writing regular blogs for a number of sought-after brands, using her position as a blogger of some distinction to draw attention to her excellent book. And so, I was keen to interview her for this chapter. However, her answers were so comprehensive and so helpful that like Nicky Kriel's interview, Bryony's interview became a chapter on its own!

Although Bryony talks about business blogging, I can assure you that her tips are just as relevant if you're writing a fiction book too. Like Bryony, I've sold many books through blogging for well-known brands and for the reasons she outlines in this interview.

Q. How have you used blogging on third-party sites to promote your book and where did you start?

A. Third-party blogging has to start with first-party blogging. I can't imagine anyone who has written a book not benefiting from writing his or her own blog. You're a writer. Write.

So, the first step is to commit to your own blog, adding something new at least weekly. Maintaining frequency is important, it forms part of what I call your Baseline Marketing Activity. It's that regular lighthouse idea, a steady and regular release of materials that keeps your message visible. Moving beyond your own blog to third-party blogs is about reach. It's about accessing a ready-made audience of people who are likely to want to read your book. It can also contribute to the credibility of your work by association.

Take some time to research what the people who you'd like to buy your book already read. Build up a list of their favourite websites, bloggers, and press titles by:

1. **Asking them.** You could do this in a specific survey, via your social media profiles, running a focus group with a few key people, or adding a field to your various web forms.

2. **Following the social scent.** Find the Twitter IDs of some typical readers and see who they follow. Find the #hashtags for a particular industry or interest area and find influential bloggers or websites using them.

3. **A simple search.** Use the words and phrases you think your potential readers would use to search online, to which your book would be an answer, and see what sites come up.

For *Watertight Marketing*, I was looking for blog opportunities to reach entrepreneurial business owners. I reached a list of around 20 sites in the UK, and decided to focus on 10 of them.

Start subtly by getting on their radar so you can warm them up to you and your material:

• Follow them on social media, both the title itself and the editor or journalists if you can find them.

• Add them to a public list on Twitter of 'Great blogs'.

- Retweet or share their articles on your social feeds.

- Leave intelligent comments on their articles.

- Join any groups they might have on LinkedIn, Facebook, etc and participate intelligently.

You have to be judicious in how many you approach. I doubt you have endless time to be writing posts. Personally, I have taken the approach of negotiating an ongoing contributor set-up with a few key sites. For example: The Guardian Small Business Network, Ingenious Britain and Smart Insights. I chose these for their credibility, national reach, and audience size. With an eye to a speaking angle, I was also mindful of building relationships with blog owners who also run events. This is supplemented by more adhoc or one-off pieces with others.

Q. What are the benefits of sharing your expertise as an author blogger when it's not blogging etiquette to promote your book in your blog? Is it not a lot of effort for a little return?

A. I talk a lot in *Watertight Marketing* about earning the right to a person's time. To read a business book from cover to cover will take somewhere between two and six hours. And this is very unlikely to be in one sitting. I don't know about you, but giving someone up to six hours of my time isn't something I'd do lightly. Time is certainly my most precious resource, and I respect the time of my readers. I see blogging as a way of giving people a taster of my material, and of my writing style. If they like what they read, they are much more likely to feel confident making the time investment it would take to read the book.

Now, let's get this out there, there are definitely ways to get higher quantity book sales than through blogging and guest blogging, and of course I also do a few of these. But, for me, it's much more about the quality. I'd be lying if I said that I don't get a buzz from watching the sales figures. But, what I genuinely love is seeing people calmly take control of their business growth by using the structured process I spent 15 years creating. If they don't actually read the book, their purchase will appear as a notch on the sales records, but nothing more.

I firmly believe that someone who finds *Watertight Marketing* via a blog is much more likely to actually read it. I can't be the only one who's bought the latest must-have book only to leave it languishing on the bookshelf unread. Someone who has gone via a stepping-stone of reading something of mine before they get the book is warmed up to it. I often get people tweeting me after reading a piece of mine and ordering their book. They're eagerly awaiting its arrival. This is tangibly different from adding an item to your basket that Amazon recommended, or receiving a book that's been bundled in with an event ticket, or whatever. If you've read a post, loved it, and then sought out the author's book, your commitment to reading it has to be increased.

The marketing of my book is about getting entrepreneurs onto their own Watertight Marketing journey. With workbooks, mentoring, and a growing community of others doing the same - buying the book is simply a gateway to an end-to-end process. It's the start of a relationship between the reader and me. That's why a more engaged route into the book is important to me. If I was simply going for high volume sales, I would probably put a heavier weighting on more transactional marketing techniques.

You need to work out the objectives for your book, and choose a mix of marketing techniques that support them. For me, this means that the relatively high time-cost technique of third-party blogging is high on my list. For others - or to kick-start sales - it might mean plastering ads all over Facebook. Whatever you choose needs to be consistent with your goals, the style of your book, and what you want the reader to do next.

Q. How can you create blog content readers will love and promote your book?

A. If you love the book you've written, and you're sure that the people you wrote it for will love it too, you already have your content. The most effective way to create content that promotes your book is to give away a lot of your book content in your posts.

This can seem counter-intuitive when it's what you want people to pay for. There's a very natural fear that putting your book content out there means people won't then go on to buy it. This is like saying that putting cheese samples on a counter means that people won't buy the cheese. You're not going to be putting the whole book out there; just tasters. Indeed, even if you do put it all out there in some form or another, it won't all be in one place. And it will never replace the value of sitting down with the content all in one place, in the sequence it was intended, and in a format you can touch, feel, smell, write notes on, etc. (Yes, I know there are eBooks too... not as good for physical stimulus - but people still feel ownership, and bookmark pages, etc).

It's highly unlikely that someone will sit for the hours it would take to piece together your book from the posts that are out there in various places and formats. If they like it that much, it will be far easier and more satisfying for them to simply buy the book.

So, my top tip for great content is to use the stuff you've written in your book. Most decent business books are somewhere in the 50,000 word region, and typically have between 10-12 chapters. Within these, you will have organised your material into headings, sub-headings, bulleted lists, etc. Each of these is a potential blog post. I'd estimate that's around 120 posts. There will need to be some tailoring for the particular site you're contributing to, and a top and tail to make it work as a stand-alone piece. But this isn't too onerous. It takes me around 30-60 minutes each time I do it. If you distributed one of these per week, that's enough content for over two years of powerful, and free, book promotion.

What you don't do is sell your book in the body of the article itself. The quality of the content, and the style of your writing, should do this for you. As much as anything, no editor would publish this. And, secondly, readers would find it annoying, which actually reduces the chances of them buying your book.

The promotion of your book is subtler. It's mostly done by your by-line, or bio. If your article is an excerpt from your book, you are almost always able to add a line at the bottom of the article too. This would say something like: *This is an adapted excerpt from Watertight Marketing, by Bryony Thomas (Panoma Press, £14.99).* Many will also allow you to enable the book name as a link. You can decide whether to make this a link to your book on Amazon, or to your own site.

For example:

The Guardian: Bryony Thomas is the author and founder of Watertight Marketing [with link to website].

Business Matters: Bryony Thomas is the author of Watertight Marketing (Panoma Press £14.99) - an entrepreneur's step-by-step guide to putting a marketing operation in place that delivers long-term sales results. www.watertightmarketing.com.

For the Smart Insights website, for whom I am contributing a monthly piece on marketing fundamentals for a year, I have been able to take this further with a bio that includes a photo of the book, a link to download a free sample chapter and links to my social media profiles.

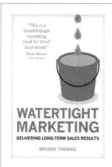

Thanks to Bryony Thomas for sharing her thoughts and opinions in this blog post. She is the best-selling Author and Founder of Watertight Marketing, and a no-nonsense marketer and business speaker, specialising in helping ambitious small businesses set things up. Her blog post is adapted from her 5-star book, Watertight Marketing, described as an entrepreneur's step-by-step guide to putting a marketing operation in place that delivers long-term sales results. You can download a free sample chapter or connect with her on LinkedIn, Twitter, Google+ or Facebook.

Q. Popular blog sites are inundated with authors keen to blog for them. How can an author effectively pitch to the editor of a popular blog?

A. Assuming you've done the subtle warming up I mentioned earlier, you shouldn't be completely unknown to the editor. From there, getting them to choose your material for their blog is about ensuring that it's genuinely relevant and useful to their readers. And then, crucially, make it easy for them to use your submission.

The initial search you did to define your target title list should mean that the subject matter is relevant. So, assuming that's been ticked, consider these things to increase your chances:

- **What heading style do they use?** Questions, bold statements, lists, shockers, etc. Craft your heading accordingly.

- **Do they use an intro paragraph?** Lots of titles have a one- or two-line intro that's pulled out in styled text at the start of a post. This is often also used in the metadata for the web page, so it shows up in search results and social shares. Make sure you include this in your post.

- **Do they use pull out quotes?** Lots of blogs will add visual interest and increase post readability by pulling out key elements as a 'quote' in a different font style. Make sure you include 'quotables' in your post.

- **Do they accompany posts with a visual?** It will definitely increase the power of your post to include an image. It can be a headache for an editor to have to find an appropriate image for your post if you've not provided one, and it might mean they don't use it, or your post ends up accompanied by a clichéd stock image. Investing in some imagery, like illustrations, can really pay off. Naturally, you need to ensure you have the rights to use it, and stamp it with your copyright if it's from your book.

- **How do they structure a by-line:** See how they by-line their articles. Is it a one-liner or a short paragraph on the author? And, is there a chance to include an image against the bio? Make sure your bio fits this structure, and provide an image. You can often make this a cover image of your book. Or a photo of you holding your book.

However, you shouldn't just pile in with your finished piece. The etiquette in contacting an editor is to give them a quick synopsis before sending a fully written piece. I would pick up the phone, and then follow-up with an email. These contact details can usually be found on their website. When sending the idea across, provide a heading and short paragraph outlining what might be included in an article, and link them to some examples of previously published pieces. If they like the idea, they'll usually give you a deadline. Meet it! There is nothing that will upset an editor more than a contributing author missing a scheduled slot, giving them the stress of filling it in a hurry. You will not get a second shot at this.

So, being reliable, easy to deal with, and respecting their editorial integrity, will go a long way. The next thing you can do to really stand out is to add some extra value, for example:

- A video that they can embed to direct, or accompany, the article.

- A set of 100 characters one-liners they could use in social media to link to the post.

- Some sites might be open to the idea of doing a competition or give-away too. Consider offering them a few signed copies of your book.

Q. What are your top tips for planning and writing a popular blog? For example, is there an optimum word count; techniques to write a great heading; tips on the perfect layout of a blog post?

A. I'd say a good blog post should take about the same amount of time to digest as a cup of tea.

Most people find blogs through social feeds - a one-liner on Twitter or LinkedIn, for example. These are short and sweet. You have less than five seconds, and about 100 characters (leaving a few for a link, and comments). If they click, you then have a few seconds more to keep them there, and if they read the whole post, it will usually take three to five minutes. So let's break this down…

A great headline for your blog post

A short headline that grabs attention might include:

- Saying the opposite of what people would expect from you, e.g. 'Three reasons not to blog' or 'Why marketing consultants are a waste of money'.

- Lists of tips can work well, e.g. 'X tips for doing Y' - I've found that lists of 3, 7 and 10 seem to travel best.

- Lists of mistakes often travel even better, e.g. '3 marketing mistakes most businesses make every day' - there's something compelling about this sort of headline.

- And, questions… e.g. 'Are you wasting money on your marketing?'

Structuring your post for success

People will scan read. Their eyes will flit from a heading, to an image, to sub-headings and up and down a list. Often people simply get the gist of a piece, and don't actually read the whole thing. You need to make this easy for them, by:

- Keeping your post below about 500 words, unless it's for a niche site of expert readers.

- Using at least one image to set the scene, ideally a few more to help cement ideas in a visual way.

- Breaking your article into sub-headings - a 500-word piece should have at least two sub-headings in my experience.

- Using bulleted lists and tabulated content to break up the text.

- Following the tried and tested set-up of an intro to say what you're going to say, a middle to say it, and a summary to say it again.

- Including a call to action, like a closing question to encourage comments.

What your post should do for a reader

The reader is giving you their time. You need to give them value in return. By the end of reading your post, they should have experienced one (or more) of the following:

- Picked up a genuine tip they can use immediately.

- Nodded their heads in happy agreement at finding a kindred spirit who sees the world as they do.

- Been challenged on a view they held, in a way that makes them think about it differently so they are open to finding out more.

Q. How can an author integrate their blogging efforts with their other marketing efforts such as social media and PR?

A. The real power of the blog is in its position at the heart of a powerful integrated set of marketing activity. Once you have your bank of posts, you can:

- Create 10-20 tweetable one-liners that link back to your piece.

- Share them as status updates on LinkedIn, GooglePlus, etc.

- Put them in your email newsletters.

- Use the images to pin the posts to Pinterest, or liven up your tweets.

- Add a link to the bottom of your email signature.

- Use them in sales follow-up.

- Use them to stay in touch with people… 'Thought you might like this recent piece'.

- Remember that if your posts are on an evergreen topic, you can keep linking back to them for as long as they are relevant… not just in the week you posted them.

A blog post is also the starting point for creating piles of additional content, simply by reformatting it. A 500-word post can usually be quite easily turned into a 10-20 minute presentation, from which you could:

- Put the presentation on SlideShare.

- Record it with a voice-over as a video for YouTube.

- Offer it as a talk at local networking events.

- Offer it as a 'lunch & learn' for a client that you want to deepen a relationship with.

- Record it as a podcast.

- Use it as the basis for a webinar or Google Hangout.

- And, of course, once these things are in place you can tweet them, link them, etc.

Once you've got some great placements of this material on other sites, you also have the opportunity to:

- Add a press archive on your website; I put the logo of the site where I've been featured, and the first paragraph, then a link to where they can keep reading it.

- Add links to the articles to the 'Publications' section on LinkedIn.

- Add the press logos to your website, marketing materials, sales proposals, etc with an 'As featured in' line.

You'll find this activity will start to build its own momentum. The credibility you gain from respected sites makes other sites more willing to feature you. You will start getting proactively approached to contribute, rather than the other way around. And, the steady flow and smart use of re-purposing means that your material is showing up frequently enough to get noticed.

Q. What are the mistakes you see authors make when blogging?

A. Stop selling; stop showing off. Imagine that your post is taking your place at a networking event. If you spent the entire time saying how brilliant you were, or asking people to buy from you every other minute, you'd soon find yourself standing alone.

Q. Please share one of your longer popular blogs and how you promoted it.

A. Here's a piece I wrote for The Guardian Small Business Network as a January feature, which I have used in the following ways:

- Tweeted, LinkedIn, and Facebook updates, using the four sub-headings as one-liners.

- Created a webinar for MDs, promoted to people tagged as 'Business Owners' on my list.

- Created a series of quote images to post on G+ and Pinterest throughout January.

- Sent out in my email newsletter, weekly round up, and to those subscribed to receive an alert from me 'whenever there is something new'.

- I also regularly use it in email follow-up after meeting with an MD to discuss their company's marketing.

Four ways to step up your marketing campaign in January

A commitment to step up your marketing campaign can be short lived, but there are ways to avoid that February slump.

So, here we are. It's January, and you're looking ahead with good intentions to really step things up for your business. Perhaps you've made marketing a new year's resolution for your small business.

The 'marketing is like fitness' analogy is an excellent one to keep in mind. There are so many parallels. But, like many a January fitness drive, a focus on stepping up your marketing effort is often short-lived. To avoid that February slump, here are four ways you can make the promise last longer than most gym memberships.

Go for a healthy diet of the right kind of work

If marketing is like fitness, then the customers you take on board are your diet. If you take on a majority of the right kind of work, your business will be in much better shape. The greasy fast-food equivalent is the kind of work that you don't really like doing… it's not that interesting, or profitable, but easy to get. Aim to make this less than 20% of what you do, with the rest made up of the kind of work that you find really stimulating, and can charge a real premium for.

An example of this might be a strategic marketing consultant writing blog posts and scheduling social media updates for their clients, rather than advising on long-term strategy.

Continually taking on work that's easy to win, but doesn't take your business forward can be a hard habit to break. But, like a healthy balanced diet, it really is worth it.

Go for a mixed routine

If there's one thing I see time and time again, it's marketing in the wrong shape. That is, with too much focus on one area, and too little in another. This is like the guy who's worked fanatically on his biceps, but does no cardio work…so, couldn't run more than a mile. In marketing terms, this typically manifests as too much emphasis on awareness activity, and not enough on conversion and loyalty.

This might mean lots of investment in SEO to get traffic to your website, but nothing engaging when they get there to encourage them to find out more. This often means that there are holes in the sales process. Holes that see your hard-earned cash wasted on generating interest that doesn't lead to real sales. By mapping a marketing tool or technique to every stage in a buying decision, your marketing operation will be in shape to support long-term sales results.

Go for little and often

We all know that yo-yo dieting is actually bad for us. It messes with your metabolism, and does about as much good for your motivation. Boom and bust marketing is about as good for your business. If you do a massive campaign one month, then nothing for months on end… you'll forgive people for having forgotten you. What's more, if you don't do something regularly, you'll never really master it. Marketing is much more effective when you commit to a consistent level of activity that you build into every day.

We've all heard that 20 minutes' exercise a day keeps the doctor at bay. Imagine if every person in your business was equipped to do 20 minutes really effective marketing every day. Keep at it, and this sort of approach really pays off.

Picture and plan

The last one on my list is being able to visualise what the effort will give you. Make it real. And, make it worthwhile. To embrace fitness, people often picture themselves playing happily and energetically with their children, or squeezing into that little black dress. Having a clear vision can be a real motivator to get started. But, standing on the scales every day to see barely any movement will put a real downer on the whole thing. The same can be true when you make a commitment to real change in your business.

For marketing to become an integral part of your business success, you need a vision at two levels. Imagine looking to the horizon to picture where your business will be in, say, three years time. Now, look to your feet and plan the next few steps in the right direction…and the metaphorical bench you'll sit on to take a breath and pat yourself on the back. I always advise planning a clear and structured process to step your marketing up over 12 months- so much more powerful than a promise to 'do more marketing'. It's only when a business owner really commits to this lifestyle change that they really see the difference.

Let me take this opportunity to wish you every success in 2014. And, if you've made marketing a new year's resolution, I look forward to hearing how you're going with it in February, and beyond.

Bryony Thomas is the author and founder of Watertight Marketing

Thanks to Bryony for her excellent tips. I hope they have encouraged you to start your own author blog and to research opportunities to blog for a few sites that are popular with your target audience.

Chapter summary.

- Consider creating your own blog and get into the habit of blogging frequently to build momentum.

- Research the blog sites that are popular with your target audience before drawing up your shortlist of the ones you would like to approach.

- Make early connections with the editors and journalists connected to the blog sites you want to write for.

- Look upon blogging as giving readers a taste of your book.

- Your book can be the basis of all the content you will ever need for writing blog posts. Study it closely. How can you turn sections, themes and topics within your book into blog posts?

- Don't ever use your blog to sell your services. Give away great information and let your attached bio do the selling.

- Study the format of blogs on the sites you want to blog for before approaching the editor.

- Don't just steam in with a blog you would like the site to publish. Contact the editor; follow up with an email. Provide links to any previously published pieces you think would be of interest.

- You should be able to read a good blog post in the time it takes you to have a cup of tea.

- Don't neglect your layout! Make sure your blog is easy to read and attractive to look at.

- Make sure your focus is always on giving great value to your readers.

- Promote your blog posts through many channels including LinkedIn, Twitter and any newsletters you send out. Put them on your website too.

- Focus on continuing to build your expert status; demonstrating you're a key person of influence with real integrity. This approach to blogging will ensure that you are rewarded with many book sales.

CHAPTER 22

How to Tweet Your Way to Book Sales Galore!

Twitter is one of the most effective marketing tools I have used to promote my books at every stage from my big idea to launch and beyond. Thanks to Twitter I've connected with many readers; found journalists, editors, bloggers, and event organisers and have been booked for paid public speaking engagements - simply by engaging in conversations on Twitter. I have built relationships with people who I've met briefly at events only for the relationship to blossom thanks to connecting on Twitter.

Whether you're writing a romantic novel, a thriller, a business book or a self help book, Twitter can help you sell books, meet your readers and make powerful new connections. It's the ultimate marketing on a shoestring tool because it's free, simply requiring a regular investment of your time. Try it out for six months. It will cost you nothing bar a few minutes here and there.

However like all marketing channels there's a right way and a wrong way of doing it. I've seen authors fail to build their following on Twitter because all they've done is go on about their book and nothing more in a series of unimaginative tweets.

The secret to success on Twitter lies in interacting with your followers, posting great tweets and engaging with your readers.

Whether you're already on Twitter but not tweeting in your new shoes as an author, or are new to it, these tips should help you get the most out of it.

The benefits of using Twitter to promote your book.

- From the minute you decide to write a book, you can share your progress with your followers and build their interest. By the time it's written, they're keen to buy it and tweet about it to their followers.

- You can find journalists, editors and bloggers on Twitter and build rapport with each one by following them and sending timely, charming and relevant tweets. By contrast it could take several attempts to contact a journalist by telephone or email before getting a response. You're more likely to get a response on Twitter provided your tweets are nicely composed and it's clear you're pitching ideas that will appeal to their readers.

- You can build relationships with people of influence on Twitter that you would find impossible to reach by telephone or email because they're protected by an overzealous gatekeeper or are too busy. It always amazes me how open and responsive these in-demand people are when you contact them on Twitter. Approach them in any other way and you'd get short shrift.

- You can build your positive reviews on Amazon by asking every reader who sends you a lovely tweet about your book if they'll take a few minutes to write one.

- Because most event organisers now promote their event on Twitter you can find the ones you're interested in speaking at and begin the process of creating rapport before offering your services as a speaker.

- You can build relationships with your readers. One of the joys of writing a book is that today you can connect with your readers worldwide from the comfort of your armchair. Twitter offers you these connections on a plate. Because of its informal nature you can chat to your readers at any time of the day or night, weekday or weekend, without it eating into your precious time.

- Incredible reach. One little tweet promoting your book can be seen by thousands of people or even more simply because some of your followers liked a tweet so much that they retweeted it to their followers who did likewise. This simple activity can result in dozens of book sales. If this happens on a regular basis it's not hard to see how book sales can soar with that bestseller status well within your grasp.

- Twitter is the ultimate flexible marketing tool. You can fit it into your schedule whether you're travelling and tweeting on your iPad, you're typing away on your laptop or socialising in the evening and using your mobile intermittently. Many of my readers contact me at the weekend and in the evening by Twitter when it would not occur to them to do so by email.

Like all forms of networking if you want to build your following on Twitter it pays to remember that behind each Twitter symbol or photo is a real person. They have to get to know, like, and trust you before buying your book or asking you to speak at their event. So you have to get into the habit of creating witty and interesting tweets. A poorly written tweet full of mistakes and clearly composed in haste won't do you any favours. As an author you'll be expected to set a high standard with your tweets. So if you're tweeting using your mobile please read each one before posting them to avoid the pitfalls of predictive text. Similarly, you can't afford to tweet when you're feeling angry or morose. Be positive, warm and welcoming on Twitter.

How I've built my following on Twitter.

Whilst Twitter should be about the quality of your followers and not the quantity, if you want to sell books you have to build a decent following.

This does take time which is why I would encourage you to follow these tips especially if you're new to Twitter or have been on Twitter for some time but are finding it hard to attract new followers. I started out on Twitter four years ago and, at the time of writing these chapters, have 3,900 people following me.

My secret for selling books on Twitter and building my following is simple.

- I tweet most days and check in regularly so I can respond promptly to any messages from my followers.

- Most of my followers are small businesses that follow me because I share marketing tips and I'm a marketing author. I make sure that a good proportion of my tweets are marketing tips for small businesses and tips for budding and established authors.

- My tweets are varied comprising a mixture of useful marketing tips, chitchat with my followers, retweeting interesting tweets, and updates on what's happening in my day and of course promoting my books.

- Before posting a tweet I imagine there's a reader looking over one shoulder and a client over the other. Will they like what they read?

- I respond with a personal message to every reader who messages me on Twitter and I invite them to tweet me their marketing questions.

- Before publishing a tweet I spend a few seconds checking it to ensure it's free from spelling mistakes, that it reads well, that predictive text has not crept in and it's interesting.

- I praise and congratulate others on their achievements and good news.

- I am patient when it comes to building my following. Quality not quantity is my aim.

Use your Twitter biography to promote your book.

With your Twitter biography you have an opportunity to promote yourself and your book. It's amazing how much you can say in 140 characters. You can include a link within your Twitter biography to your Amazon page, website or blog. So use the full character allowance. You can change your Twitter biography as often as you like too. This means that in the run-up to your book being published, you can use it to promote the name of your book and its imminent launch and can change it once your book is on sale. Keep on changing your biography to include useful snippets that generate sales. For example if your book wins an award or is well received by a critic add this information. Spend a little time composing it because it will help you attract new followers. Look upon it as a mini elevator statement.

This was my Twitter biography during the first few months of my third book being launched:

Multi award-winning author. Latest book *The 15 Essential Marketing Masterclasses For Your Small Business* voted *Talk Business Magazine* Best Biz Book 2013 www.themarketinggym.org.

Whereas at the time of writing this chapter it is:

UK's #1 bestselling small business marketing author | Now published in China | Professional speaker | CIM Fellow | Won 7+ writing awards for highest responses.

And here is Nicky Kriel's Twitter biography:

Social Media Coach & Trainer, Author of *How to Twitter for Business Success*, Speaker & mother. Social Media strategy for SMEs. Visit my blog for useful tips. nickykriel.com/blog.

Don't stuff your Twitter biography with hash tags and keywords so that it means nothing and looks unappetising. You're not writing for robots so compose something that promotes you and your book.

A nice smiling image helps too! Your book cover does not have to be your Twitter avatar. It can seem impersonal when you're hoping to engage in a friendly dialogue on a social media site. A smiling image of you will encourage people to follow you. You can use your Twitter background wallpaper to promote images of your book cover and of you speaking at an event.

Getting started.

If you're not already using Twitter rest assured that within minutes of setting up your account, you'll understand how it works. It really is that easy.

But if you're unfamiliar with it, here's a brief explanation of the basics:

1. Your tweets are restricted to 140 characters. You'll have to get used to composing concise messages without resorting to text abbreviations. You can include links within your tweets to videos, blogs, websites, your Amazon page and more.

2. You can send open messages to virtually anybody on Twitter using the @ symbol with their Twitter address after it (e.g. @deeblick). A person does not have to follow you for you to send an open message to them.

3. If a person is following you, you can send them a private message using the direct messaging facility which means your message will only be seen by that person. However, if you're not following them back, they cannot send you a private message. They'll have to send you an open message instead which may not be appropriate, so make sure that you follow any person you want to send a private message to.

4. If you really like a tweet you can use the Favorite button. This will be saved on your Twitter dashboard and it will show your followers that you highly rate this tweet and you can use this tool to build a list of readers.

5. You can block anyone on Twitter. Equally you can be blocked too!

6. You can use the notifications symbol to read open messages sent to you and find out who has retweeted your tweets or is talking about you using your Twitter address in their tweet. It's worth checking this every time you go on Twitter. Your readers will welcome your prompt response as will an editor or an event organiser responding to a tweet from you. I sent a message to one of my followers recently. They didn't respond to it until four weeks later. I'd invited them to contribute to an article I was writing. They missed the boat and so lost out on the opportunity of some valuable PR.

7. You can use free tools such as Hootsuite to schedule your tweets which can be useful if you want them to be seen by followers in other countries with a different timeline and you want your tweets to be spaced out over a day. This works well for many people on Twitter. I have never scheduled any of my tweets so if you see me tweeting on Twitter I am actually present. So please say hello.

26 simple ways to promote your book on Twitter.

The power to promote your book on Twitter is literally at your fingertips - and it's free! But if all you do is pump out the same tweets about your book several times a day you'll come across as boring and won't sell many books. The secret lies in promoting your book with a series of imaginative tweets. Here are 26 ways that I promote my books on Twitter and how you can too. Below some of these tips I've shared examples of tweets I have composed or retweeted. I usually post a couple of tweets on most days promoting my books. This is not overkill. Most of your followers will not be avidly reading every one of your tweets. It's more likely they will read your tweets if they happen to pop up in their timeline when they're on Twitter.

1.   Tell your followers where you're writing from today.

     'Ensconced in my little log cabin writing my fourth book on how to write and market a bestselling book. It's really coming together...'

2.   Post images of where you're writing. Most of my writing takes place in my log cabin which makes for a nice image. When I visited my brother in Yorkshire to finish a book I posted some images of the Yorkshire Dales, explaining how the beautiful surroundings were inspiring me.

3.   Share your progress with your book.

     'Great day. With a client working on a seminar then seeing the sublime cover visuals for my new book + having cover photos taken.'

     'Back from a meeting with my fabulous book cover designer @thecoloursuite Loving the designs.'

'Good day. Written 4000 words for my latest book *The Ultimate Guide to Writing and Marketing a Bestselling Book*.'

4.   Share the title of your new book.

'Feels funny seeing my fourth book on Amazon when I'm still writing it. What do you think to the title? http://www.amazon. co.uk/Ultimate-Guide-Writing-Marketing- ...'

'The title of book four *The Ultimate Guide to Writing and Marketing a Bestselling Book: on a shoestring budget...*'

5.   Share the cover of your book. You can include a link to the cover on Amazon or if it's in the early stages why not share your designer's images?

'What do you think to the initial design of my book cover? Colourful isn't it!'

6.   Ask readers to send you a tweet when their book has arrived. Share this with your followers but don't forget to thank each reader with a nice message.

7.   Ask readers to post a picture of your book when it arrives, thank them for doing so and share their tweets with your followers.

8.   Retweet the tweets from readers praising and/or promoting your book and add a word or two or even a smiley face symbol.

@deeblick My son @mattpark22 loved your book *15 Essential Masterclasses For Your Small Business* which I won @HorshamMicrobiz. '☺'

@monsheabutter: @deeblick reading masterclass book thorough but easy to read I will be able to pass an exam in marketing soon! 'Great!'

@thisiscapstone: Thanks @deeblick another amazing seminar #TBS2014. Everyone loved you & your book. No one knows small biz promo like you. '☺'

Top Marketing author @deeblick signing books at CIM Herts Small Business #Marketing event. Got my signed copy!

@rebeccagraceee: Nice to meet you today @deeblick :) Can't wait to read your book! 'Let me know how you get on!'

@MarketingVC: @deeblick Read your first book in Sydney 4 yrs ago so fab to be here today & meet u @TheBusinessShow. 'Amazing!'

@whatyousow: Watching @deeblick at #tbs2014. Have implemented loads of suggestions from her fantastic book & ALL helped What You Sow. 'Wow x.'

9. Retweet the tweets from event organisers who are tweeting about your book and explain that you're speaking at their event.

10. Share any news about organisations that have ordered copies of your book.

    'Lovely email from the Channel Manager for Stannah Lifts; he's bought 30 copies of The 15 Essential Marketing Masterclasses'

11. Ask your readers to share their favourite excerpts from your book.

    'Calling my readers of 15 Essential Marketing Masterclasses! Tell me the masterclasses you've found most useful'

12. Ask the readers who tweeted their appreciation of your book if they will share their favourite bits.

13. Promote the position of your book on Amazon. You can send a tweet from your book's dedicated page on Amazon and add a personal message too. I do this on a regular basis but I vary each tweet slightly as you can see.

'My 2 small business marketing books currently at 1 and 3 in the bestsellers; all shoestring marketing tips http://www.amazon.co.uk/gp/bestsellers/books...'

'My 2 small biz marketing books still rocking the bestsellers at 1 + 2 http://www.amazon.co.uk/gp/bestsellers/books... and 76 5 stars for my latest book'

'No 1 in the bestsellers *The 15 Essential Marketing Masterclasses for Your Small Business* http://www.amazon.co.uk/ ... via @AmazonUK'

'My 3 books are currently #1 #3 #5 in the bestsellers. Told my son who said "Mum tell me when they're 1, 2, 3" Kids keep you grounded'

14. Share a reader's review of your book with an interesting tweet, including a link to the page on Amazon or your website.

'Thrilled with this review from a serving British officer in Afghanistan using my book to start his biz in July...'

'Love this review from a reader in business for 30 years saying he's got bruises on his legs from reading my book!'

15. Share a critic's review of your book.

    'Read what the book review critic at *Elite Business Magazine* thought about my latest book here...'

    'Here's what the book reviewer at *The Sun* has to say about my latest book. All 5 stars too...'

16. Share the number of reviews on Amazon.

    'Just had the 150th review added for *The Ultimate Small Biz Marketing Book*. Look I promise I'm not fibbing! http://www.amazon.co.uk/Ultimate-Small-Business-Marketing-Book...'

    '90 reviews, 87 5 stars *The 15 Essential Marketing Masterclasses*... Reply w/ #AmazonBasket to add this via @AmazonUK'

17. Share the details of a book signing and/ or event you're speaking at.

    'I will be @horshammicrobiz on Saturday running 2 masterclasses + signing copies of my latest award-winning book'

18. Share the details of any awards your book has won.

    Thrilled that *The 15 Essential Marketing Masterclasses* has won @ thebookbag non-fiction book of the month award'

19. Promote the special anniversaries of your book for example its launch day, the first month, first six months, one year and so on.

    '3 years today since I launched *The Ultimate Small Business Marketing Book* + still #1 in the bestsellers'

20. Promote the number of books you've sold. Your first 100, 500, 1,000 sales and so on should be celebrated with a tweet!

    'Celebrating 20,000 sales of *The Ultimate Small Business Marketing Book*'

    'Told by my publisher we've hit 1000 book sales for *The 15 Essential Marketing Masterclasses For Your Small Business*'

21. Run a competition giving away free copies of your book. In the first tweet that you can see below I promoted a book giveaway. This was part of my marketing plan to promote my speaking engagement at The Business Show. As you can see from the second tweet The Business Show also supported the competition which was a real bonus. I retweeted all of the Business Show's tweets about this competition to my followers too and we jointly announced the winners on Twitter.

    'Giving away 3 copies of my latest book @TheBusinessShow Tweet me your top marketing tip + you could win one!'

    '"@TheBusinessShow: Fancy winning a fab @deeblick book? Tweet Dee a marketing tip with @TheBusinessShow in the tweet & you could do!" Go on!'

22. Promote every publication and blog that is featuring your book. This works really well if the blogger or publication is on Twitter too. They will retweet your message to their followers giving it even more exposure.

    'In the Dec issue of *@talkbusinessmagazine* my latest book has won their Top Business Book 2013 award. Over the moon!'

'If you're based in Northern Ireland you can read a review of *15 Essential Marketing Masterclasses in Business First Magazine*'

'Today's issue of *The Sun: The 15 Essential Marketing Masterclasses* has been reviewed as "essential reading for any budding entrepreneur"'

23. Send a tweet to a person you think will be interested in your book with a link to its Amazon page.

24. Share any good news about your book.

   'Taken 16 months but *The Ultimate Small Business Marketing Book* has completed translation into Chinese'

   'Working long distance with my publisher in China on the PR launch of *The Ultimate Small Business Marketing Book*. Pinch me moment'

   'Thrilled that the eminent + respected book PR guru Jeff Scott of @platypuspr is writing the foreword to the book I'm writing now'

   'Fab contributors to my 4th book on how to write a bestseller + market it are @bryonythomas @BradBurton @NickyKriel @NoRedBraces'

25. Post a promotional tweet but include a compelling benefit about your book with or without a link to your website or Amazon page.

   'Struggling with your marketing? Have a look at my latest jargon free award winning book packed with tips...'

'Terrified of public speaking? You'll love the masterclass in my latest book sharing all my public speaking tips'

26. Post a screen shot of your book showing its bestselling status on Amazon.

'Here are my last two books currently at 1 and 2 in the Amazon bestsellers small business marketing category'

'Proof that *The Ultimate Small Business Marketing Book* is currently at position 150 on Amazon out of 7 million titles!'

Promoting your book on Twitter is easy and, if you can set some time aside on a daily basis to tweet, you'll be rewarded with book sales.

How one little tweet generated an immediate book sale.

A few days ago I found myself with 10 minutes to spare before meeting a client. I used that time to tweet some marketing tips. I also promoted one of my books with a link to its page on Amazon as follows…

'20,000 copies sold! Rising daily: *The Ultimate Small Business Marketing Book* http://www.amazon.co.uk … via @AmazonUK'

This resulted in one of my followers, Todd, (@SocialMediaTodd) a social media manager and online marketing specialist, tweeting back that he was going to buy it which he duly did. Knowing I was in the middle of writing this chapter, I asked Todd if he would explain what made him respond to my tweet and buy my book.

This is what he told me:

"I've followed you for a while and I like your inspirational tweets in the morning. Because they're good, I read them. Because I like them I figured

I'd like your book. You tweeted about your book this morning and it all came together! You're always in my timeline so I don't forget you or skim (because you're interesting). You mentioned your book was doing well - social proof - so I decided all the things were right for me to buy then and there. (Plus your bio link went straight to your website page with the book link on). I'm a keen marketer and I like your passionate style. If you're in my timeline when I'm on Twitter (like this morning) then I will read your tweets and your presence is grown some more."

Now Todd has been following me for some time now but he didn't buy my book when he first found me on Twitter. It was a few months after he started following me that he decided to buy it. Todd's case study shows why it's important for you to tweet about your book regularly. A follower will buy your book when the time is right for them. This may be when they see your very first tweet about it or it could be many more tweets down the line! Tweeting regularly and consistently pays off.

17 things you can tweet about to be interesting and engaging.

We would be dull indeed if all we did was post tweets about our books. So, get into the spirit of Twitter and be affable and interesting. Here are 17 ways in which you can build your following by posting appealing and sociable tweets.

1. **Tweet about what you're doing right now.** Make it witty and humorous. Tweeting *"in a cafe eating toast"* is boring. But *"tackling some tough toast washed down with weak coffee"* is likely to raise a smile and some of your followers will identify with your experience. Consider how you can use alliteration and humour to make an everyday situation interesting.

2. **Tweet any mishaps that befall you.** For example when I tweeted: *"That embarrassing moment when you choke on a piece of toast in*

a café and can't stop spluttering and coughing for 5 mins..." six followers immediately tweeted back. Sharing your human side warts and all is endearing.

3. **Share your plans for the day** but remember to be upbeat and ask a question to encourage a friendly dialogue with your followers. *"Looking forward to meeting a new client then lunch with a local business editor. And you?"*

4. **Share what you've just done.** *"Fantastic 4N networking meeting in Horsham this morning. Great to meet @noredbraces at last"*

5. **Tweet about the weather.** Even on Twitter we love talking about it especially when we're in the throes of extreme weather.

6. **Share your love of a particular food** or, if you're eating at a nice restaurant or café tell your followers where you are and describe the experience.

7. **Share regular tips that show your expertise.** For example I make sure that many of my tweets are marketing tips because they're appreciated by my followers. If you can share your expertise in bite-sized nuggets of wisdom your Twitter following will grow because you'll be regarded as a reliable source of useful information. Here are three tips I posted recently. I've only used 130 of the 140 characters for each tweet so my followers can retweet it without having to abbreviate it.

'When appraising your marketing effectiveness customer service should be included. A well nurtured customer is a great ambassador'

'It's a fresh new week for putting marketing at the centre of your business + watching sales soar as a direct consequence of doing so'

'Awesome customer service is about making customers feel valued + cared for at every touch point from pre-sale to after care'

8. **Share some lovely images.** For example, I've posted pictures of my log cabin, my hens, the Yorkshire Dales, my book covers, the adverts I've spotted with spelling mistakes and selfies with readers at events I've spoken at.

9. **Tweet about any travel delays you're experiencing.** You might just help one of your followers embarking on the same journey.

10. **Share inspirational quotes from people you admire.** Add a few words explaining why you love the quote to make it more personal.

11. **If you've found a useful video, podcast, article, infographic or blog** tweet about it and include the link.

12. **If you're reading a great book** recommend it to your followers and tell them why it's so good.

13. **Share a review you've written for a book** or a comment you've made on a blog.

14. **Share your thoughts on something topical and relevant to you.** For example when I was approached by BBC Radio Sussex to share my thoughts on International Women's Day I tweeted about this experience.

15. **Tweet about your everyday life.** You might have decided to give yourself the day off or perhaps you're going out for a nice meal. Your tweets don't have to be highbrow, deep or meaningful to be engaging and interesting.

16. **Send tweets congratulating your followers.** When one of your followers shares their good news why not send a nice tweet back congratulating them. What you give out, you get back.

17. **Invite your followers to ask you questions** on the subject you're considered an expert in. This can be informal or you can set aside a particular time every week.

Make sure your tweets comprise a nice blend of chit chat, of tweeting about your expertise, sharing your knowledge, responding to others and promoting useful resources, links and ideas. If you can get to grips with these simple guidelines you'll have no problem promoting and selling your book on Twitter.

How to get your tweets retweeted.

A retweet is when a person shares one of your tweets with their followers. If you want your reach on Twitter to increase and to become known as a great author then having your tweets retweeted to hundreds, often thousands of people will help your cause. If you implement the tips you've read so far many of your tweets will be retweeted.

Here are some further tips on getting your tweets retweeted:

- **Give out what you want to get back!** Be generous in retweeting the tweets of others but only the ones that are worth sharing. Filling a follower's timeline with banal and poorly composed retweets will do you no favours.

- **Respond to the tweets you enjoy.** Send a nice message and retweet the tweet and you'll encourage these followers to do likewise.

- **Tweet about something topical that's within your area of expertise.** What's happening on the news, online or in the world at large that you can tweet about? If the debate is already happening on Twitter, join in. Because you're sharing your opinion as an expert with an obvious connection to the topic you're more likely to have these tweets retweeted.

- **If you have a blog** don't just share a link with a few words, let your followers know how they will benefit from reading your blog which should encourage them to retweet it to their followers. "*12 tips on getting your tweets retweeted. My latest blog*" has more impact than "*My latest Twitter blog.*" Look upon the tweet you are using to promote your blog as the headline of an advert. It needs impact. Include the link in the middle of your tweet. Tweets with a link are retweeted more often than tweets without one.

- **Within your tweet include the Twitter name of a follower you would appreciate retweeting your message.** If they can see the connection they may retweet your message to their followers.

- **Ask a question.** *'What's your top tip to promote a book on Twitter? Please tweet back.'* You should receive many answers and some followers will retweet your question to their followers.

- **Thank the people retweeting your tweets.** A genuine, warm message goes a long way in building rapport and getting those retweets.

- **Send a direct message to a follower you'd really like to retweet a particular tweet.** Explain why. For example when I want a follower to retweet the latest news about my book I will ask them in a direct message which pretty much guarantees a retweet.

- **Make it easy for people to retweet your tweets.** Restrict your tweet to 130 characters so it can be retweeted in full.

- **Ask for a retweet.** Adding the words 'Please retweet' or 'Please RT' has been proven to increase the likelihood of your message being retweeted. Overplay it and you'll irritate your followers but it works well if you're tweeting a question or tweeting good news about your book.

Why you may be unfollowed on Twitter.

You can be the most amazing tweeter in the world but some people will still unfollow you for no apparent reason. But, if you find yourself in the position of losing good followers on a daily basis you may need to tweak your Twitter strategy.

Here are the most common reasons why people will unfollow you.

1. A person followed you on the basis of one tweet you posted but your subsequent tweets were very different. Don't worry about losing these followers. It's impossible to be all things to all people.

2. They were unscrupulous with a dubious Twitter strategy! They followed you (and many others too) with the intention that when you followed them back, they would immediately unfollow you. They do this to puff up their ego by showing to the world they are followed by many but follow very few.

3. You don't tweet often enough. If you haven't tweeted in the last month that can be a good enough reason for some followers to unfollow you.

4. A person followed you hoping you'd follow them back. When you didn't return the favour they unfollowed you.

5. You're tweeting too much in too short a space of time. Flooding your followers' timelines with dozens of tweets in minutes can be irritating. Consider spacing your tweets out.

6. You're broadcasting most of the time with your tweets consisting of words prefaced by a hashtag and links to information but little else. There's no hint of a real person behind the tweets. After a while these tweets are boring.

7. You're not responding to your @ messages and direct messages or if you are it's too little too late.

8. You're using Twitter to sell your books and nothing else. As mentioned before Twitter is a great medium for promoting your book but if all you're doing is selling you'll turn people off.

9. You've fallen into the trap of sharing dubious jokes and dodgy humour that should be restricted to friends and family.

10. Your tweets are full of spelling mistakes and written in text talk.

If it's clear you're losing too many followers review your last five days of Twitter activity to find out where you're getting it wrong.

I hope this chapter has inspired you to get stuck into Twitter. If you say hello to me on Twitter and follow me, I will follow you back.

Chapter summary.

- Twitter is ideal for helping you promote your book from your big idea to post launch promotion.

- The benefits of Twitter include finding and creating rapport with journalists, building relationships with readers, securing Amazon reviews and finding events to speak at.

- It pays to check every single tweet before posting it.

- Always be friendly, helpful and charming on Twitter.

- Build your following on Twitter by tweeting regularly, sharing great advice and interacting with your followers.

- Your Twitter biography will help build your following. Use those 140 characters.

- There are many ways in which you can promote your book on Twitter including sharing your progress, revealing your title, asking readers to post pictures of your book and promoting its position on Amazon.

- Readers will buy your book when it's right for them and that's why you should tweet about it regularly.

- Don't just broadcast on Twitter, interact and join in with the conversations.

- Don't just tweet about your book - that's boring! Talk about the weather, what you're doing, congratulate your followers and invite readers to ask you questions.

- It's easy to get your tweets retweeted if you're tweeting interesting, topical, and sometimes humorous tweets or even asking for a retweet.

- If you are being unfollowed on a regular basis, review your last five days of tweets.

CHAPTER 23

How to Pull Off the Perfect Book Launch

Your launch gives you an amazing opportunity to put your book on the map. That's why it should ideally take place within the first few weeks of your book being published. At your book launch you will be surrounded by people only too willing to support you by reading your book, promoting it to their circle of contacts and friends, and reviewing it.

And yet I am always surprised when I speak to an author and find out they've decided not to have one. My good friend, Nicky Kriel, the bestselling author of *How to Twitter for Business Success* was not going to have a book launch until I persuaded her to change her mind and offered to speak at it. Nicky found a lovely venue - a local hotel that offered their function room at no charge because she had used them for her social media workshops. One of Nicky's friends, a baker, made some delicious cakes, and on the day more than 50 people turned up with many buying several copies of her book. The local papers covered her launch and many of the guests tweeted about it afterwards. Nicky's book launch was in the morning. By contrast, my book launches have been evening events but, like Nicky's, are always very well attended. What's more, I've not paid a penny for any of my book launches and at each one have sold more than 100 books.

So, how do you ensure that your book launch is a roaring success too?

1. Put a date in the diary for your book launch when you're at stage two of your marketing plan so it's unlikely to be cancelled because you hit a production delay. Nothing beats having a date to encourage you to stick to your deadlines. It also gives you ample time to warm up the people you would like to invite and find a

sponsor (more on this later). I would avoid having your launch on a Monday or Friday or at the weekend for obvious reasons.

2. Start your guest list and keep on adding to it. I begin mine with the people I really want to attend. This includes members of my family, my clients, journalists, business people I've built a great connection with on Twitter and at networking events, some of the readers I've built a special rapport with, and my guest contributors. You may want to encourage your guests to bring a colleague or friend depending on the size of your list. I have never offered this because I've always had more people than places. I've had to let guests know they can't turn up with a friend because there won't be enough seats.

3. What I have learned is that it pays to invite people who don't live or work miles away from the venue of my book launch. At my last book launch which was well attended, my final guest list had 140 confirmations and 138 people turned up on the night including people I was not expecting! Six guests confirmed their attendance only to cancel in the run up to the event. They all lived a few hours' drive away from the venue. If you want a big turnout make sure that most of your guests are local.

4. Your invitation list will change which is why you have to keep on adding to it with new people taking the place of those that can't come. And people who have confirmed their attendance will cancel for perfectly good reasons in the run-up to your launch. If you're aiming for 100, I would encourage you to invite 125 people but check beforehand that the venue can cope with a last minute surge of unexpected guests. Some people will not have confirmed their attendance with you but they'll turn up anyway.

5. I have always chosen an attractive, easy-to-reach venue with plenty of free onsite parking and good rail links. I book a room for

the launch and the book signing with an area close by for networking beforehand. Because I struggled to be heard at my first book launch I have since requested a microphone. People absorb sound at an alarming rate so unless you're planning an intimate gathering, it's best to use a microphone. You may have several potential venues you're interested in. For example if you're writing a children's book, your local library may be perfect. If you're writing a cookery book, a local restaurant may have a nice function room. As well as considering conventional venues such as purpose-built conference centres think off the wall too, but ensure the space gives you, your guests and your speakers some privacy.

6. It pays to negotiate. I've managed to reduce the price of the room hire by agreeing to promote the venue in my invitations and launch press releases and I have held my book launches in the evening when room hire rates tend to be at their lowest. I've also kept costs down by only providing tea, coffee, juice and biscuits. You won't be expected to provide free alcohol and food. Whether you have your book launch during the day or the evening comes down to your personal preferences and any special offers you can take advantage of. But think about your guests. What do you think will most appeal to them and, encourage them to turn up?

7. I put my requirements in writing. This is a précis of what I sent the event organiser for my last book launch with my order of play for the event which you can see a little further on.

   - Access to the room required at least 30 minutes before the pre-launch networking to check it out, test the microphone, place programmes on each seat, and arrange books on the selling and signing table.

- Guests to be allowed to stay on for 45 minutes after the book signing for informal networking without the risk of being asked to leave.

- Two tables and two chairs with white cloths to be provided in the main room - one for selling the books, one for signing the books.

- 140 seats to be in rows with the first row allocated to VIPs (guest contributors, sponsor and family members).

- Microphone to be provided and tested by the organiser the day before.

- Tea, coffee, juice and biscuits to be ready 15 minutes before the scheduled networking, served from three areas so people don't have to queue. Refreshments to be available after the book signing too.

- A paying bar to be open during the pre-event networking and when the book signing is taking place.

- Final confirmation of the guest list will be supplied by me two days before the event.

I have always met with the organiser a few weeks before my book launch to ensure that everything is going to schedule and as requested. This is highly recommended. You don't want to turn up on the day only to discover that the room has not been set up to your brief or is still occupied because of confusion over timings.

8. **How to get your book launch for free!** I've had three lovely book launches and not paid for any of them. For my first book launch, which was held at a local football club, the room was offered at

no charge because the venue organiser was a member of the networking group I belonged to. One of my clients paid for the refreshments and a local photographer offered his services at no charge in exchange for some promotion. Because I had appeared on the BBC with the celebrity Saira Khan who starred in the first series of *The Apprentice*, she offered to say a few words.

For my second book launch, which was held at a lovely purpose-built training and conference centre, one of my clients offered to pay for everything in exchange for being the event sponsor. I secured a free photographer, printer, designer and videographer in exchange for promoting each one of them. I repeated the same successful formula for my third book launch. Of course, I had to make these launches attractive to my sponsors. For example at my third book launch, which was sponsored by Perrys Chartered Accountants, I offered the following promotional opportunities:

- Promotion of Perrys in the invitations sent to guests.

- Name checking Perrys in all pre-event and post-event press releases.

- A five-minute speaking slot for the CEO Stewart Pope.

- Perrys pop-up banners to be on display in the main room.

- Five guest places.

Who are you connected to who would benefit from this level of exposure in exchange for sponsoring your book launch? If you have negotiated the cost of the room hire and refreshments you should be able to offer a cost-effective sponsorship opportunity. Look for ways in which you can make sponsoring the event appealing to a potential sponsor by identifying just as I have done the different ways in which you can promote them.

How to get your guests to attend and buy your book.

I follow a strict process when inviting people to my book launch because I want as many people as possible to turn up on the night ready to have a good time and of course to buy a copy of my latest book. And - touch wood - so far my book launches have been packed to capacity. Book sales have been plentiful too. However it had not occurred to me that I had a winning book launch formula until Megan, the marketing manager at Wiley, told me on the evening of my last book launch that it was the most successful one she had ever attended. Apparently a few days earlier she had gone to a book launch that was attended by 100 people and only 11 books were sold. At my launch that evening we sold 120 books.

So here is my book launch planning process - how I ensure the room is packed and people come keen to buy! I hope you find the accompanying email invitations that I sent useful too.

- As outlined earlier, once I have a firm date for my book launch, I begin the time-consuming but much-needed process of picking up the phone and asking each guest to put the date in their diary. People get booked up in advance so it's worth doing this.

- Approximately six weeks before my book launch, I send a PDF invitation and an email to each guest so I can include a personal message. Again, this does take time but it enables me to tweak the content of the email to reflect my relationship with a person. This increases the likelihood of them not only wanting to come to my launch but actually turning up on the night.

Here's the wording for the PDF invitation. It spells out the fact that my book can be bought at the event. I didn't do this in the invitations for my first book launch and many people asked if I was selling my book at the event or not.

Your exclusive invitation to the Book Launch and signing of *The 15 Essential Marketing Masterclasses For Your Small Business*

Thursday 12th September
17:45 - 20:30

Roffey Park Institute, Forest Road, Horsham, West Sussex, RH12 4TB.

Informal networking will be followed by speeches and the book signing. Payment for the book (£12.00) can be made by cheque or cash. A receipt will be provided on the night if required.

Tea and coffee will be served and a cash bar will be available.

Dee's book launch has been very kindly sponsored by Perrys Chartered Accountants.

I sent this confirmation email within two working days to every person who'd responded to my invitation:

Hi Nicola,

I am delighted that you are attending my book launch on 12th September at Roffey Park. If for any reason you are unable to attend the book launch, please could you let me know at the earliest opportunity as we are approaching a full house! It should be a lovely evening with networking aplenty, some fabulous speakers and of course the book signing itself.

In addition to complimentary tea, coffee and soft drinks there will be a cash bar should you want something a little more exotic.

The event will be videoed and there will be a photographer taking pictures.

I very much look forward to seeing you on the evening.

Kind regards
Dee

Perrys Chartered Accountants are the proud sponsors of Dee's book launch.

I sent this email to everyone who hadn't confirmed their attendance within two weeks of receiving their initial invitation:

Dear James,

I hope you are well and that you received the invitation to my book launch sent to you a few weeks ago. As I have not heard from you I am sending a gentle reminder.

The launch of *The 15 Essential Marketing Masterclasses For Your Small Business,* which is being very kindly sponsored by Perrys Chartered Accountants, is on Thursday 12 September at Roffey Park. (Details attached).

Kick off is 5:45pm and the event itself should end around 8:30pm. Lots of lovely networking, some amazing speakers and of course the book signing itself. My book will be on sale on the night for £12 and we will give you a receipt. You can pay by cash or cheque.

It is not available on Amazon until 20 September so you will be one of the first people in the whole wide world to get a copy!

I'm looking forward to seeing you but please could you confirm your attendance in the next 10 days as the event is nearly full and I don't want you to miss out on what should be a fantastic evening.

Kind regards,
Dee

There will always be some people who are planning to attend your book launch but don't get round to telling you without a few gentle reminders.

A week before my launch I reminded each one of my guests with this email:

Dear Peter,

With just one week to go to my book launch on Thursday, 12 September at Roffey Park I'm emailing to say how much I am looking forward to seeing you.

As you know from my previous invitation the event starts at 5:45pm and will end around 8:30pm.

The event is now full so you should have a fantastic time with plenty of networking, some amazing speakers and of course the book signing itself. My book *The 15 Essential Marketing Masterclasses For Your Small Business* will be on sale on the night for £12. It is not being released on Amazon until 20 September so you can grab an early copy.

If for any reason you are unable to attend, please could you let me know as soon as possible so that I can advise the venue, but otherwise it will be lovely to see you at what is set to be an amazing event.

Kind regards,
Dee

Dee's book launch is very kindly being sponsored by Perrys Chartered Accountants.

Be prepared in the week before your book launch for some of your confirmed attendees to drop out. This is bound to happen so don't take it personally. If you have built a good guest list and followed this invitation process, the room should be full to bursting.

In the weeks leading up to your book launch make sure that you're talking about it on social media. Share images of your book and retweet some of the messages that guests are posting. These are small simple steps that will lead to book sales.

How to make your book launch magical.

Your book launch should be an exciting and entertaining event for you and for your guests, so don't be content with just a little networking followed by the book signing itself. Put on an event that will have your guests talking about it for many days afterwards - not just with each other but on social media too. This will of course result in even more book sales. Creating a buzz is not as challenging as you might think.

Here's what happened at my last book launch:

4.30pm Interview with local papers at the venue.

5.00pm Meet the organiser, check out the room/set up.

5.30pm Guests arrive, register and mingle.

6.00pm Master of Ceremonies (my brother) calls guests to the main room.

6.05pm MC welcomes guests, says a few words about me and introduces the first speaker, sponsor Stewart Pope.

6.10pm Stewart explains why Perrys are sponsors.

6.20pm MC introduces the first of the four expert contributors to my book. Each one shares for 10 minutes why they were keen to be involved in *The 15 Essential Marketing Masterclasses For Your Small Business.*

7.05pm MC introduces me to the audience. I talk for 15 minutes on why I wrote the book and what it's all about.

7.25pm The book signing. Allow 60 minutes for guests to chat to me and take pictures.

9.00pm The last guests leave and we head off for a curry.

You can have several smaller book launches in the wake of your big official launch. In fact I would encourage you to arrange as many mini book launches and signings as you can possibly handle within the first month or two of your book being published. This will have a very positive snowball effect. At every launch, you will attract people keen to buy your book and to share their positive feedback about it on social media and on their blog. So look out for opportunities at local and regional networking events and offer talks and book signings. Revisit your target audiences and where they hang out and, if they're gathering at a place that's close to home suggest a book signing.

Enjoy your book launch and savour every moment.

I look back fondly on my book launches because each one gave me the opportunity to spend some time with a lovely group of people and to christen my book at long last. After months of writing, it's the most amazing feeling in the world to be sitting at a table signing copies of your book. So make sure that you enjoy your book launch and that you thank your audience and the people who have supported you on your journey to becoming a published, soon-to-be bestselling author. Your book launch is just the first in a long line of successes. Invest your time and energy in making it an event that really does justice to your incredible book.

Chapter summary.

- Put your book on the map by celebrating it with a book launch.

- Your launch is a fantastic promotional vehicle for your book.

- Make sure the venue is easy to reach with good transport links and space for networking, speaking and the signing itself. Negotiate!

- Start your guest list as soon as you have a date and a venue. Keep on top of it because it will change.

- Don't invite too many people that will have to travel from afar unless you're confident they will turn up.

- Confirm all your requests to the venue in writing.

- Consider a sponsor. Prepare a document with all the benefits they will gain from sponsoring your launch.

- Make sure guests are aware that you will be selling books at your launch.

- Phone each guest, invite them, confirm their response and remind them.

- Plan a sparkling event with networking, guest speakers and the signing itself.

- Ask for Amazon reviews and encourage guests to take to social media afterwards to post pictures and talk about your launch.

CHAPTER 24

How to Get Positive Reviews *and* How to Get Professional Reviewers to Review Your Book

How many times have you been persuaded to buy a product or a book on the strength of its great reviews alone? Quite a few I should imagine. And this is going to happen to your book too. A person may be aware of your book, even interested in buying it, but the tipping point, what makes them go ahead and buy it, are those positive reviews. They underpin the good work of your book cover. And whilst a person might not have heard about you before going online and being recommended your book, it's the positive reviews that will persuade them they've found a book they can buy with confidence.

Sometimes however positive reviews can backfire and cause more harm than good.

To illustrate this point, a few years ago I was approached by an author who asked if I would review her book on Amazon. After browsing the introductory pages and reading a few chapters, I looked it up on Amazon. One five-star review in particular stood out. It was from her designer. I knew this because in the acknowledgements page of her book she thanked her designer by name and now here was the very same name heading up the review. In this review, the designer praised the book in gushing terms and concluded it by saying she hoped one day to meet the author. Oh dear. False reviews like this can count against you and could lead to a barrage of negative publicity, especially if another author fighting for the same turf gets wind of these tactics. So, whilst I would encourage you to ask for reviews of your book, be squeaky clean and avoid any dubious tactics. Trust your genuine readers to support you. I'm often asked by other authors how I have managed to get so many positive five-star reviews of my books. Whilst it pays to write a good book in the first place, that's not enough. You have to encourage your readers to post reviews.

Here's how I do this:

1. **Review copies.** In the two months leading up to my book being published, I will approach a handful of people I know and trust and ask if I can send them a copy of my book as soon as it is published on the proviso they read it and then review it on Amazon.

2. **My book launches.** I always ask the members of my audience if they will review my book on Amazon after reading it. This pretty much guarantees that within a few weeks of my launch, there are half a dozen reviews from people who have actually bought and read my book.

3. **Twitter.** Twitter is by far the most effective channel I use to ask my readers for reviews on an ongoing basis so they don't dry up after a few months. A reader will contact me on Twitter with an open tweet telling me how much they're enjoying reading my book or, if they have just finished reading it, how it's helping them to grow their business. I will respond with an open tweet thanking them for their lovely message. But I will also send a private message asking if they will review my book when they have a spare moment. Many readers are more than happy to oblige and a review usually follows, but I steer away from chasing them if they don't post one. I don't want to be seen as a pest!

4. **Book signings and public speaking engagements.** I often meet readers at book signings and public speaking engagements who have read my previous book(s) and are now buying my latest book. Again, I will ask if they will review my book(s) on Amazon. Sometimes a reader will post a couple of reviews at the same time; a double bonus. Some write to tell me when they have posted

a review which is such a thoughtful gesture. I respond to every reader who contacts me and thank them for taking the time to write a review.

5. **Reviews from professional reviewers and influential publications.** I realised just how powerful professional reviews were when the book reviewer from *FSB Magazine* posted a glowing review of my book which, as I covered previously, resulted in it reaching number one in its category on Amazon. For my third book, Wiley commissioned a specialist book PR consultant, Jeff Scott from Platypus PR. (You will recognise Jeff's name. He has written the foreword of this book and also shares his publishing tips in Chapter 12). Jeff sent a number of review copies of my book to be reviewed by popular business publications and professional reviewers. This resulted in several glowing reviews within a few months of my book being launched and it won two awards. I used these reviews and awards to promote my book further still and asked one of the reviewers if he would reproduce his review on Amazon which he did. Of course I can't claim any credit for this and I realise how lucky I was to have Jeff in my corner but there's nothing to stop you from emulating Jeff's approach by sending copies of your book to influential professional reviewers. Sue Magee's tips at the end of this chapter show you exactly how to accomplish this.

What I've learned is that you have to ask for reviews and keep on asking for them. A reader eulogising about your book and recommending it won't automatically think to write a review, but once you've asked them they'll be happy to support you.

How to handle negative reviews.

It's not nice being on the receiving end of negative or unflattering feedback about your book, especially when the person dishing out this feedback does it in the form of a one- or two-star review on Amazon or on another review site. Now this unpleasant review is there for the world to see. Unless you have a thick skin, it's an upsetting experience. However, as your book becomes more popular so does the likelihood of it attracting negative reviews. Have you heard of the 'Tall Poppies' syndrome? Sadly some people will be only too keen to dish out a negative review simply because you have so many positive ones. They want to chop you down to size!

Once you've got over the shock of a negative review you have to see it for what it is; one person who has not enjoyed your book and has decided to use the review system to tell you and others. It may seem unfair but this person is as entitled to their negative view as your fans are to sharing their positive opinions. It's not the end of the world. A few negative reviews amongst dozens of great ones won't put people off from buying your book.

Should you respond to these negative reviews?

There's no black-and-white answer to this. It really depends on what this person has said about you and your book and if you feel that a response is required or that remaining silent is your best strategy. At the time of writing this book, I have amassed a grand total of five one-star reviews and three two-star reviews out of 294 in total for my three books. I have only responded to one of the one-star reviews - the first negative review I received - and I only did so because the reviewer asked a question I felt was important to answer. I've chosen to ignore the others even though some are unpleasant and incorrect. I didn't want to enter into what could well have turned out to be a never-ending unpleasant and petty dialogue. I have seen authors respond to their negative reviews in a hasty, defensive and angry manner. This has resulted in other readers joining the debate to defend the negative reviewer. The only 'winner' in this sorry situation is the person who posted the negative review. By now they'll have a growing audience to spur them on to become even more critical in their responses.

One negative review that's handled badly by you can open up a floodgate of unseemly and unflattering comments and there you are stuck in the middle of it trying to defend yourself to no avail. So if you want to respond to your harsh critics, it pays to consider the implications beforehand; what can happen as a consequence of your response.

That doesn't mean to say that you should not respond to your negative reviews if you feel it's important to set the record straight. Sometimes you should. Here are my tips to keep your good name intact and to take the sting out of a negative review.

- Take some time to read the negative review, even printing it off, so you can reflect on it with a clear mind. Talk it over with a person you trust before deciding on your response. Take the initial emotion and heat out of the situation so you can think clearly and rationally.

- Decide which parts of the review you're going to respond to and which parts you'll give a wide berth. If the reviewer is saying they did not enjoy reading your book there's nothing you can do about this. They're allowed to dislike it. However, if they're making factually incorrect statements, your response should focus on these. You don't have to answer every negative point nor do you want to come across as defensive and immature.

- Draft your response and ask for a second opinion before posting it. Make sure it's concise, grammatically correct and you're coming across as a helpful, balanced and objective person. Resist the temptation to point out any spelling mistakes and inconsistencies in the review. Be the bigger and better person in this.

- Don't ever lose sight of the fact that you're the author and as such will be expected to conduct yourself in an altogether more mature and civilised manner than your reviewer. You're going to be judged by the tone of your response and how you present it. A block of hastily written text looks poor whereas a thoughtful narrative with paragraphs, even bullet points, demonstrates that you have taken some time to respond and are neither emotional nor bitter. People interested in buying your book will read the negative reviews and the positive ones before making their decision. If it's obvious you have responded defensively with a poorly written rejoinder they may decide not to buy your book. However, if your reply is balanced and well written, it will count in your favour and the power of the negative review will be significantly eroded.

- If the reviewer responds to your response with more unflattering comments, close the debate down. Provide your email address if you're happy to clarify any further points or simply leave it at that. Some reviewers will enjoy becoming even more negative and will cling to their original position no matter how reasonable your response. They will be determined to have the last word and nothing you say will make them reconsider their opinion and back down. You don't have to have the last word and you may find that some of your readers will join in the debate and defend you.

- If the reviewer makes some good points acknowledge them with good grace. I read a two-star review of a book recently where the reviewer said she was marking down the book because it had many spelling mistakes. The author responded defensively saying there weren't that many! I felt she should have shown some humility and thanked the reviewer for pointing out these mistakes.

- If you believe the review is damaging or libellous and should be removed, you can complain to Amazon through your author pages or to the host of the blog on which the review was posted. Don't be disappointed if they decide to keep the review. Move on. There are many five-star reviews down the line for you.

Remind yourself that you can't please everyone all the time and that every bestselling author has their critics; thankfully in the minority.

How to get your book reviewed by a professional reviewer.

Sue Magee co-founded the hugely popular www.thebookbag.co.uk book review site which includes over ten thousand reviews of fiction, non-fiction and children's books. You'll also find her @TheBookbag on Twitter.

I was chuffed to say the least when Sue offered to contribute to this book. Her tips show you exactly how you should approach the task of getting your book reviewed by a professional book reviewer. They are solid gold and of immense value to any author. Follow them to the letter! I will...

Before approaching a reviewer:

1. Make certain that your book is listed with the major online booksellers and that the details are correct. Ensure there's an image of the cover and that stock is available. Many online review sites rely on the money they get from affiliate sales to run the site, so having the listing as it should be with stock available can be a deciding factor when a reviewer considers whether or not to read the book.

2. You will need a press release. Even if you plan on sending all the details in an email it's good practice to send a press release with the book. It has immediate impact when the package is opened and it's invaluable when the book is actually going to be sent on to someone else to review. The person with the responsibility for publishing the review then has a clear statement of the title of the book and the author's name. You'd be surprised how often reviewers get these wrong! Include the date of publication, the

ISBN number, a short (and hopefully interesting) biography of the author and a brief synopsis of the content. Don't give spoilers - you want a reviewer to have the same reading experience as someone who picks the book up in their local bookshop.

3. If the book has been reviewed elsewhere give short quotes from reliable sources. Don't print your Amazon reviews. An experienced reviewer might look at Amazon reviews, but the first thing they'll do is disregard those where the reviewer hasn't written any other reviews, or where the reviews look suspiciously similar - and it's surprising how often what's left doesn't amount to much. You might not have set out to deliberately manipulate the star ratings, but mum, dad, the relatives and all your friends are not going to be honest about the book. They love you too much. Remember too that you're approaching a reviewer for his or her opinion of your work and not for free publicity. Sending a stack of other reviews suggests that they might not know what to think unless they were told and no reputable reviewer is going to like this.

4. Carefully select the people you would like to review your book. Do your homework. Have a look at the type of book which they - or their site - generally cover and find a good fit. It's not essential to sign up for the newsletter or follow them on social media, but it does give you an insight which you might not otherwise get. Have a look on the site for any advice given to authors and publishers.

5. Approach reviewers as you would want to be approached. Spamming them with emails or buttonholing them on social media and pushing your book will not endear you to a reviewer. Being friendly and interesting before you make an approach is a good start. Ask if you might email the reviewer about the book rather than just ploughing in.

6. Be careful if you use a template for emails which you're going to send to reviewers. There's nothing wrong with developing a really

good email, but do make certain that you change any names before you send them out. Sending one with the name of another site or another reviewer does rather give the game away. You want the reviewer to feel they were carefully selected and not just a name on a list.

7. Offer to send the book to a reviewer. Don't say that you'll include an SAE so they can return the book when they've read it, or send the copy your mother-in-law read, complete with dog ears and a light sprinkling of fag ash where the pages meet. (In fact if you're a smoker, keep your review copies somewhere uncontaminated - non-smokers can be very sensitive to the smell and the book might well end up in the bin before it's even been looked at.) Be flexible about the formats you can offer and investigate the possibilities of sites such as Smashwords or NetGalley so that you can offer free downloads.

8. Publicity for a book is most valuable in the six weeks immediately following publication so it's helpful if you can get copies to reviewers at least a month before. Finished copies are preferred but if you're sending advance reading copies make it clear that the book is being professionally proofread. Don't send uncorrected proofs after publication, you can leave a reviewer feeling slightly insulted, or (and probably more likely) concerned that the book has not been adequately proofed and the words 'uncorrected proof copy' are just a cover.

9. I've probably laboured the point about being polite to reviewers before you have a review. But what about afterwards? If you're happy with the review a note of thanks is always appreciated or even an acknowledgement that you've seen the review. A surprising number of authors/publicists don't bother - and it's human nature to go the extra mile for those who do.

10. If you're not happy with the review the first thing to do is to stand away from your computer and count to a thousand. When you've calmed down... consider whether the problem is that there are factual inaccuracies. Send a polite email explaining that the hero's name is A not B and that it's set in X not Y. Most online reviewers will be only too pleased to change inaccuracies and a publication could print a correction if it's material.

11. If the reviewer didn't like the book, accept that you can't win them all. Don't wade in, all guns blazing and definitely don't ask your friends and relatives to do the same. Don't create a storm on social media. Ultimately you will make yourself look foolish. And there could be a knock-on effect.

Why?

Think of book reviewers as a community. We meet at book launches, publishers' presentations and we chat online. You might think we're in competition but it's more collaborative than you might expect. We support each other and we share contacts. We also share information. It almost certainly won't be a deliberate attempt to blacken someone's name but we spot what's happening on social media, we see the comments under fellow bloggers' reviews and just occasionally a blogger will approach another and ask if they'd look at a review and tell them whether they think their review is reasonable. And knowing that an author can be difficult doesn't mean I'll be extra kind about their book - it means I'll probably avoid them altogether.

Ultimately, reviewers need books and authors need reviews. Approached correctly the combination can work well.

Chapter summary.

- Positive reviews sell books for sure but they should be genuine. A fake positive review can come back to haunt you.

- If you want dozens of positive reviews you'll have to get into the habit of asking for them.

- Use Twitter, your book launch, book signings, public speaking engagements and business networking to ask for reviews.

- Negative reviews are disconcerting and upsetting but they are a fact of life for most successful authors.

- Some negative reviews are unfounded and lacking in credibility and some may be perfectly legitimate. You will have to decide on the ones you will respond to, the ones you will report and the ones you will ignore.

- Don't ever respond to a negative review straight after reading it. Give yourself time to calm down and reflect on your response.

- As an author you have to take the moral high ground, so avoid sarcasm and any other negative emotions in your response and review what you've written before posting it.

- Aim for professional reviews of your book but treat the professional reviewer with respect and go the extra mile, thanking them afterwards.

Conclusion

I hope you have enjoyed reading this book as much as I've enjoyed writing it. Has it inspired you to write the book that's been inside your head for ages? If you have already written a book do you now feel you can promote it with confidence? I hope your answer is a resounding yes!

The success of your book project is all about taking action. So think about the secrets I've shared with you and promise yourself that you're going to put what you've learned here into practice.

I've deliberately written this book to give you an abundance of practical advice and a list of specific and eminently achievable actions. I know they work because they've kept my books at the top of their category for years and have helped me sell books all over the world.

But there's more work to be done!

If you want to achieve your full potential as a bestselling author you have to be passionate about your subject. You have to live and breathe it every day. You have to be constantly on the lookout for opportunities to talk about your book and to positively influence others. When you're on fire with enthusiasm, people will travel for miles to see you and they'll talk about you with real passion afterwards. Don't let a day go past without doing something to raise your profile even higher. You want to be seen as the go-to expert and key person of influence in your field.

When I was writing this book I was approached by several authors asking if I had plans to write a fifth one. I haven't. I'm now using my free time to create a series of author workshops and an author mentoring programme. After being asked to do this for many years I've finally decided to bring the tips, tools and tactics in this book to life. So please watch this space. It goes without saying that I would really like to hear from you. One of the highlights of writing a book is connecting with my readers, so please get in touch. I'd love to hear how my book has helped you and to hear all about your book too. If you're interested in my author workshops and author mentoring programme I will send you the details when everything is in place.

I wish you many happy and productive hours of planning, writing and, of course, marketing your book all the way to the bestsellers.
Success and happiness always, one word at a time.

Kind regards,
Dee

Email: dee@themarketinggym.org

Twitter: @deeblick

Mobile: 07845 439332

www.themarketinggym.org

About the Experts

Brad Burton
Author, 4Networking Founder and Motivational Speaker

Websites: bradburton.biz and 4networking.biz
Twitter: @bradburton

Brad is the author of 3 bestselling books; *Get Off Your Arse* (which is the highest reviewed/ rated motivational business book on Amazon) and *Get Off Your Arse Too* both of which he self published. His third book *Life: Business Just Got Easier* was published by Wiley, sells globally and is a WH Smith bestseller. Brad is also the founder of 4Networking and the UK's number one motivational speaker. Without fail every year Brad is voted the most inspiring and engaging speaker at The Business Show. He never fails to deliver!

Bryony Thomas
Speaker, Author and Creator of Watertight Marketing

Website: watertightmarketing.com
Twitter: @bryonythomas and @watertightmkg
Facebook: WatertightMarketing

Bryony is a captivating professional speaker and award-winning author of *Watertight Marketing* - described in one recent review as "a work of sheer, unparalleled marketing genius" and, in another as "the marketing book that makes sense of the rest." Bryony developed the powerful methodology for this bestselling book over 15 years, and across 200+ businesses. She's a proven marketer, working first in marketing agencies on clients like Microsoft and Dell, and then as client-side director of marketing within FTSE-100, Experian. Since 2008, she has been working hands-on with owner-managed businesses as they follow her 12-month process for putting a structured marketing operation into their business; a process that delivers long-term sales results. No fluff or padding, Bryony Thomas always delivers practical ideas that make a real and measurable difference.

Chris Day
Publisher, Authorcraft Founder and Author

Website: Filamentpublishing.com
Email: chris@filamentpublishing.com
Twitter: @ChrisDayFP
LinkedIn: LinkedIn: https://www.linkedin.com/in/ChrisDay
Telephone: +44 020 8688 2598

Chris founded Filament Publishing Ltd in 1999 having worked for a decade with one of the world's largest publishers, Encyclopaedia Britannica. He is a journalist, ghost writer, and the author of '*Turning your Knowledge into Income*'. Chris now mentors authors on marketing their books through AuthorCraft - a community of writers groups he set up in 2012. He believes that every new book is a start up business and must be looked upon in that way if it is not to end up an expensive hobby. Chris lives in Croydon and holds author workshops in London every month.

Jane Mallin
Book Editor, Copywriter and Copy Editor

Email: janemallin1@gmail.com
Twitter: @Jane_Mallin
Mobile: 07784 214237

I started reading and writing aged four and never stopped so it made sense to make words and stories my profession. I've been a writer and editor for 20 years, working on magazines and newspapers and with corporates and SMEs. I've written everything from annual reports and White Papers to case studies and sales and marketing literature.

I most enjoy working with authors (fiction and non-fiction) editing their books whilst retaining their unique style. I love helping them to achieve their goals and meet their publishing deadlines!

I'm a member of SfEP (Society for Editors and Proofreaders) and an NLP Practitioner so I'm good at helping writers of all genres blast through their blocks.

Janice B Gordon
Author and Business Transformation Consultant Mentor

Website: theproblem-solver.co.uk
Twitter: @janicebg
Telephone: +44 020 7175 0877

Janice is the author of *Business Evolution, Creating Growth in a Rapidly Changing World*, endorsed by Lara Morgan who writes: "Janice cuts through the clutter and noise with her 'Essential 4Ps', making it easy to create growth in your business." Janice is a visiting Fellow of Cranfield School of Management, with 20 years' business experience gained working with blue chip organisations, SMEs and growing her own businesses. Having generated £6 million+ sales in the last 12 months, Janice creates mind-set shifts and practical customer experience strategies to help businesses get incredible results.

Jeff Scott
PR Book Publicist, Author and Writer

Twitter: @PlatypusPr
Email: info@platypuspr.com

Jeff Scott inherited his mother's love of people, delight in ideas, curiosity about life, pursuit of laughter and also her love of reading - almost anything, mostly books (of any type). Over 30 years into a varied often high flying publishing career, Jeff's love of books and reading have allowed him to travel the world (in person and in his mind). Jeff has delivered eye catching media publicity and PR book campaigns for publishers including: Anthem Press, BBC Active, Blackwell, Bloomsbury, Cambridge University Press, Capstone, Clairview Books, Continuum, Duncan Baird Publishers, Imprint Academic, Kogan Page, Miles Kelly, Myrdle Court Press, Pearson Education, Policy Press, Portfolio Penguin, Prentice Hall Life, Profile, Routledge, Rowman & Littlefield, Simon & Schuster, Solis Press and Wiley. Jeff's fourth (self published) book was nominated for British Sports Book of the Year 2008 (Biography).

Nicky Kriel
Social Media Consultant, Trainer and Author

Website: nickykriel.com
Blog: nickykriel.com/blog
Twitter: @NickyKriel

Nicky is a social media consultant, speaker and author of the bestselling *"How to Twitter for Business Success"*. She is one of the UK's top social media trainers and has been featured in the *Guardian* and *Daily Telegraph*. Nicky uses her background in corporate marketing to help companies integrate social media into their own marketing strategies. As a Master NLP Practitioner, communicating is her strength, teaching people to engage with the 'social' aspect of social networking; it's not all about tools and technology, but about people and relationships. She has worked with businesses ranging from solopreneurs to multinational companies - in the UK and internationally. Nicky was selected by Scredible as one of the Top 20 influential Social Media people in the UK who 'walk their talk'.

Richard White
Author and Sales Improvement Consultant

Website: theaccidentalsalesman.com
Twitter: @richard__white
LinkedIn: https://www.linkedin.com/in/richardjwhite

Richard is a sales improvement consultant who's helped thousands of experts and trusted advisers feel more comfortable with sales and become more effective. Richard developed his sales methodology as a result of his struggle with sales as an IT consultant. In his latest book Consultative Selling for Professional Services Richard shares the same structured methodology that's helped him to enjoy selling and build a thriving IT consulting practice with many blue chip clients including Unilever, First Choice, and British Airways.

Stefan Thomas
Director of 4Networking and Author

Website: noredbraces.co.uk
Twitter: @NoRedBraces
LinkedIn: https://www.linkedin.com/in/noredbraces

Stefan had to make networking work for him and out of desperation, refined his approach over seven intensive years and at over 800 networking events.

The techniques and strategies he perfected during those years led him to be at a networking event with Wiley, the publishers of the *"For Dummies"* series of books. They needed no convincing as to his pedigree and expertise as the UK's renowned networking expert and so commissioned him to write *"Business Networking for Dummies"*, an Amazon and WH Smith bestseller. The book has been described as "the definitive guide to business networking".

Suzanne Dibble
Lawyer

Website: suzannedibble.com
Twitter: @smallbizlawexp
Facebook: smallbusinesslawexpert

Suzanne is a multi award winning business lawyer with vast experience ranging from acting for Plcs on billion pound projects to helping micro businesses with their day to day business law requirements.

Having worked with Richard Branson, Simon Woodroofe and other famous entrepreneurs and been a board director of a £100m+ company, Suzanne is commercially minded and entrepreneurial in her outlook. Clients appreciate her practical, jargon-free advice.

Suzanne was runner up in the prestigious Solicitor of the Year Award at the Law Society Excellence Awards 2011 and also shortlisted in the Excellence in Client Service Award.

Acknowledgements

Once I had made the decision to write this book I surrounded myself with a group of immensely talented and supportive people.

They are:

Chris Day, from Filament Publishing, the publishers of this book. Chris is one of those people who you can ring at virtually any time of the day or night, weekday or weekend, and you will always get a warm and helpful response. His support in helping me bring this book to fruition has been fantastic. Chris has gone far beyond the traditional remit expected of a partnership publisher.

Jane Mallin, my editor. For this book I broke with tradition and gave my husband Malcolm a rest from wielding his red pen. Jane has polished my manuscript, ironed out my writer's idiosyncrasies and been an absolute joy to work with.

My incredibly talented expert contributors. Without their support this book would not have justified the word 'Ultimate' in its title. They are: Jeff Scott, Janice B Gordon, Richard White, Brad Burton, Stefan Thomas, Nicky Kriel, Bryony Thomas, Suzanne Dibble and, of course, Chris Day.

Sue Magee and Susan Mears – world class experts in their field.

Louise Lucas who designed my eye-catching, attention-grabbing book cover in her usual cheery and 'nothing is ever too much trouble' manner.

My amazing husband Malcolm for many reasons but not least because he never complains that when I'm writing a book it becomes an all-consuming task that completely takes over my life and impacts on his.

My lovely mum Ann who never tires of talking with pride about my book writing successes to anyone within earshot.

My brother Andrew with whom I have a very special bond. Andrew has been on the sidelines encouraging and supporting me for many years. He's the one person who knows how to keep me grounded and sane when my head is going into overdrive and I'm panicking that I've bitten off more than I can chew.

Alice Chambers and Sarah Payne for being two special friends and such great fun. Our regular coffees and chats were so welcome when I needed a break from writing.

I am also indebted to the many thousands of readers from all over the world who have helped me become a bestselling author. Without their support, this book would not have seen the light of day.

And finally, thank you for buying this book.

With love and gratitude,
Dee